Stage It and Stream It

Plays for Virtual Theater

Stage It and Stream It

Plays for Virtual Theater

Edited by John Patrick Bray

APPLAUSE
THEATRE & CINEMA BOOKS
Essex, Connecticut

APPLAUSE
THEATRE & CINEMA BOOKS

An imprint of Globe Pequot, the trade division of
The Rowman & Littlefield Publishing Group, Inc.
4501 Forbes Blvd., Ste. 200
Lanham, MD 20706
www.rowman.com

Distributed by NATIONAL BOOK NETWORK

British Library Cataloguing in Publication Information available

Library of Congress Cataloging-in-Publication Data Available
ISBN 978-1-4930-7289-7 (pbk. : alk. paper)
ISBN 978-1-4930-7290-3 (electronic)

♾️™ The paper used in this publication meets the minimum requirements of American National Standard for Information Sciences—Permanence of Paper for Printed Library Materials, ANSI/NISO Z39.48-1992

Contents

Full-Length Plays

Introduction
Plays for Virtual Theater

The idea of streaming a live performance is not new; nor is watching a recorded performance of a live event. For example, The National Theatre in the United Kingdom has had a series of their productions recorded and distributed to movie houses around the globe.

During the coronavirus pandemic, theatre artists found ways to use new media to continue creating their art and sharing it with audiences. These innovations were in response to extraordinary, unexpected circumstances, but they arguably helped to give birth to a new form of theater, with its own taxonomy, its own dramaturgical approaches, and even its own prizes, the Young-Howze Theatre Awards (and I am indebted to Ricky and Dany Young-Howze for their suggestions as I compiled this anthology). This genre is most often referred to as "*Zoom Theater,*" but that term is not quite appropriate, not only because Zoom is but one of many platforms used, but because some of the works found in these pages featured performers inhabiting the same space. (This is very true for Brendan Powers and Rachel Burttram, the husband-and-wife team comprising the company tiny_Theatre.) For the sake of this volume, we will simply call these Plays for Virtual Theater, which allows for a multitude of approaches when creating and experiencing works specifically using an online platform.

In this book, you will find different styles of theatrical works: monologues, short plays, one-acts, and two full-lengths that were originally performed online. You will find marital and other family dramas, mysteries, science fiction plays, and fantasy—in other words, the same gamut of styles and genres you will find with any other approach to theatrical performance.

Thank you for purchasing this book and supporting our new theater!

Monologues

98 People on Live

Audrey Cefaly

Production History

98 People on Live was developed as part of Alabama Shakespeare Festival's *#22HOMES* Project. It was devised with tiny_Theatre cofounder Rachel Burttram and directed by the author. It was then made available on You-Tube: https://youtu.be/KNEWGdhrU8E. *98 People on Live* (Copyright © 2020 by Audrey Cefaly. All rights reserved. Reprinted by permission of the author).

The cast was as follows:
HENRI KILGORE   Rachel Burttram*
with a special appearance by Brendan Powers* as GUS KILGORE
*Member Actors' Equity Association.

Characters

HENRI KILGORE
GUS KILGORE (optional)   Henri's husband

Time

2020 pandemic times

Place

The Alabama home of Henri and Gus Kilgore

[Henri Kilgore stands in her kitchen in central Alabama some four feet away from the camera. She walks toward it, squinting slightly to read the screen. She talks absently to her husband Gus who is doing the filming.]

Did it go? Lemme see. It looks . . . do I need to—Oh, that's Billy! Oh, it's on? I'm on live? Hey Billy! I was gonna do a thing right here, a recipe, you need to call me—hey Tina—but not right now, I'm on live—Hey Tina!

[Holding up a sack of potatoes.]

Y'all look what I got, this is all they had at the Kroger, I was gon' make y'all a potato salad but what's eh-body drinkin'? I get the reds too, Tina, you see 'em out there lemme know, y'all lemme know, okay, y'all got toilet paper, Billy, y'all got paper, we got 30 cases in the shed, hey Foster—

[Arguing with Gus now, the camera strays out of focus, as they whisper-squabble.]

(to GUS) Oh, stop it. Gus! Well, why can't I—there is NO WAY you need that much paper, you are unbelievable, this is a panDEMic.

[Back in the frame now, but still whisper-yelling at Gus.]

(to GUS) I can talk louder, you want me to talk louder?!

[To the camera—sweetly now.]

Tina, how you doin', I can't even believe this, yes, I got my hair back 'til they let us out, but that's the style now, showin' your roots—hey Donna, hey Fellicia, is that Cotton, Hey Cotton—Gus, get me a drink—can we drink on live, y'all, is eh-body holdin' up okay, oh, we have 23, Gus it's 23 people on live, Hey Phil, oh hey Nancy, you promised that casserole Nancy—showin my roots, yeah, showin my roots, the bee-bops love it—KK was like, "you look like Nancy Pelosi" *(reading the screen)*, she's seven—hey, Bob—she's seven, Tina *(reading the screen)* I know, how is she watching CSPAN, Gus, give it—

[He hands her the phone, it falls on the counter.]

Shit, Gus, no, damnit, hand it to me, what are you doin, good Lord, *(to Tina)* well, I don't know if they were just tryin' to make me feel better, but I do feel better—

[During the following, Henri sets the phone down on the counter and exits the kitchen yelling at the grandkids at the TOP OF HER LUNGS. The audience now sees a shirtless Gus wandering around the kitchen making Henri's drink. HENRI's tone calibrates based on the age of the grandchild. (FLETCHER is the baby of the two.)]

Y'ALL KNOCK IT OFF, I WILL BEAT YOUR ASS, Fletcher, baby, what have you got?? Put that down—Ridley, what has he got? Leave him alone, Ridley, I will BEAT YOU, take him out, ooooh, Fletcher, don't touch Meemah's lotion, okay, that's special lotion, Ridley, take him out, what on earth, he is COVERED, he used this whole lotion, where were YOU, Ridley? He smells like a prostitute—take him in that bathroom, the front one, just wipe him down, I told y'all I was on live! Well, what else, a towel, a wash rag! *(while picking the phone back up)* This is a damn disaster! Hey, y'all.

[Henri now has the camera—if possible—even closer to her face than it was before; only half her face is visible in the frame. She reads some of the comments.]

Oh, y'all saw Gus? He's naked from the waist down. Just kiddin'. He's got socks on, Alice! I do have your sweater, yes Millie, it's in my mudroom, you want me to put it out there?

[Henri retrieves the sweater from the mud room and then goes to her closet in search of a bag or a box. The camera is no longer on her face but catching glimpses of her footsteps and the inside of her closet, her hangers, etc., her looking under the bed for a box . . . her glasses fall to the floor, she retrieves them. We may also catch a glimpse of the family pet, ad lib.]

Let me see. I had a box. You know what, I'm just gonna put it in a bag.

[Henri hands the phone to Gus.]

(to GUS) Honey will you hold this phone, while I . . .

[Henri puts the sweater in a plastic grocery bag.]

(to GUS) Oh, you got my drink for me. Thank you, Sugar.

[Henri takes the sweater and her drink through the mudroom to the backdoor. Again, she has no awareness that she is no longer in the frame, we see her slippers and footfall.]

(to GUS) Oh, this drink is nice and strong. *(calling)* I love you!

[Henri steps over the sleeping cat, exits through the screen door onto the patio.]

(to the cat) You gotta stay inside Milo, I know you were born to be wild.

[Henri closes the screen door behind her and walks to the swing where she deposits the sweater.]

Okay, Millie. It's out here.

[We hear the unmistakable sound of Gus having a coughing fit in the kitchen. Henri puts the phone down, face up, and we see the night sky for a few moments, maybe 10 seconds. Henri picks the phone back up as she takes another big sip from her drink.]

(nervously—to Millie) Yeah girl, any time. *(pause)* Sure. Hey ya'll look at what I got.

[Henri points the camera at a house plant out on the porch.]

That man from the nursery left that for me, isn't that nice?

[Henri makes her way to the seating area and sits.]

[Long pause. The sound of WINDCHIMES.]

Y'all. I gotta tell ya somethin'. *(pause)* Gus isn't feelin' so good.

[Long silence while Henri drinks little sips from her glass. She touches a nearby windchime, maybe, looks up at the sky. We sit with her in a prolonged silence as she quietly drifts through all the horrible scenarios, all the images of COVID, an image of Gus through a tiny square pane of glass in a room she will never enter to say goodbye to her husband of 33 years, knowing he is hours from death, her hand on the glass, her husband drifting in and out of consciousness. . . . She may cry, she may throw a glass, she may break down, she may hold strong, she may drift out of the frame, but eventually she remembers there are people watching.]

He's got a little—

[She points to her throat, to indicate coughing.]

n'fever. . . . *(pause)* And he won't—

[Long silence.]

[Looking down at her cell phone now . . .]

98 people on live . . .

[Henri lets the phone rest in her lap for a moment as she finds the "stop" button.]

END OF SCENE

Disappearance of an Activist as Documented by ClassPass Customer Service

Joyce Miller

Production History

Disappearance of an Activist as Documented by ClassPass Customer Service first premiered live over Zoom video conferencing software at the first Planet Connections ZOOMFEST, produced by Glory Kadigan and KM Jones, stage managed by Taylor Mankowski, and directed by Padraic Lillis.

The cast was as follows:

CUSTOMER   Issa Best

Characters

CUSTOMER   A Black activist who is just looking to stay fit on a budget while devoting all their time and resources to fighting systemic injustice. Super socially conscious, tries to be as upbeat, kind, and polite as possible to all essential workers and customer service representatives, whose lives are now surely turned upside down by the pandemic.

Time

Beginning summer 2020 during the coronavirus pandemic lockdown

Place

A Brooklyn apartment, as seen from the camera of a computer. Later, the trunk of a moving vehicle, as seen through the camera of a smartphone.

Scene 1

[CUSTOMER is typing an email to Customer Service while speaking it out loud. Some burn marks on the wallpaper from a small stove fire.]

Dear Customer Service,

First of all—WOW! Thanks so much for giving me a way to stay in my self-care routine on a budget as I work from home and devote my resources to social justice. I'm so grateful ClassPass immediately transitioned into virtual fitness at the start of the pandemic. At the same time, it seems like possible assassination efforts against me by various governments and shadow groups have also made the switch to online.

I signed up for the ClassPass free trial (so grateful for this!) and spent four of my credits on Barry's Bootcamp 5:00 AM Wednesday morning class via Zoom. The instructor was amazing! I was totally sweating by the first three minutes and my glutes felt like they were about to fall off! "Yeah everybody!" Barry screamed, "Let's set this workout on fire!!!" But then, assuming his name was actually Barry, Barry's tone shifted. The music became a low hypnotic throb and Barry's words were, "Now we're gonna bring the heat . . . for real. . . . I want you to look around the room, and grab a lighter, or a candle, or a gas stove, and set your home on fi-ire so you can feel the burn!!! DO IT! OR I'LL GET YOU! I KNOW WHERE YOU LIVE!"

The thing is, Barry was so inspiring that I totally did everything he said. I know that's on me, in a sense. At the same time, culturally, we put a lot of trust in fitness instructors, and I feel Barry may have violated a boundary. I'm not sure how I'm going to explain this to my renter's insurance, but somewhere, a line was crossed, and it's unclear who's responsible.

Now, maybe Barry was using a fitness metaphor, or I'm new to the branded language (I know Barry's has a cult following). If so, I apologize for the long email and appreciate your clarification. Otherwise, if you find

I am correct in suspecting that Barry did not adhere to ClassPass expectations and protocol, I would love to have the credits refunded.

Thank You!!!

[BLACKOUT.]

Scene 2

[CUSTOMER is typing an email to Customer Service while speaking it out loud. Some burn marks on the wallpaper from a small stove fire. Some shattered, crooked photographs of an ill-fated romance hang from the walls in the background.]

Dear ClassPass Customer Services,

I hate to write a second time, as I'm only a free trial member, but wanted to touch base. I don't normally do this, but at a holiday healing breath workshop that I booked through ClassPass, the instructor and I obtained consent, in our mutual joy, to spend mindful company with one another outside the class.

After a period of finding this to both of our liking, we chose to consciously couple and raise a child together. One week ago, my partner suddenly announced that they were leaving me and taking the child. Since then, I have been unable to discover their whereabouts. *(Takes moment. Devastated.)* Looking back, I came to the realization that all of our interactions consisted of my response to leading statements about various underground movements, insistence I always be the one to initiate our meetings, and no digital paper trail of communication. I am now attempting to determine whether this is an indication that we weren't sufficiently communicating our needs to one another, or that in fact my ClassPass instructor was a secret police honeytrap using advanced psychological warfare to engage me in a romantic relationship in order to gather information on my political affiliations. Wow. You really do teach others how to treat you.

As I take the time and space to regroup, I feel I ought to let ClassPass know, as well as see if I can extend the free trial from where I left off, and possibly get those eight credits refunded.

Thanks!!!

[BLACKOUT.]

Scene 3

[CUSTOMER is typing an email to Customer Service while speaking it out loud. Some burn marks on the wallpaper from a small stove fire. Some shattered, crooked photographs of an ill-fated romance hang from the walls in the background. Portions of the wall are covered in aluminum foil.]

Dear ClassPass,

I decided to give Barry's At-Home a second chance. It got me right into my cardio zone, and I was just feeling this release from all the stress, about, you know, my ex and stuff. Then, Barry's voice switched from motivational to menacing. His head swiveled around until he was directly facing me, somehow able to make eye contact right through the screen, and I was locked together with him in an unblinking stare. "Execute the kill mission without fail," Barry hissed. The next thing I remember is that I awoke to a low frequency sonic pulse that obstructed my hearing for a full ten minutes. Either this was one of the most intense full body strengtheners I've ever had, or Barry's Bootcamp is attempting to use me for MKUltra experiments. Unless the strange echoes were because my Netflix unpaused during a bout of dehydration.

Not sure if this would merit the return of my 12 credits. My leg muscles are very sore, in a good way. I'm putting it out there, depending on the ClassPass credit refund policy.

The best advice I can glean from the MKUltra survivor activist community is to cover the inside of my apartment in tinfoil and try not to react in any way that gives the CIA an excuse to discredit my sanity.

[Looks around suspiciously, pulls a tinfoil helmet or hat from off screen, secures it on head]

Physical fitness is a pillar of the people's autonomy and, though it needs to be decolonized, I appreciate the work you do in making it accessible. I am also curious if you are able to refer me to an attorney, in the event that my roommate's sudden disappearance is related to this workout.

Best.

[Covers webcam with a piece of tape]

[BLACKOUT.]

Scene 4

[CUSTOMER is typing an email to Customer Service while speaking it out loud. Some burn marks on the wallpaper from a small stove fire. Some shattered, crooked photographs of an ill-fated romance hang from the walls in the background. Portions of the wall are covered in tinfoil. Computer printouts of racy photos with CUSTOMER's head photoshopped onto the body are visible.]

ClassPass,

It has come to my attention that there are screenshots of my recent Class-Pass experience photoshopped into disturbing images on a Romanian fetish site.

I am unsure whether the Zoom Room was hacked on my end or the studio's. Luckily, a friend happened upon the pictures through a series of coincidences that I won't bore you with.

I am informing you for the sake of future students. *(Sound of a text message alert. Glances at phone.)* I also wonder if there is a way to keep BogdanMoldovaTrapKing666@gmail.com from asking me to be his friend. I was definitely hoping to have the 16 credits refunded on this one.

Thanks.

[BLACKOUT.]

Scene 5

[CUSTOMER is typing an email to Customer Service while speaking it out loud. Some burn marks on the wallpaper from a small stove fire. Some shattered, crooked photographs of an ill-fated romance hang from the walls in the background. Portions of the wall are covered in tinfoil. Computer printouts of racy photos with CUSTOMER's head photoshopped onto the body are visible. Something like The Red Army Choir plays in the background.]

ClassPass Customer Service,

I did not realize that Jivamukti yoga is the yoga where the Red Army Choir is played on repeat, with students encouraged to alert the instructor of any injuries or anti-American sentiments. I was blown away by poses I'd never heard of, like "The Guillotine," "The Pitchfork," and "The Death of the Middle Class Pig." We ended with a "Dancing Among Our

Comrades Upon the Burning Pyre of Capitalism Guided Aromatherapy Visualization." I will make sure to give the teacher a five star review for vigilance—but figured I should check in with ClassPass to verify I clicked the right link.

Best, and please stay safe!

[BLACKOUT.]

Scene 6

[CUSTOMER is typing an email to Customer Service while speaking it out loud. Some burn marks on the wallpaper from a small stove fire. Some shattered, crooked photographs of an ill-fated romance hang from the walls in the background. Portions of the wall are covered in tinfoil. Computer printouts of racy photos with CUSTOMER's head photoshopped onto the body are visible. Something like The Red Army Choir plays in the background. Something small and flying whizzes by CUSTOMER's head.]

Dear ClassPass Customer Service,

At first, I got really into the first fifteen minutes of Pure Barre Home. The teacher even called out my name, in a manner that was harsh, yet chipper. She demanded that I move my head three inches to the left, then a little to the right, then told me to hold still.

I thought, "Oh, rad. The video instructor is giving me a posture adjustment."

It was then that a miniature drone bearing a small syringe came whizzing towards me through the open window. Could be Pure Coincidence. Apologies if it was part of the class, because in the moment I was so startled, I smashed it out of the air, and wanted to ensure that I won't be fined for any damage.

Thank You!

[Tries to capture the mini-drone.]

[BLACKOUT.]

Scene 7

[CUSTOMER's face is seen up close through the camera of a smartphone with the shadow of light through burlap cast across their face. They are in the locked compartment of an unspecified moving vehicle and the screen jostles a bit.]

Hey ClassPass,

I just want to say that my fitness journey with ClassPass has really been transformative, and that your customer service department went above and beyond. I took your advice and invoked the Freedom of Information Act, and while government agencies can "neither confirm nor deny" that I am the target of an investigation, my endorphins are giving me such an amazing high right now.

While I am aware this isn't normally allowed, I wonder if it would be possible for the remaining credits from my free ClassPass trial to rollover one more month, since some of my ClassPass experiences do not reflect all that I feel ClassPass has to offer. Unless you can confirm that my being in a locked compartment of this moving vehicle is part of the CrossFit class I began live streaming 45 minutes ago. Perhaps studio reps are collecting students individually to conclude our workout in the park as a group.

Also, there's a bag of coarsely woven fabric that was placed over my head, which I'm not sure is in accordance with Personal Protective Equipment guidelines. If you could let me know whether this seems normal and I'm just being weird, or if I should have my credits refunded. I need to make sure my card on file isn't automatically charged once the free trial ends.

Sincerely,

[CUSTOMER is interrupted by the sound of a phone battery dying and BLACKOUT.]

END

BRIG

J. Merrill Motz

Production History

Independently filmed and released through papersoul.org, October 1–31, 2021. Editing and titles by Derek Lee Miller, poster artwork by TJ Turner & TJ Turner Pictures.

The cast was as follows:

BO'SUN   J. Merrill Motz

Characters

BO'SUN   The boatswain of *Searcy*, in charge of hull maintenance and all below decks. 30s–40s, bedraggled and grizzled from years at sea. Long hair and beard.

Time

The Golden Age of Piracy, live on Zoom.

Place

The *Searcy*, adrift in the Atlantic Ocean somewhere between Cornwall and Antigua. Specifically, below deck of the *Searcy*. More specifically, locked inside the brig of the *Searcy*. Most specifically, only one visible corner locked inside brig of the *Searcy*.

NOTE: This script was conceived, written, memorized, and filmed in less than ten days on a zero-dollar budget in the summer of 2021. Due to the tight (self-imposed) time constraints, the author made the decision to not spend any precious and dwindling time researching the accuracy of his nautical terms or jargon, siding instead with his own limited knowledge of ships and sailing, far too many sea shanties bouncing around in his head, and the old adage of "if it sounds right, be confident, and say it convincingly." So many details will appear off. In the grander theme of the piece and the character, it felt more fitting to simply be close enough. All of this to say, yes, the author is aware you don't "trim the mains" to go faster. Roll with it!

SCENE 1—DAY ONE

[The video comes to life. A wall is seen, bars shadowed upon it. This is the brig, below decks of the Searcy. *Strange noises are heard above. Eventually, heavy breathing. A bedraggled face comes into view. Far, far too close to the camera. Basically all that can be seen is an eyeball, long gray hair, and a shaggy brown and gray beard. This is BO'SUN, locked inside. He whispers, shaking, terrified.]*

Shh! Shh! They're still up there . . . they're still walking the deck! They look like the crew . . . they look like me boys . . . but they don't live. They're dead! Stab me eyes, they're all dead! Shh! Shh! *(pause)* They still stand, they still walk . . . but they don't speak. They just stare. They stare, but they don't see . . . they hear, but they don't respond. I'm the only one left . . . what will they do with me . . . what will they do with ol' matey the Bo'sun. . . . Shh! *(pause)* I'll tell the tale. If they find me here, I'll at least have the tale told. These will be me messages in a bottle. . . . Shh!

There be no one else. Not one. Cap'n Archambault . . . Sully the cook . . . First Mate Stanyard . . . even that bastard Blacketer . . . there be no one left. I snuck below decks, barred the trap behind me. Hugged the hull and crept through the cargo holds, quieter than any bilge rat stowin' away in the bread stores, and made me way to the brig. Locked meself within. No one knows below decks better than ol' matey Bo'sun. They've not left the top decks. So here I'll wait.

They have to sleep eventually . . . maybe I can . . . maybe I can make me way topside once they sleep . . . but do the dead even sleep? How does that old story go. . . . Shh! I hear them! Shh!

[SHIFT]

SCENE 2—DAY EIGHT

[Bo'sun sits, as before, sucking on his pipe.]

They don't sleep. I could hear them shuffling about all night, and I hear them still. I don't know where they're going or what they're doing, but they never. Stop. Movin'. I haven't ventured out of this cell in at least a week. Luckily I can reach Sully's barrels of dried meat from here. *(He reaches off and brings back a piece of jerky and eats it.)* And luckily . . . *(He shows a bottle of rum.)* Let no man be wanting that has grub for his hunger and grog for his thirst. *(He takes a pull.)* 'Tis a good thing ye can't see the bucket I use when I'm done with both of these. But the stench is enough to keep them dead bastards away from this cell, I gather. *(He sucks his pipe.)* I still puff on me pipe here, even though I ran out of matches three days ago . . . which is fine, as I ran out of anything to burn five days ago. But it gives me comfort, it does. *(pause)* They've not found me yet. They're all still topside. Let them rot in the sun, say I. Only me ol' matey Bo'sun can be king below decks. I'd make a fine second mate, I would, but I can still be king below decks. *(pause)* It's all that bastard Blacketer's fault. It must be. Never trust no silver spoon lime juicer, says I. Can't even grow a beard. Never trust any salt that can't grow a proper set of whiskers after seventy days asea, says I. *(pause)* Aye. It's all that bastard Blacketer's fault. I've no idea how, but I've naught but time to parse it out. *(pause)* They're not even trying to get below decks. They're not even trying to find me. Me! Ol' matey Bo'sun! Have they forgotten me so soon?

[SHIFT]

SCENE 3—DAY TEN

The *Searcy* set out from Cornwall with thirty-six souls aboard. Cap'n Archambault, his first mate Mr. Stanyard, second mate Blacketer, Sully the cook, Wyatt at the helm, myself as the Bo'sun, ol' matey the Bo'sun . . . eight hands below deck, twelve above, and ten upon the rigs.

There's not one left alive now.

Was it a storm, ye ask? There's always a storm in these stories, they say. No. Not a storm. Brigands, then? Pirates? Corsairs? We'd be so lucky. Was it a plague? If it were plague, do ye think I'd be spared to relate the tale? Some fell beast of the deep? A kraken to squeeze our hull to pieces, knock our masts asunder like kindling? Or some giant leviathan to swallow grown men by the score like so many kippers? Don't be daft. Those are only stories!

Was it a . . . was it a curse, then? *(pause)* A curse? *(pause)* Aye, there's the rub . . . when I went topside that morning to find every member of this crew dead on their feet, the sails unlashed and flapping in the breeze, the *Searcy* all but dead in the water, weeks from any shore . . . I knew it could only be a curse. But how? I still need time.

[SHIFT]

SCENE 4—DAY FIFTEEN

[BO'SUN leans against the wall, looking pensive. He takes a deep breath. It is time.]

'Twas near dawn on the eighth day when I was woke by the all hands. We scrambled topside to see what was spied. "Sails, ho!" came the cry from the nest. "To the fore! Sails, ho!" Every man stood in a line, pressed against the rail, scannin' the horizon, but there was naught to be seen but the gray light of the dawn upon the waves. I shoved Blacketer aside to get a better spot, even though there was naught to see even closer, but it felt good to remind him of his place.

Cap'n Archambault was at the fore deck, his glass to his eye. "It's the *Threnody!*" he finally said. And all the men along the rail began to mutter . . . the *Threnody?* She's our sister ship, she should be forty days ahead of us on the return leg from Antigua! "The signal bell!" said Cap'n Archambault, "Mr. Stanyard, let her ring out!" First Mate Stanyard was quick to spring to the main mast and gave the bell six long, loud peals. We stood stock still, craning our ears to hear any bell in response. "Again!" ordered the Cap'n, and Mr. Stanyard gave six more rings. Still, naught but the lapping of the waves. "Again!" came the order, and again the ringing, and again naught in return.

"Cap'n," came the reedy voice of Blacketer beside me, "perhaps we are still too far off for the bell. Perhaps a cannon blast can travel the distance better?"

"Oh, 'perhaps,'" I scoffed and spat over the rail. "Perhaps a waste of good powder and shot, says I."

"One cannon, then, sir," Blacketer added.

"Surely we can spare one ration of powder, without shot,"—oh, the look he gave ol' matey Bo'sun!—"for the sake of our sister ship?"

"Surely!" Scoffed and spat over the rail again, did I. "Surely no less a waste, Cap'n Archambault, sir."

Cap'n Archambault stood still as a statue, the glass still to his eye. Finally, "A fine idea, Mr. Blacketer. One report, starboard alee. Lively now, lads."

And it was Blacketer that then turned to the men and called "You heard the skipper, boys, set one cannon to call!"

Who is he to give orders? Thinks he's suddenly First Mate, does he, Mr. Stanyard himself, does he, sitting at the Cap'n's right hand? Wash, says I.

But the boys set to work, and it was only a few moments before the dawn was split in half with the crack from the cannon spewing fire to the skies.

Damned things always set me ears to ringing, they does. But as the echo faded, and the *Threnody* made no reply, we looked to Cap'n Archambault. Finally, he took the glass from his eye. "Trim the mains, lads! We need to get closer!" And Blacketer, again, was the one to call "All hands, all hands! Full speed ahead!" Who does he think he is . . . but away went the lads, and the *Searcy* took to the breeze and all but flew as the gray of dawn began to lighten. Now we could spy the *Threnody* on the horizon, a tiny speck growing larger as we grew closer, closer.

"The signal bell, Mr. Stanyard!" cried the Cap'n, the glass glued to his eye once more. "Let her ring again!" there was something in his voice I did not like, I didn't, so I went to his side.

"What is it, sir?" says I. "What do ye see?"

And the Cap'n didn't reply, as is his right, says I, as skipper of the *Searcy*, but instead called out "Again, Mr. Stanyard! Ring again!"

I waited for the usual no response from the *Threnody* before asking again, "What do ye see, sir?"

It took a third and then a fourth and then a fifth repeating before he finally replied, "They're all topside."

"Sir?" says I, not understanding.

"All of the crew. Cap'n Marksbury. His mate Mr. Swan. They're all just . . . standing on the deck."

"What," jokes I, "you're saying every man aboard the *Threnody* has lost his hearing at once? Going about their duties on deck without hearing a cannon rip the morning in twain?"

The look the Cap'n gave me chilled me to me very soul. He shoved the glass to my chest.

"Not deaf," says he. "Not moving," he extended an arm and finger to point, "Spy for yourself."

I put the glass to me eye, to see what he meant.

Upon closer inspection I could see that . . . there was something wrong with their sails. They weren't lashed to catch any breeze, but, no! No! they were hanging in tatters . . . holes bigger than a man covering their whole surface. They'd never catch a breeze with those again. And all upon her deck . . . every man aboard the *Threnody* stood in a line, pressed against the rail, as we had been only moments before, silent, still as the grave, all their eyes fixed upon the *Searcy*, upon us, as we approach.

"God's bones," says I. And Cap'n Archambault ran to the prow of the *Searcy*, his hands cupped to his beard. "Ahoy, *Threnody*!" he called. "Ahoy, Cap'n Marksbury! Mr. Swan, ahoy! Answer me true, boys, anyone aboard! Ahoooy!"

No voice answered. But the ship drew closer, closer.

And no man at the rail made any move, gave any sign that they could hear us or could respond.

And I knew, lads. I knew staring at their stone faces watching us get closer, closer, until we'd be too close to escape . . . that ship was cursed. That ship was cursed and soon we too would join them!

"The signal, Mr. Stanyard," cried the Cap'n, "let her ring out!"

But I heard me own voice cry out, "Not the bell! The cannons! Ready the cannons, boys! Blow the damned ship out of the water!"

"Belay that!" roared the Cap'n, "Mr. Stanyard!"

"The cannons!" says I, "Ready the cannons!"

"No swab to lay hands on them guns!" roared the Cap'n. "Mr. Stanyard, ring the signal bell! Mr. Blacketer, relieve the bo'sun of his duties!"

Oh, ye should have seen the look upon that bastard Blacketer's face! The pleasure he was going to take in finally clapping me in irons and finally throwin' me ol' matey bo'sun into the brig, but I was fit to be damned fore I let that lily white banker's son stop me from sending that cursed ship to splinters.

Before he could lay hands upon me, I took the Cap'n's glass, and I swung it with all the might the lord god gave me, and struck the second mate across his pate sendin' him staggerin' to the deck.

I didn't need the glass no more . . . we were close enough to see all the crew standing as gargoyles watching us get nearer, nearer.

"Fire the ship!" cried I, "Don't let them near! Come on, lads, ready the guns!"

But before Cap'n could say otherwise, there was a flash aboard the *Threnody*, and all three of her masts erupted in flames . . . those hangin' sails now alive, flappin' and spreading fire from stem to stern. None of us saw how the fire could have started so quickly, but it was mere seconds before the entire deck of the *Threnody* was ablaze, the flames so high you couldn't even see the crew pressed against the rail. Almost. The fires were so high and so bright that the only dawn we had that day was red sky and smoke.

By the time the *Searcy* pulled alongside her sister ship, there was nothing left of the *Threnody* to save.

"Full stop!" cried Cap'n Archambault. "Drop anchor!"

"Sir?" asked First Mate Stanyard.

"Someone might yet live!" replied the skipper. "We have to wait," and he went back to calling into the smoke "Ahoy! Anyone alive! Ahoy!"

Mr. Stanyard called to us, "Look to the water, lads! Look for anyone alive!"

And the boys pressed to the rail again, the necks craned downward, their throats coughing in the thick smoke.

Not I, though. Not ol' matey Bo'sun. I knew that no survivor should set cursed foot upon the decks of the *Searcy*. If that blasted Blacketer hadn't stopped me, I could have fired the guns and destroyed the ship before we even got this close, I just know it, lads.

We were there for hours, it seems. I'm not sure how long exactly, but long enough for Blacketer to come to his sense and join in the search, for it was his reedy voice that called out "Here! Here! It's first mate Mr. Swan! Drop a line, boys, bring him aboard!"

And I was running to his spot at the rail, "No!" cries I, "he's cursed, he is! Don't bring him on the ship!"

But Cap'n Archambault answered, "Belay the Bo'sun! This is your Cap'n! Bring him on board!"

And so Mr. Swan was laid upon the deck. His shirt was gone, and all upon his chest and arms and back and face and neck were a map of tattoos, hundreds of painted pictures of sailin' ships, and waves, and islands, and sea serpents, from a hundred different ports of call. But his eyes were open. And his painted chest rose and fell with breathing. Cap'n Archambault knelt beside him.

"Mr. Swan," said he, "Paddy, me lad, it's Cap'n Archambault of the *Searcy*. Where is Cap'n Marksbury, man? What happened? The *Threnody* burns, why didn't you tell us you were in need?"

And Mr. Swan fixed his eyes on Cap'n Archambault, and though he breathed, he spoke not a word.

"Speak, Paddy! Tell us what happened aboard the *Threnody*!"

And still Swan said nothin'. But he shook with some sort of tremor, maybe a shiver from being in the brine for so long before we hauled him aboard, but I knew different.

I knew he was already dead, damn him, his damned body just didn't know it yet. Cursed to live long enough to bring his death aboard the *Searcy* for all of us.

He shook with tremors again, and Cap'n Archambault clasped his hand tight, and Swan drew him close.

"What is it, lad? Speak, lad, please!"

But Swan only raised his other arm, and trembling, pointed a finger at all the tattoos covering his chest and neck and arms, tracing a line from one shoulder down his trunk across and up his chest, before he shook once more, and the arm dropped limp to the deck.

Cap'n Archambault stayed at his side a moment longer before taking to his feet, saying loud enough for all to hear. "He'll have a sailor's farewell. I'll have the Bo'sun make the arrangements. Weigh anchor, boys, we sail for Antigua. There's nothing more to be done here this day."

Now, I would protest this assignment, but know better than to question my Cap'n's orders, thank ye, and am just grateful enough he's forgotten he wanted Blacketer to clap me in irons only an hour before. So I knelt beside the body to prepare him for his final swim.

"Why," I heard Blacketer's reedy voice say beside me. "Why didn't he say anything?"

I looked up at his lily white face, streaked with blood from where I brained him with the spyglass, and could not help but grin at him.

"Because he no longer has no tongue, sir," says I, turning Swan's gaping skull to face him, "he's chewed it off, he has."

And Blacketer somehow grew even paler, put a hand to his mouth, and ran to lose his supper over the rail.

Perhaps that's why he doesn't wear a beard.

But now you see . . . you see how this is all that bastard Blacketer's fault. I tried to destroy the ship. I tried to tell them to leave Swan off the ship. But Blacketer interfered. And now he's as dead as the rest of them. Good riddance, says I.

[SHIFT]

SCENE 5—DAY TWENTY

[BO'SUN is drunk, singing, gesturing with the rum.]

(sings) Put him in the brig until he's sober . . .
Put him in the brig until he's sober . . .
Put him in the brig until he's sober . . .
(yells) EAR-LY IN THE MOR-NIN'!
WAY-HEY, AND UP SHE RISES!
WAY-HEY, AND UP SHE RISES!
WAY-HEY, AND UP SHE RISES!
EAR-LY IN THE MOR-NIN'!

[Pause. He listens.]

Nothin'. Bloody bastards . . .

[SHIFT]

SCENE 6—DAY TWENTY-FOUR

[BO'SUN puffs his pipe. He is sober again. Mostly.]

When I was . . . a lad, a wee lad, me father took me on a trip to London town. I'd never seen so many people crowdin' the streets. And on a corner near the market there was a lady from the Apennines singin' to the people. She wore a massive dress, covered in drapes and folds. On each of the folds were painted pictures, pictures of sailin' ships and islands and voyages upon the sea. And she sang in a language I couldn't understand, but as she sang, she would sweep the dress and unfold the drapes, and show different pictures underneath, and twist, and turn, and dance, and twirl, showing new images all the while, and I could tell the pictures she was showin' us were telling the story of what she was singin', even though I couldn't understand the words she was sayin'.

When she got to the end, I asked me father for a copper to give her, and he gave me instead a silver, and told me, "that's Cantastoria, lad. Story-singing. Why don't you stay here and listen to her tell her story a few more times, see if ye can't parse it out. There's a good lad," and he disappeared into the crowd. Cantastoria . . . I rolled the word over in me head a few times. Cantastoria . . . I watched that woman sing her story over and over, and I do believe I was able to parse out the story, even though I knew they were just pictures upon a dress and not the words she was singin', her story was still passed to me, even in my ignorance.

The story of the second mate of a ship who was torn in his love for a woman on shore, and his love for the sea. But while the woman loved him dearly, he would keep spurning her to return to the sea, even though the sea is vast, and indifferent, and cares not for any man that sails her surface any more than it cares for any fish that swims in her depths.

If only the sailor would stay, said she, they would be together in her home on the beach, and he could see his true love's waves from her window every mornin', but he could be safe on dry land, with her, and happy, and they could be buried side by side when the day would finally come.

But of course, the sailor could not choose such a mundane life on land, and returned to his ship, where his ship hit a storm—there's always a storm in these stories, they say—and all souls aboard were lost. And instead of being buried next to his love on land, he became just another countless soul lost forever to the depths . . . nameless, futureless . . . for the sea is always hungry. You could empty every graveyard, open every crypt, scatter the ash of every man, woman, and child, from all of recorded time and you would never fill her up.

I added this last bit meself, even as a lad, I had a bit of a morbid streak.

When I paid her my father's silver, she was so excited, chattering on in that Apennine tongue, but I wanted to know if that's what her story was actually about, but she did not ken the King's English, and I could tell she was only excited for the silver more and not the questions from some whelp.

Shortly me father returned, drunk off his heels, as usual, to gather me for the long journey home to Padstow. And I asked me father if he thought that's what the story was about, he cuffed me behind the ears and told me

I'd be so lucky to ever make second mate upon a sailing ship. "Ye'd probably fail at bein' a bo'sun, ye would."

Still.

It's her story I keep with me, true or no, even as I could hear the sea calling to me just as it did the second mate in the story. I've no idea what happened to that lady from the Apennines, but I'd like to think her story lives on in my remembering. But I guess . . . I guess now it dies here with me in this brig.

Hmm.

Wonder why I thought of that story now, after all this time. Hmm. All in good time.

[SHIFT]

SCENE 7—DAY TWENTY-SIX

[BO'SUN looks anxious, restless, paranoid.]

I think I understand. When I was preparing Mr. Swan to be returned to sea, I couldn't help it, I read his tattoos. I remembered him pointing to his tattoos as he died in Cap'n Archambault's arms and I thought the tattoos must hold some sort of answer. In reading the pictures on his body, a story began to take shape.

Even though there was no singin' lady from the Apennines, there was only the *Threnody* burning off our stern. Still . . . I saw a story.

The story of a sailor coming to port and visiting a soothsayer, and the soothsayer saw his future. A future of doom and ruin. For the sailor was cursed, and there was no escape. But the sailor mocked the curse, and the soothsayer, and returned to his ship, where the ship hit a storm—there's always a storm, they say—and all souls aboard were lost . . . except the sailor, who was left alone, adrift, clinging to the ship's mast for dear life, a tiny speck on the endless tides of the hungry sea. This last image, of the sailor clinging to the mast, was a fresh tattoo on Swan's back . . . the flesh still raw from receiving it likely in port at Cornwall before we caught up to them. But here it was, plain as the red dawn around me as I knelt over his fresh corpse . . . Swan had finished the story of the curse and then brought that story aboard his ship for all his crewmates.

And that night . . . that night, I relayed the tale of Swan's tattoos to all me boys in the mess over grub . . . all me boys who laughed at ol' matey

Bo'sun, makin' up tales from a dead man's skin . . . tales I meself had brought aboard the *Searcy* . . . for it was I that spotted Swan's tattooed body bobbing in the waves alongside us and called for him to be brought aboard, me head still splittin' from where Blacketer had brained me with the spyglass, because I tried to stop him from firing our cannons on our sister ship. . . . *(He breaks down. He recovers.)* No. No. It's that bastard Blacketer's fault. It must be.

[SHIFT]

SCENE 8—DAY THIRTY

[BO'SUN looks as if he hasn't slept in days.]

Why was I spared? Why did the curse take everyone aboard the *Threnody* and the *Searcy* both but it spared ol' matey Bo'sun? Because dead men tell no tales. How can a curse survive if no one knows about it? How can a story be heard if there's no one alive left to tell it? A story needs to be told to be heard. What if a story is just as hungry as the sea?

[He chuckles. He rubs his head. His arm is covered in bloody cuts resembling hash marks.]

And here be I . . . prattlin' on . . .

[SHIFT]

SCENE 9—DAY THIRTY-THREE

She wasn't happy for the silver. She was happy because someone had heard her story. The story. The Cantastoria. The story in pictures even if the particulars aren't correct, if things, details aren't correct, it matters not . . . the story is still told. The curse is still passed. Across language. Across time. Across tattoos. Pictures in tattoos or pictures you see in your mind Pictures taken in me closet . . . a closet that looks nothin' like the brig of a ship . . . across a shoddy pirate accent. Even if I didn't even live in the times of the story . . . I felt just as alone as a sailor locked in the belly of his own ship. . . . *(He breaks down. He recovers.)* I needed to share this story that has cursed me . . . for this story has cursed me . . . *(He taps his head.)* Up here . . .

[He points through camera to the audience watching.]

And now all of you have heard it, too . . .

[SHIFT]

SCENE 10—DAY THIRTY-EIGHT

[The back wall. BO'SUN is heard laughing. Maniacally, nearly inhuman. His face comes into frame, streaked with blood. His eyes mad, his teeth red. He makes no attempt to lower his voice anymore.]

I know how it ends! I know how it ends! *(yells)* Do ye hear me, top side!? All watch on decks! All watch ahoy! I KNOW HOW IT FUCKING ENDS!!

[SHIFT]

SCENE 11—DAY FORTY

[The back wall. Silence. Strange noises above. BO'SUN is nowhere to be seen or heard. Camera fades.]

[END OF PLAY]

Short Plays

Baby's Breath

Arlene Hutton

Production History

Baby's Breath was developed as part of New Circle Theatre Company's 7 Over 7 project in June 2020. It premiered online for New Circle Theatre Company and was directed by Melanie S. Armer.

The cast was as follows:

WENDELL   William English
DENISE   Debra Kay Anderson
KENDRA   Kimmarie Bowens

Characters

WENDELL   a retired fireman living in the woods near Palatka, FL, white, 50s, 60s.
DENISE   his younger sister, lives in Charleston, SC, white, 50s.
KENDRA   Wendell's ex-wife, lives in New Orleans, Black, 50s

Time

Early summer, 2020.

Place

Online. (Palatka, FL; Charleston, SC; and New Orleans, LA)

[WENDELL and DENISE, mid-conversation, in separate spaces: live in separate pools of light or viewed through an online platform, as if they were talking on FaceTime or Zoom or whatever is current. WENDELL is at his home in Palatka, FL. DENISE is at her home in Charleston, SC.]

WENDELL You know, my picture is out there on the Facebook now and. . . . Here's the thing, I keep getting friend requests from women. I swear, Denise, every single one is just gorgeous! Well, you know me, Baby Sis, I can be friends with anyone. So some of the requests I accept, thinking I might have an enlightening conversation.

DENISE You said you were going to come visit me this weekend.

WENDELL It's a dry weather alert, Baby Sis. Fire season in Florida. Have to keep the brush all cleared. Have to watch for smoke. Not that I'm on call any more. I miss fighting fires. Miss my buddies.

DENISE I'm only four hours away.

WENDELL Charleston didn't treat me and Kendra very well.

DENISE About Kendra—

WENDELL Haven't talked to Kendra in years. Feels like I haven't talked to a woman in forever, unless her kitty cat was stuck up a tree. But these gals on the Facebook, every time so far—and in a very short time—they are talking about a far more personal relationship than just "friends"!

DENISE Wendell. It's a scam.

WENDELL I promise you I have not said the first suggestive word. I know I'm not some young good-looking guy. And there's all these other guys in and out of the Facebook way more stylish, more inclined to have more in common with these lovely ladies. You gotta see their pictures. Wish I could show you. You know, you could come visit me.

DENISE You live in the woods in a trailer.

WENDELL It's a doublewide.

DENISE Wendell, we have to talk.

WENDELL We sure do have to talk. I need some advice on these Facebook women.

DENISE These "women" are not who they say they are.

WENDELL   Oh, it's real. Just before you zoomed in I was messaging to one young lady, thirty-four, she said. That's her age, not her bra size. Look at me, Little Sis, I'm messaging and Zooming! What about that! Well, almost right away this gal begins calling me "dearest." Then she up and wants me to be her husband! I told her I'm married—I wonder if Kendra is on the Facebook—you know I never signed those divorce papers—

DENISE   Wendell—

WENDELL   If I sound in any way like I'm gloating, I'm not. I know I'm a homely looking country guy. The fire department kept me too busy to think about women, but now I'm retired. . . . I'm telling you, Baby Sis, these women are beautiful.

DENISE   They may not even be women, but people posting fake photos.

WENDELL   One gal asked, "what do you want from me?" I had to nicely remind her that she contacted me first. I said, "I was just hoping for a friendly and enlightening conversation." She asked me for three hundred dollars. I told her if it was an emergency to go to her local church for help. I haven't heard any more from her.

DENISE   Did you send them money?

WENDELL   I'm not an idiot. But I talk to them. I talk from the heart—give them some good words, compliment them, listen—

DENISE   Don't feel bad. We've all been taken advantage of while trying to do a good deed.

WENDELL   Have never been in such a situation before.

DENISE   You're a naturally kind person and you believe what people tell you and you want to help them. You're always trying to do the right thing. Always. So let's talk about—

WENDELL   When these women tell me their stories I really feel for them. So what if some of them just need someone to talk to?

DENISE   I'm telling you not one of these women is who she says she is.

WENDELL   Well, sure seems like wanting to be my way of friendly is not what they want.

DENISE   You've got to delete all these people.

WENDELL   You never trust anyone, do you? That's because you're Miss Independent. You never need any help.

DENISE   I need help now. I need you to come live with me.

WENDELL   I'm fine.

DENISE   Well, I'm not.

WENDELL   What are you talking about?

DENISE   I need you to . . . to think about where you're going to live now. Now that you're retired. Wait. There's someone calling in who I think wants to talk to you.

[The light or screen reveals KENDRA, a Black woman. A long pause.]

WENDELL   Well, if it isn't Kendra.

KENDRA   Hey, Wendell.

WENDELL   Well. Kendra. How the hell are you? You're still beautiful. You look the same.

KENDRA   You sure don't. Are you doing okay, Wendell?

WENDELL   I'm just an old man living alone in the woods. Near Palatka.

KENDRA   The woods sounds like a nice place to be these days.

DENISE   I have a beautiful garden here in Charleston. *(No one speaks.)* So, Wendell, Kendra and I were talking a few minutes ago—

WENDELL   Didn't know you two were in touch.

KENDRA   Denise called me out of the blue.

DENISE   Found her number on the internet. Kendra lives in New Orleans.

WENDELL   New Orleans. Mighty fine honeymoon. Remember?

DENISE   Were you there during Katrina? My lord, did you wind up in that stadium? What a horrible thing. Wendell, Kendra and I want to talk to you about—

WENDELL   *(to KENDRA)* You still a nurse? I'm retired from the fire department. When you're retired every day is Saturday.

KENDRA   Denise thinks you need to come live with her.

WENDELL   Kendra, I wasn't much of a man to you and your folks back in the day, but I found my calling.

DENISE   And now he deserves a comfortable retirement. Tell Kendra about all your awards and commendations.

WENDELL   I looked for you on the Facebook.

KENDRA   I'm not on—

DENISE   *(interrupting)* Wendell, remember how you always said that Kendra was the smartest person you knew?

WENDELL   I never could figure women out. They're all smarter than me.

DENISE   Then you need to listen to us. Remember how you always said, "I'll ask Kendra." *(to KENDRA)* He doesn't listen to me.

KENDRA   You never listened to him.

DENISE   I listen.

KENDRA   You know, Denise, I thought you reached out to me because you'd been listening to your TV. That you heard my brother was finally exonerated. It's been all over the news. Especially in Charleston.

DENISE   I've been sick.

WENDELL   Terrell got out of prison?

KENDRA   So let me get this straight. You were just calling to ask me to say "hey, Wendell, I know I haven't talked to you or your sister in years, but I think you should move in with her in Charleston, a town you hate." *(a beat)* I'm going to say good-bye now.

WENDELL   Don't go.

DENISE   I always said your brother was innocent.

KENDRA   No, you didn't. No, you didn't, Denise. You never once said that. And you know what else? You never liked me. *(DENISE starts to respond.)* Let me finish. You never liked the fact that Wendell married someone who looked like me.

DENISE   Well, thank goodness you didn't have a child together.

KENDRA   Same old Denise.

DENISE   You used to be kind.

KENDRA   I used to hold my tongue.

DENISE   Wendell, I need you to come take care of me. Kendra, I had the virus. With pneumonia. Maybe some heart damage. I have trouble catching my breath. Sometimes I have to be on oxygen. My doctor says I shouldn't live alone. You're a nurse, Kendra, you know what I'm going through. Tell Wendell it's time for him to come back to Charleston.

KENDRA   I can't help you.

DENISE   Sometimes it's like I can't breathe.

KENDRA   I know how you feel. I really do. But you never bother to listen to how I feel.

[KENDRA's light (or screen) goes dark.]

WENDELL   For a moment I thought I had a chance again.

DENISE   She was never good enough for you.

WENDELL   Baby Sis, you always treated her bad. Surprised she took your phone call. Weren't for you I might still be living with that fine woman. Smartest woman I ever knew.

DENISE   I need my oxygen. I can't breathe.

WENDELL   Me, neither. Seeing Kendra knocked the wind out of me, that's for sure. Never will figure out you women. It's all gonna be okay, Baby Sis. *(He's suddenly distracted by a pop-up on his computer screen.)* Oh, look! I got a new Facebook message. From Kendra.

[Blackout on Wendell.]

[Denise is trying to catch her breath.]

[Blackout on Denise.]

[End of play.]

Life in the Hard Drive

Greg Lam

Production History

Life in the Hard Drive was commissioned by Pork Filled Productions as part of its "Resilience!" event in 2021.

Characters

> SADIE   a lawyer
> VINCENT CHAO   the defendant
> MAXI   Vincent's girlfriend

Synopsis: A man is offered a new method with which he can serve his criminal sentence.

Note: This play was originally written for Zoom presentation and takes advantage of scene-change fluidity and other effects. Character names can be changed to reflect the backgrounds of the actors.

[Sadie and Vincent appear. Vincent is in prison gear; Sadie is dressed professionally.]

SADIE   I'm sorry, Mr. Chao. I'm here to help you get through this.

VINCENT   I can't . . . I can't believe it. This is a mistake.

SADIE   I know. This is awful, but it's reality now and we have to deal with it. What are you going to do? Juries these days. They come to trials with their minds already made up.

VINCENT   I know you did your best.

SADIE   It doesn't matter that those guys started the whole thing, that they instigated it. It's a shame.

VINCENT   Twenty years. I don't believe it.

SADIE   There is a new option, though. One that I do not recommend but I would be remiss if I didn't present it to you. Do you want to hear about it?

VINCENT   Why not? Hit me.

[Maxi suddenly appears. She is Vincent's partner. Sadie has disappeared.]

MAXI   Vincent, do you think I'll make a pretty old woman?

[Vincent is surprised by this sudden shift in setting. He tries to roll with it.]

VINCENT   Excuse me?

MAXI   Do you think I'll be pretty, old?

VINCENT   You're not pretty old. You're young. We're young. We have a long way to go ahead of us.

MAXI   No, silly. When I'm old, do you think I'll still be pretty? Some people grow up to look good old and some look like trolls. I want to be a good looking grandma.

VINCENT   It's too early to think about that, Maxi.

MAXI   No, it isn't. I mean, look at you. I think you're going to be a really foxy old guy. I can see it in you. Time will be kind to that face of yours.

[Vincent smiles. Shift to Sadie suddenly appearing and Maxi disappearing.]

SADIE   A new facility is opening up. Very experimental. Funding up the wazoo. People can volunteer to go there for a reduced sentence instead of their full term at a traditional prison.

VINCENT   What's the catch?

SADIE   It's very different.

VINCENT   How different?

SADIE   It's "totally disrupting the prison industry," according to *Wired*.

[Maxi suddenly appears. Sadie disappears.]

MAXI   Hon, will you hurry up? We're going to be late!

VINCENT   Right, yeah. Don't want to be late. Um . . . Where are we going again?

MAXI   To our work party, silly! It's downtown. I don't want to miss the Yankee Swap again.

VINCENT   Right, yeah. I'm . . . I'm ready when you are. Wow, you look incredible.

MAXI   Please. It's just an old dress.

VINCENT   What if I told you I wanted to be with you, forever?

MAXI   I'd say, "Are you really sure about that?" Forever is a long time.

[Sadie suddenly appears. Maxi is gone.]

SADIE   Don't say you're ready to jump at this just yet, Mr. Chao. I want you to think about it carefully. It's less time but I worry that this form of incarceration may actually be more taxing on you than traditional prison. Mentally.

VINCENT   How can that be the case? I won't be getting into fights in a prison yard all the time. Right? No communal showers or strip searches or solitary. It's all simulated.

SADIE   It's relative time. Sure, it'll only be five years, but with their methods it's . . . I wouldn't recommend it.

VINCENT   It's my choice though, isn't it?

SADIE   Of course. It's always your choice.

[Maxi suddenly appears. Sadie is gone.]

MAXI   You have to choose.

VINCENT   It's hard.

MAXI   I can't do it by myself.

VINCENT   Can't you?

MAXI   Look, we can put your uncle along with your work friends at this table in the corner. I think that makes the most sense.

VINCENT   My work friends are not going to gel with my uncle.

MAXI   But your uncle would totally get into a fight with your dad.

VINCENT   It's not that bad.

MAXI   Please. Look, I think this works, but if you want, you can try to figure out a better solution. You can work it out.

[Maxi disappears. Sadie appears.]

VINCENT   Well, how does it work?

SADIE   You spend most of your sentence in stasis, basically a medically induced coma. While unconscious, they hook you up to a machine that broadcasts certain stimuli into your brain. It'll trigger a very vivid series of memories. Both ones that you've actually experienced and others that have been manufactured for you. It's said that they simulate time at four times the actual rate.

VINCENT   So, I'll get out four times as quickly.

SADIE   But it won't feel like less. It'll feel much longer. You'll be there five years, but it feels like 20 or even more. It's constant.

VINCENT   This is the first I've ever heard of it.

SADIE   It's brand new, all the rage in tech circles. They call this place "The Hard Drive."

[Sadie disappears. Maxi appears. The sounds of a struggle.]

MAXI   No!   Get away from me!

VINCENT   That's my wife, you scumbag!

MAXI   Vincent, he's hurting me! What did we ever do to you?

VINCENT   Let go or I'll . . . That's it! I'll— I'll—

[Vincent starts punching out of frame.]

MAXI   Vincent! I think you're really hurting him.

[Vincent looks at his bloodied hands or a weapon.]

[Sadie appears, reading a pamphlet. Maxi disappears.]

SADIE   Happy memories, sad memories, boring memories . . .
"Designed to reinforce the sense of reality to each inmate." There's
no rhyme or reason to the simulation. I don't know how they expect
this to be rehabilitative, but here we are.

VINCENT   I . . . I just think that this will save me time. Years of my
life. I'd be able to get out while I'm still young. Rebuild. I'll still be
young, I can still bounce back. I just have to keep at it, keep hoping.

SADIE   I want you to be certain of your decision Mr. Chao. They claim
that this will be a more efficient method of criminal rehabilitation. I
worry that this is just a cheaper way of cramming inmates into
smaller-boxes.

VINCENT   As long as there's a chance to . . . come out the other side.
With Maxi. I think this makes it more likely, don't you think?

[Sadie disappears. Maxi appears.]

MAXI   I hope you understand, Vincent.

VINCENT   Maxi, I—

MAXI   No, I know. It's terrible, but . . . I hope you understand.

VINCENT   This is one of the times. This isn't real. I can feel it.

MAXI   What are you talking about?

VINCENT   So it's strange. Sometimes I realize when it isn't real. Like,
usually they draw from my own experience and I can't tell the
difference, but sometimes it's just some made up situation and I
realize I'm in the simulation.

MAXI   I'm not your imagination.

VINCENT   That just makes it worse. I can feel the time crawling and
my body rotting away underneath me. I can feel the shackles, and

they're in my mind, and that's terrifying. We've been here so many times before. It's just going to go on forever, isn't it? It's just going to go on and on and—

MAXI   I can't do this, Vincent. I can't be the one that waits for you. It's too much to ask. Life is going on out here, Vincent, at normal speed. Life is passing me by as I wait for you.

VINCENT   Don't. Don't do this, Maxi.

MAXI   I . . . I can't do this. Goodbye.

VINCENT   This isn't real! This one isn't real!

[Maxi disappears.]

[Sadie appears. We return to the beginning scene.]

SADIE   I'm sorry, Mr. Chao. I'm here to help you get through this.

VINCENT   I can't . . . I can't believe it. This is a mistake.

SADIE   I know. This is awful, but it's reality now and we have to deal with it.

[The End]

Protocols

Vince Gatton

Production History

Protocols was written for Kitt Lavoie's Scene Study Emergency Pack in March of 2020. It was first produced professionally by the On and Off Theatre Workshop in June 2020, directed by Daniel Gee Husson.

The cast was as follows:
SHON   Matt Biagini
ARI   Nathaniel Moore

Protocols was also produced by Theatre Three in October 2020, directed by Jeffrey Sanzel.

The cast was as follows:
SHON   Eric Restivo
ARI   Jae Hughes

Characters

SHON   Mid-to-late-20s, the older sibling: sharp-minded, impatient, capable, direct, and weighed with the burden of responsibility.

ARI   Late-teens-to-early-20s, the younger sibling: somewhat more vague in disposition, less driven and way less direct, but with a surprisingly solid emotional center and wisdom.

Note: SHON and ARI can be cast as any race, ethnicity, or gender.

Setting

A video call. Shon is in a work setting, Ari at home.

[SHON, at work, answers a video call from ARI, at home.]

SHON *(to Ari)* Hey—*(to someone off-camera, there in the office)*—Frank! Over there! *(to Ari)* Hold on, one sec—*(to Frank)* There, yes! *(to Ari)* Hey.

ARI Hey, Shon.

SHON What's up? *(nods at Frank, mouths "yes")*

ARI Oh, not too much . . .

SHON Ari, I— *(to Frank)* No, Frank, that goes to Rachel, she's handling the—yes, yes. Jesus. *(back to Ari)* What's up?

ARI How's your day going?

SHON Ari, what? There's a lot going on here. *(He shakes head "no" to Frank off-camera and points.)* What is up?

ARI I just, you know, just wanted to check in . . .

SHON Ari.

ARI . . . see how you're doing . . .

SHON *ARI*. We've got two outbreaks going on right now, TWO, and I'm one of the few people who still has a freakin' job, so it's kind of stressful here right now—

ARI Yeah, no, I get that—

SHON People still need toilet paper, Ari.

ARI Oh, yeah, totally—

SHON *LOTS* of toilet paper. So it's kind of crazy here right now, so can you please just—No! Frank! There!—please just get to the point?

ARI Oh, no, yeah, sure, I don't mean to bother you—

SHON It's not a bother, Ari, I just need you to get to the point!

ARI OK, yeah. Something just came up here, and I could use some, you know, advice . . .

SHON Ari, I need you to handle stuff with mom and dad, OK? You're there, you need to be responsible.

ARI Yeah—

SHON I can't be there, you're the one who's there. You need to handle things.

ARI Yeah, I know, so, but, that's the thing. We just couldn't remember, like, the different protocols. *(Shon sighs.)* Like, which is the thing for which.

SHON Ari.

ARI We just want to make sure we have it right.

SHON Ari, didn't you ever read a book? See a movie? Watch TV? It pretty much lines up!

ARI Right, but—

SHON OK: Protocol Z is, any damage to the head and brain. Like, bash in the skull, decapitation, gunshot between the eyes, any of that will work. Protocol V is much more specific: you have to use wood, and it has to go through the chest cavity and into the heart.

ARI But does it have to be like, a stake?

SHON No.

ARI Because we were like, what even counts as a "stake," you know? Dad and I are trying to figure out what we have that can count as a stake.

SHON Anything wood will do, Ari.

ARI Like, could a baseball bat work?

SHON You'd have to sharpen it, whittle it down or something.

ARI OK, cool.

SHON It just has to be sharp enough to get through the chest.

ARI Cool.

SHON Why?

ARI Huh?

SHON Why are you asking?

ARI Oh, just . . .

SHON Did something happen?

ARI Well, mom's friend Jackie came by.

SHON . . . Came by?

ARI Yeah.

SHON Jackie "came by"?

ARI Yeah.

SHON What does that mean, Ari?

ARI This morning Jackie was at our back door. And she was . . . well, she was all, you know . . . like that.

SHON Oh, no.

ARI Yeah.

SHON Damn.

ARI Yeah. And they look the same, at least at first, right? So we weren't sure which was the right thing, the right protocol.

SHON Yeah, that's a problem.

ARI Because if you do Z, right? But it's really a V? Then you have them getting back up later, with their head all messed up, but still coming at you with the teeth and stuff.

SHON True.

ARI And like, the V protocol won't even slow a Z down.

SHON Yeah, they look the same at first. It's a little later on you can tell, later on with Z they do that gurgly, raspy sound thing. V they get really quiet. You gotta know which is which.

ARI So, it's hard.

SHON Yeah.

ARI But fire works for both, right?

SHON It's on both protocols, yes.

ARI It works for both?

SHON *[To Frank, off screen]* FRANK, NO. There! *[To Ari]* Yes, fire works for both.

ARI OK, good. That's good. 'Cause I had to do something about Jackie, and all I had close was lighter fluid, so that's pretty much what I did with Jackie.

SHON Oh.

ARI But if fire works for both, at least, you know, I know she's not gonna get back up. Right?

SHON Yeah. Yeah, that's right.

ARI So that's good.

SHON Oh, OK. Wow. *(beat)* You're OK?

ARI Yeah, sure.

SHON I mean, that's . . . that's a lot. *(Ari shrugs.)* So, wait. If you already torched Jackie, what's the stake for? *(silence)* Ari? *(Ari still does not answer.)*

ARI You got a lot on your plate . . .

SHON Ari, tell me, tell me right now. WHAT IS GOING ON?

ARI OK. Shon. OK.
Mom and Jackie. You know how mom and Jackie are. And mom just . . . she just couldn't . . . not. She couldn't not open the door.
Dad and I were trying to figure out the right protocol and she just . . . she opened the door. And Jackie got in. Dad and I got her back outside onto the patio, and that's where the lighter fluid was, there by the grill, but . . .

But mom got bit. Before we could get to her, mom got bit.

So.

So she's in the bedroom now. We've got her in the bedroom. And we, you know, we had time to you know, talk to her and stuff, there were a few minutes there when we could talk to her. But now she's gone quiet and we really just have to do it. We just have to do it, and we wanted to make sure we were doing it the right way. And I think, given how quiet she's being, that well, that V is the right way.

So. Yeah.

SHON   *(after a beat)* You weren't going to tell me.

ARI   Dad didn't want me to call you at all, but—

SHON   Were you?

ARI   —but I said we should at least call and see where your head was at—

SHON   YOU WEREN'T GOING TO TELL ME?

ARI   . . . Shon. You get upset. You get upset real easy. So sometimes I gotta, we gotta, think about how we tell you things. I try to . . . you know . . . protect you. Where I can. Sometimes I get it wrong. And I'm sorry about that. But listen. I'm gonna go. I'm gonna go and take care of this now. So I'll go do this . . . and then we can talk again later, OK? OK, Shon?

SHON   . . . Tell her I love her?

ARI   She won't understand.

SHON   Please?

ARI   Yeah, yes, I will. But Shon?

SHON   Yeah?

ARI   She knows. You know she knows.

[A long beat.]

SHON   Do you?

ARI   Do I what?

SHON   Do you know? That I . . . ? How much I . . . ?

ARI   Yeah. Yeah, Shon. I do, too. *(Shon nods.)* You go to work. You do
that work. It's important. I got this. OK?

*[Shon nods. Ari gives a little wave and ends the call. Shon sits for a long moment.
He glances off-camera.]*

SHON   Frank, that doesn't . . .
Never mind. It's OK.
Thank you, Frank.
No, really.
You're doing great.

[END OF PLAY]

The Last Supper

Lindsay Adams

Production History

The livestream premiere of *The Last Supper* was Saturday, May 2, 2020, with Dramatic Distancing. It was directed by Darby Rae.

The cast was as follows:

MAN   Curtiss Johns
WOMAN   Gabriel Brown

Characters

MAN   Twenties–Thirties. Any Race.
WOMAN   Twenties–Thirties. Any Race.

Setting/Time

A Zoom Call. At the height of an outbreak.

NOTE: If the actor playing Man does not have facial hair, there is substitute dialogue that follows this script that may be used.

[The Man and the Woman are on a Zoom video chat together. Each has a plate in front of them.]

MAN   So, this is it.

WOMAN   I guess it is.

MAN   The last supper. See?

[He briefly makes Leonardo da Vinci's "The Last Supper" his background.]

WOMAN   Geez that took it to a dark place.
Who's Judas in this scenario?

MAN   Well dibs on Jesus.

WOMAN   So I get to be Judas then.

MAN   Maybe nobody's Judas. Maybe you're Peter. Or Paul. One of the P's.

WOMAN   Somebody's always the Judas. . . . So . . . What do you have?

MAN   I have cooked tofu that has been breaded with stale potato chips. Topped off with a soy sauce reduction. I even plated it.

WOMAN   Very nice.

MAN   I do what I can.

WOMAN   And that's everything you have?

MAN   Yeah. What about you?

WOMAN   I just made a sandwich.

MAN   Of?

WOMAN   Bean sprouts, apples, and Tabasco.

MAN   What?

WOMAN   Sweet and spicy you know. I have one extra piece of bread, so I'll have that for dessert.

MAN   But how is that a sandwich? The bread has to be so soggy.

WOMAN   A little bit. We should eat soon.

[She touches her face. Maybe she scratches. Or maybe just one of those involuntary touches.]

MAN   Hey. Wash your hands, don't touch your face.

WOMAN   Sorry, I feel like I've gotten even worse about that since . . . somehow. Like by thinking about it I touch it more. If you were here, I could just touch yours.

MAN   Bon appetit?

WOMAN   Yeah, sure.

[They eat.]

MAN   How . . . is it?

WOMAN   It's not half-bad. You know. The Tabasco really takes over.

MAN   Makes sense.

WOMAN   Yours?

MAN   Turned out alright.

WOMAN   Nice.

[She finishes. She waits as he keeps eating. She seems unsettled. He is contentedly still eating.]

WOMAN   Is this fine?

MAN   Is what fine?

WOMAN   This.

MAN   Yeah, it's fine.

WOMAN   Okay good. . . . Like you don't seem fazed at all. You just seem fine, with being stuck at home.

MAN   Well, I like time to myself. And I can get more done around the apartment.

WOMAN   Sure, yeah.

MAN   I'm fine.

WOMAN   Okay . . . good . . . I just . . . miss you a lot. . . . Like not even just touching me. I mean yeah also that. But just like you being around. Smelling the stuff you put in your beard to make it soft. When you're reading or thinking about something. You do that absent-minded thing where you stroke your beard, even though you hate it when I stroke it.

MAN   I don't hate it.

WOMAN   Sure, okay, you just wince every time. But anyway, it makes it smell more when you touch it, the stuff.

MAN   Beard balm.

WOMAN   What?

MAN   That's what I use. To make it soft.

WOMAN   Okay yeah. That. I just . . . I don't know what I'm saying exactly now . . . I lost my train of thought.

MAN   It feels like you're petting a dog sometimes.

WOMAN   What?

MAN   I just wish you would be more . . . still. Just, you're always moving.

WOMAN   Okay.

MAN   I just . . . that's what I don't really like.

WOMAN   So basically, um, you don't like how I touch you.

MAN   . . .

WOMAN   Let's just have a nice dinner. Eat. Finish . . . eating.

MAN   Are you okay?

WOMAN   It's fine, I'm alright.

MAN   Clearly it's not alright, you're about to cry.

WOMAN   Sometimes I'm just sad. I get to be sad too . . . sometimes. I know you're dealing with everything with work. And now you're stuck in that and the economy is shit and will be shit probably for . . . a while. But everything is shit okay? Right now. And I still get to be sad. Even if you're having a bad time and you're unhappy.

MAN   I'm fine.

WOMAN   No you're not. No, you're not and I can tell, but you won't say anything.

MAN   What am I supposed to say? Talking about things doesn't help me.

WOMAN Well, it helps me and it lets me know what's happening. I literally don't know where you are.

MAN I'm in my apartment. You know, the only place any of us get to be right now.

WOMAN You know that's not what . . . I mean like emotionally.

MAN . . .

WOMAN I just want to be there for you, and you won't let me.

MAN I do, too.

WOMAN Okay, then you'll let me get groceries for you, like I offered to.

MAN . . .

WOMAN Is that a yes?

MAN I . . . um . . . I don't need groceries.

WOMAN I'm sorry, what?

MAN I got off early today so I already went to the store.

WOMAN You're fucking kidding me. You said that was it. The meal was all you had left.

MAN I really wanted this to be a good night.

WOMAN By lying? I can't believe you did a grocery run. It is so unsafe for you.

MAN I was fine.

WOMAN You're at risk.

MAN I was safe.

WOMAN You only have hand sanitizer because I made you take mine.

MAN I wash my hands.

WOMAN This was the last meal. The last supper as you put it. We were making the whole not having food left into a game. It was supposed to be fun and like something like a date or . . . What are we doing?

MAN   We're still having dinner together.

WOMAN   You really don't care?

MAN   What do I not care about?

WOMAN   You like having dinner over a screen. It's like you wanted this all along.

MAN   I wanted a pandemic. I wanted to not be able to see people.

WOMAN   You wanted this. With us. You have been so distant with me. And with all of this, I already feel pretty fucking alone right now. I don't know what . . . I try really hard to be happy and upbeat and to be your cheerleader and to make things better. And not to bring anything else in to make this situation worse. But I can't just keep . . . Please say something. You know I just keep talking when you don't RESPOND to me.

MAN   What am I supposed to say to that. Sorry I'm the awful person who doesn't care about you enough.

WOMAN   It's not that you don't . . . But you don't say it or show it or—

MAN   How am I supposed to show it right now?!

WOMAN   No, but before.

MAN   I don't remember before. All my life is just Zoom meetings and putting out fires at work. And now having to have conversations about our relationship. It feels like it's been fucking eternity here. So I don't know what I did or what I wasn't doing.

WOMAN   It isn't just about me. Like you don't go to things when I invite you when other people invite you. And then like even when we were still seeing each other. In person. But not seeing anyone else. When the group has Zoom parties. You would always make up something. So then I wouldn't either because I was with you. I'm really worried about you. Like have you been talking to anyone else?

MAN   I want my keys back.

WOMAN   What?

MAN   I want them back. I want you to give them back to me.

WOMAN   We're sheltered in place. What do you think I'm going to do? Like I'm gonna go pour bleach on your clothes or something?

MAN   I want you to get them to me.

WOMAN   Is this seriously how you're breaking up with me? . . . Are you going to say anything after that?

MAN   I just need some space.

WOMAN   All you fucking have is space.

MAN   I've just been thinking about this a lot, about what I need, and I'm not sure that this is what I need right now. I need someone who cares about me.

WOMAN   What the fuck does that even mean. How about you care about yourself? You don't even keep yourself safe. You won't even let me get you groceries.

MAN   I need someone who isn't always critical of everything that I do.

WOMAN   That's it. You're not going to even yell or . . . Just yell at me, something. Like any of this mattered to you. Like I mattered . . .

MAN   You really like playing the victim, don't you?

WOMAN   No, I don't. You make me that. You're Judas.

MAN   What?

WOMAN   You're the Judas.

MAN   Wow, okay.

WOMAN   You are. You're Judas. Way to fuck up the Last Supper dude.

MAN   I'm not having this conversation with you.

WOMAN   Just like every other one you refuse to have.

MAN   I want my key back. I'll come over there if I have to.

WOMAN   No! You aren't!

[She gets up with her phone and moves into the kitchen.]

MAN   You don't get to give me permission.

WOMAN   Well, there won't be any purpose if you do.

[She has found the extra piece of bread.]

MAN   You won't let me in? I will make a scene if I have to.

[She pulls the key off the key chain.]

MAN   Are you saying something? Are you talking to me? I can't hear you if you're talking.

[She places it on the bread. Making a sandwich.]

MAN   You . . . wouldn't.

WOMAN   Time for dessert.

[She eats the bread.]

MAN   Are you crazy?

WOMAN   You aren't getting your silver Judas.

MAN   You're acting crazy.

WOMAN   Happy Last Supper to you too.

MAN   You're fucking insane.

WOMAN   You can get a new key in June!

MAN   You . . .

[He logs off the Zoom call. She spits the key out of her mouth and looks at it.]

WOMAN   Just stay inside.

[She starts crying. End of Play.]

NOTE: *Substitute dialogue to use if actor playing Man doesn't have a beard.*

WOMAN   Okay . . . good . . . I just . . . miss you a lot . . . Like not even just touching me. I mean yeah also that. But just like you being around. Smelling the stuff you use in your hair, when you're reading or thinking about something you do that absent-minded thing where you run your hand through it, even though you hate it when I do.

MAN   I don't hate it.

WOMAN   Sure, okay, you just wince every time. But anyway it makes it smell more when you touch it, the stuff.

MAN   Tea Tree Oil.

WOMAN   What?

MAN   That's what I use. To make it soft.

This Is Not Business as per Usual

Sharece M. Sellem

Production History

This Is Not Business as per Usual was developed during the COVID-19 pandemic in response the protests surrounding the case of George Floyd in Minnesota. It premiered at B Street Theatre's *Virtual New Play Brunch*—a virtual showcase of short plays by playwrights from around the United States.

The cast was as follows:

GINA   Stephanie Altholz
BRIAN   Peter Story
CHLOE   Heather Gibson

Characters

GINA
BRIAN
CHLOE

Time

End of May 2020

Place

A virtual Zoom meeting

[CHLOE is over it. She decides to take this moment during a staff meeting to put in her resignation. GINA, BRIAN, and CHLOE log onto Zoom for their

regularly scheduled Tuesday meeting in the morning. BRIAN comes in first, then CHLOE.]

GINA   Hey! Hey there Brian!

BRIAN   Good morning!

GINA   Look at that sun! Sheeeesh! I can barely see you! Can you move your computer a little or maybe this way? Geez, I didn't expect us to jump into summer this quickly!

BRIAN   I know! It's amazing how mother nature just flips the switch on ya. You never know when it'll happen. It just does. It's like I felt it in the air . . . I knew it would creep upon me. It was just a matter of when.

[CHLOE enters.]

GINA   Right!? How's your doggie? *(makes annoying dog baby noises)*

BRIAN   She's a good girl! *(talking to his dog across the room)* Isn't that right, Bella!

(He also makes annoying dog baby noises.)

CHLOE   Good morning.

GINA   *(Still focusing on the dog. Pretty much forgets she has a meeting)* Aren't you a good girl, aww!

BRIAN   That's right, she's my good girl! *(He gets up, still talking in baby dog voice.)* Excuse me, I just have to give her a treat. She looks sad like she's missing me since I'm all the way over here and this meeting is taking away all of her Papa's attention, awwww.

GINA   You do that! Awww, the baby. *(sees Chloe)* Oh! Hi there! How are you, Chloe!?

CHLOE   Great.

GINA   How's everything going in your world? You know, I thought about you this morning when they were talking about all of the students and how they have to give them their degrees in their car.

CHLOE   Yea.

GINA   Such a shame. So sad! I can't even imagine being a college graduate in 2020. It's just, my god, so many things are happening and it's just a sucky time, ya know?

CHLOE   Yup.

GINA   *(feels the tension, but playing it off)* So! I got the report. *(sing song voice)* Thank you sooooo much! I really don't know what I'd do without you!?

BRIAN   *(sits back in his seat)* Hey Chloe! How's it going?

[CHLOE sighs, there are more important things to discuss.]

BRIAN   *(cont.)* Ok! So uh, yea! Gina sent me the report everything looks good. The only thing we're missing is the section about the deliverables.

CHLOE   What about it?

BRIAN   There's an entire page missing explaining what we've done in the fiscal year.

CHLOE   What exactly have we done?

[BRIAN and GINA know that she's getting ready to make a point they don't like or want to admit.]

GINA   Oh! There was the 5K run for Black & Brown Communities in the Hill.

BRIAN   Yea, that's a great one. We had tons of sponsors and like 200 people showed up. That event alone brought in, how much was it, Gina?

GINA   *(proud)* $30,000.

BRIAN   30K. That was great. Oh! And the Make Lives Better conference. That was awesome. We had that woman from that diversity consulting firm, what was her name? I forgot. It was like super long.

GINA   Oh, Geez, if I remember. I just remember that the cost per plate was $50 and we barely had enough seats left. That was a great one too. That event was an easy 50K.

BRIAN   Oh Chloe, don't forget we need to include the backpack drive for back-to-school this past fall.

GINA   OOOOooooohhhh yes! That was great PR! We were right in the street with our tables and cars with banners. We had the radio station there . . . what's the name of that radio station?

BRIAN   Right, they play hip-hop and R&B?

[CHLOE sighs. They both look to her to give them the answer. She doesn't.]

GINA   Well, anyway. It was awesome. Everyone showed up. Everyone in the neighborhood just gathered around the table like kids in a candy store. It was like Christmas!

CHLOE   The backpacks were made out of paper-thin fabric. You wouldn't be able to hold one regular schoolbook in it without it ripping on the sides. It literally crumbled in my hand when I dropped water on the extra one I had.

BRIAN   Well, we got them donated, Chloe. The sponsor was nice enough to give us those. I mean geez, we got them for free ya know?

[CHLOE sighs. BRIAN and GINA look at each other and pause for a moment. They collect their thoughts.]

GINA   Alright! Well, Brian you said we were missing information on the report, so Chloe, can you have that completed by Friday? I need to get it over to Pam as soon as possible. She's backed up with grants since COVID hit and I don't want her to feel too overwhelmed.

CHLOE   Overwhelmed. Hm.

BRIAN   I'll also need you to like really jooz it up as well. You want to really fill it up with all of the other little stuff we did along with the big stuff, like the Zoom meeting we held for parents on SNAP and how we helped Latino families when COVID hit, when we brought in a bilingual puppet show for Zoom to teach kids how to eat healthy while on SNAP.

CHLOE   Guys. I'm done.

GINA   I know you're tired and have a lot to—

CHLOE   Like done, done. Over it done. Like I'm leaving.

GINA   What? What are you talking about, Chloe?

CHLOE   I wrote something, and since I have you both on Zoom I might as well do this right here, right now. I was going to send you all this letter in an email saying (*reads the nice resignation letter*), "thank you for the experience I've gained working here. I've learned so much. I will have wonderful memories of my time here, blah, blah, blah and thank you so much for this opportunity and best of luck . . . please consider this as my two weeks' notice, yadah yadah. But since my most recent episode of unfortunate events here, I've decided to go out with some hot truth. Why not? Right? What do I have to lose? We've made it this far, right?

[She's ready to unleash.]

Today is June 2, 2020. Exactly one week after George Floyd died in front of America's eyes for an entire excruciating 8 minutes and 46 seconds. I know some of you are not a fan of mine—

[They try to act like it's not true.]

—and that's ok. I have no hard feelings towards you, trust me—I want you to just hear me out. Like actually listen to what I have to say this time. Some of you know me beyond our surface level conversations prior to meetings where we all settle in and make small talk to feel some sort of normalcy as we prepare to delve into a meeting about how we can better serve our Black and Brown communities. Being one of the only other people of color besides Natasha who is half Puerto Rican half Italian—

[GINA raises her hand and tries to interject "Wait!". . . pulls back as she realizes this is a train going full speed]

—I can't help but to think about the funding we've received, or I should say YOU received year after year to serve communities of color and as I would look around the table, every single one of your staff members is a white person. A white face. A white body. A white voice. And worse, a white thought. Now before you say, "Oh Chloe, it's not about that. As you know, black people die every day in the streets. And it's not just because of the cops. They are murdering each other too. And this is why our organization is here to help. We are here to provide them with the resources they need."

BRIAN   We talk about this all the time and its—

[She continues her thought running him right over.]

CHLOE   I can't help but to wonder why I've been sitting in these meetings and never spoke up, until now. This is not simply just another day at the office. This wasn't just another Black death. We are experiencing a revolution. The whole world protested this weekend on behalf of the 400 years of fatigue, brutality, rape, slaughter, mistreatment, and downright work of attempted genocide. These public demonstrations were and are in response to the call to action, to reform the police departments, to change the slave patrol model that still exists today. Gina, your son is mixed like me. His father is a Black man. How can you possibly think this organization gives a damn about Black people when you can't send an acknowledgement email to your own staff!? This is NOT business as usual! Everyone should be outraged, and everyone should hear that call to action, but no. You don't see yourself in the problem. You believe that this is a Black problem when really this is EVERYONE's problem. How long will you knowingly apply for funding to serve communities of color and not hire management staff that represents them? When will you acknowledge that we have a 400-year-old problem? When will you acknowledge that Black people were brought here to be labor and not expected to survive in a land the white people claimed as their own—your ancestors—your homes—your bank accounts—your institutions—your lineage— your wealth all sits on the blistered and beaten backs of Black folx. I stayed quiet because that is the culture. YOUR culture. And it's toxic. And I've had enough. So no, I will not finish out my two weeks. I will gracefully exit the company today. And no, I don't want to hear I'm sorry. I don't want to hear "I have a friend or relative who is a nice cop."

[GINA sits back raising both hands in frustration. Her husband is Black and is also a cop.]

I don't want you sending me superficial apologies. All I ask is that you acknowledge the blood money on your hands and put it where it counts—if you even have a conscience. I don't need anything from you. I just want my damn dignity. *(starts to stand)* And by the way, I'll be starting my own company. And when your Black and Brown clients no longer need your services, you can give me a call. We know what we need.

[She exits the meeting. Both share a long pause in shock.]

BRIAN   What in the hell just happened? *(yells)* Chloe!?

GINA   I don't think, ever, in my 15 years working in this organization, that I would've heard the words she used. How dare she?

BRIAN   I don't even know what to say?

GINA   I got her this job.

BRIAN   You did? I didn't know that.

GINA   I thought it would be good because she was a recent graduate, she worked really hard on her own to get her degree, she understood our work and our mission and I just knew she'd uh, fit right in, I guess.

BRIAN   Fit right in?

GINA   Well yea! She's articulate, she really knows how to speak to the cause. I was even talking about promoting her and adding "diversity coach" to her title so she could facilitate meetings on diversity instead of us paying someone else to come in. It would be like two for the price of one *(catches herself)* oh and it would be good for her resume!

BRIAN   You know, between you and I, I'm really getting tired of them making it about that.

GINA   About what?

BRIAN   It's like, people need to be held accountable for their actions. You know, in my house, we say all lives matter. It just sounds selfish to say Black Lives Matter. Even my friend Jeff, who's Black, agrees. I mean, isn't that why we do this work? Because all lives matter, including other people.

GINA   Honestly, this is an old problem. The truth is *(almost whispering)* we just don't know what to do about it.

BRIAN   I think she was rude.

GINA   I get why she's upset. I just don't have the answers, and honestly Brian, by acknowledging the stuff that happens to them, it makes us accountable. Like we should do something. I wouldn't even know where to begin.

BRIAN   Does Natasha know anything about grants?

GINA   Ha! Hardly. I can't even get her to do a simple intake with a client. I wouldn't put her anywhere near grant documents. You're going to have to take over for a while until I find a replacement.

BRIAN   I mean, I can manage grants, obviously, but that's above my pay grade. I'd need a raise if I'm going to take on Chloe's work. That's a lot. And I wouldn't be able to do everything she did, just like a quarter of it.

GINA   *(sighs)* We're screwed.

[End of play.]

Humans

Mrinalini Kamath

Production History

Humans was written for the Theater Breaking Through Barriers (TBTB) Starchangers series.

It premiered via Zoom and was directed by Stuart Green.

The cast was as follows:

BENJI   Ben Rauch

LADY HALO   Lisa Riegel

MISS OTIS   Jessika Carter-Ross

CATTLEYA   Rhianna Basore

Characters

BENJI   adolescent dog

MISS OTIS   adolescent cat

LADY HALO   tween dog

CATTLEYA   young cat, just out of kittenhood

Time

The present

Place

Zoom

[At rise: a screen with four Zoom boxes, featuring BENJI, CATTLEYA, MISS OTIS, and LADY HALO, mid-Zoom.]

BENJI   I'll hear him far away, like on the stairs, and my heart starts to BOOM BOOM BOOM. I mean, it's always been like that, but now it's REALLY like that, and I start jumping the second I hear his key in the door, and I almost knock him over so I can lick his wonderful face, and I just miss him soooo much now, it's horrible. It hurts.

MISS OTIS   But . . . isn't that how it's always been for you? It's just part of what you are, right?

BENJI   Well, yeah, but it's never been—

LADY HALO   Let me, let me—you know, explain, because I totally get where he's coming from. Before it was like, "Yay, he's home!" or "She's home!" before she moved out. . . .

[LADY HALO appears to lose her train of thought in the sadness.]

CATTLEYA   Oh no, she moved out?

[LADY HALO sadly nods.]

BENJI   Mine too, mine too!

LADY HALO   I guess she just didn't love him, anymore? I hope it wasn't anything *I* did—

CATTLEYA   I'm sure it wasn't.

MISS OTIS   But you were trying to explain how things are different now?

LADY HALO   Oh yeah. Yeah. Yeah. Yeah. I was always happy when they came home, but now . . . now it feels like my heart is about to burst, IT WILL BURST, if he doesn't come through that door fast enough. Because he was—they were—home ALL the time before, and now, he's just gone sometimes. Until he comes home.

CATTLEYA   I don't feel like *that*, exactly, but I . . . I actually do go to the door when I hear noises in the hallway, because I think it might be one of them.

BENJI   Really? Really? I didn't think your kind did that.

MISS OTIS   We *don't*.

CATTLEYA *(ashamed)* I know, it's not normal—but I can't seem to help it. They both were around all the time before, and then she was there at least, and now, they're both gone.

I tell myself that it's just curiosity, that it's just me being nosy, when I think I hear people and get excited . . .

MISS OTIS Okay—curiosity is good, that's normal—

CATTLEYA But I think I really do miss them, especially her, when she's out during the day. Like, my heart doesn't feel like it's going to burst or anything like that, but . . . there's this little . . . pull? I adjusted my naps so I wouldn't have to think about her too much while she's gone, but I miss her.

LADY HALO I thought there were two humans?

BENJI Yeah. Yeah. Two.

CATTLEYA There are, but he's gone most of the time—he's been leaving every day and coming back at night for a while. I guess he goes and hunts? I don't know, he doesn't seem to bring anything home.

MISS OTIS Males aren't that great at hunting.

BENJI Hey. Hey. Hey. Hey.

MISS OTIS Well, mine isn't, anyway.

BENJI Cattleya—does *she* hunt?

CATTLEYA I think so. She'll be gone and sometimes she'll bring back these big boxes—

MISS OTIS Oooh—I love a good box!

CATTLEYA Me too! And some of these boxes are SO big—they're better than what's inside.

MISS OTIS See, that's good. You appreciate a good box. That's *normal.*

CATTLEYA But the way I want to see her so much—and even him— it all just makes me feel so . . . wrong. Not normal.

BENJI You seem perfectly fine to me.

LADY HALO   Me too, me too!

MISS OTIS   *(sighing)* She's not.

BENJI   Hey. Hey hey hey hey—

LADY HALO   Hey hey hey hey hey—

MISS OTIS   FOR US, I mean. She's not fine for who she is. You all are so lucky that your humans go OUT—I wish mine would. I mean, she does, but he hangs around the place all the time, now. And then she comes home and is there ALL night—they're both there, SO MUCH. I can't get any rest from them.

BENJI   I will never understand that.

MISS OTIS   I just—I need *space*. My own space. We had a good time-sharing thing going on, you know? I could walk around and own it most of the time—they were just there for a few hours in the morning and to sleep at night. Then all of a sudden, they were there ALL. THE. TIME. And so . . . *needy*. Like, I get that they sometimes want to cuddle or pet me, but so much? It's just not who I am. And how am I supposed to exercise—

BENJI   Oooh, I love EXERCISE!

LADY HALO   Walk! Walk. Walk. Walk.

BENJI   Walk. Walk!

MISS OTIS   If I could finish—how am I supposed to exercise my independence? Where is my privacy? These are things you don't quite get, Cattleya, because you found your furrever home when you were young and things just started being weird, with the humans at home all the time. You've got cat instincts trying to claw their way out of you, but you were put into a kind of situation that a dog loves, and I guess that made a real impression. I mean, it's almost all you've ever known. Maybe now, maybe the way things are going now . . . maybe this will make you more normal, and—

[She stops abruptly, as we hear the sound of a mourning dove. She is gone from her Zoom box.]

LADY HALO   Miss Otis? Where'd she go, where'd she go?

[CATTLEYA's eyes are wide and she appears to be on the verge of drooling.]

CATTLEYA   BIRD.

[MISS OTIS reappears.]

MISS OTIS   Sorry, I was a little distracted—

CATTLEYA   BIRD.

MISS OTIS   Well, yes, but it flew away. Very good, Cattleya! That's exactly how you should be.

[MISS OTIS starts to groom herself—CATTLEYA does as well, the dogs do the dog equivalent. MISS OTIS pauses.]

MISS OTIS   Did your humans change the way they look?

BENJI   Mmm . . . I don't think so?

MISS OTIS   One of mine grew a winter coat on his face. He's home all the time now, and he's always stroking that coat on his face, like he can't believe it's there. His head fur is long, too. It's like he wants to be more like *me*.

LADY HALO   Mine did that, but then I think he cut it off? Or maybe she cut it off, before she left? I think he used to go to a groomer, but then when they were at home all the time, he did it himself. I never saw a groomer come over.

CATTLEYA   Mine didn't get a coat, but he got a belly. Used to be so flat. Now when I sit in his lap, I can make *so many* biscuits on his belly.

[She giggles. LADY HALO looks wistful.]

LADY HALO   Everything's changed again. My human has someone come during the day to take me out when he's not there—

BENJI   Mine does too! Mine does too! Just like before.

LADY HALO   Mine didn't before. My humans used to take turns. One would be home one day, then the other the next day. But now there's just one.

[She sighs and puts her head down.]

BENJI   Ohhh, don't be sad. I hate when dogs are sad. It's even worse than when the humans are sad.

[He suddenly stops, as if listening to something off-screen.]

Hey. Hey. Hey!

ALL   What?

[He disappears from the screen.]

CATTLEYA   Benji?

LADY HALO   Where'd he go?

[BENJI reappears.]

BENJI   Sorry—thought I heard him. Or the walker human.

LADY HALO   Do you like your walker human?

BENJI   Yeah. Yeah. Yeah. He's nice. Sooo nice.

LADY HALO   Mine's nice. I'm with, like 4 other dogs, and I like them, b . . . but—I miss it just being me and my human. And this other human, he likes me, we walk around the place, he feeds me, he tells me I'm a good girl, but . . . it's not the same as going on a walk with *your* human.

MISS OTIS   Do the other dogs you walk with have the same . . . issues?

[LADY HALO nods.]

LADY HALO   A couple do. One is actually going to stop coming— she's moving. Her human keeps telling her that there is going to be a YARD, where they're going.

BENJI   Ooo . . . a yard . . .

[CATTLEYA also looks interested; MISS OTIS looks uninterested.]

CATTLEYA   She must be moving far away.

LADY HALO   She doesn't know. She just knows that her human started leaving every day and coming home at night and was sad, but now he's happy. He keeps telling her that once they move to the place with a yard, he'll be home with her all day. He's happy, so she's happy.

BENJI   I wish that were me. My human—he seems really unhappy, when he comes home. He looks sad and even though he smiles at me, I can feel . . . the things coming out from him . . .

[He swipes his paws around.]

. . . you know how you can just sense what they're feeling?

LADY HALO   Yeah. Yeah. Yeah.

CATTLEYA   Yeah.

MISS OTIS   Yeah.

BENJI   And I don't know . . . what to do.

MISS OTIS   What do you mean? Didn't you just say that you want to knock him down and lick him?

BENJI   Yeah. Yeah. Yeah. But he's sad. I jump, and I lick, and I wag my tail, and I think it helps a little, but . . . he still seems so sad. When he takes me out to walk at night, he's started smoking again. He stopped for a long time, but after she left, he started doing it again. I'm on the sidewalk, doing my thing, and he pulls out that smelly fire stick and just looks soooo sad.

CATTLEYA   Maybe they don't like leaving home, either.

LADY HALO   Or maybe he just misses her? I know my human misses my other human, even though they yelled a lot.

CATTLEYA   *(sighing)* I miss my other human. She still takes care of me in the morning before she leaves, but . . . I miss her when she's gone. I'm actually kind of mad at her.

MISS OTIS Do you give her the cold shoulder when she comes home? Show her that you're mad?

CATTLEYA Kind of.

MISS OTIS You should lean into that feeling.

CATTLEYA Really?

MISS OTIS Yes. It means you're a little closer to being normal.

LADY HALO Hey. Hey. Hey. Hey.

BENJI *(overlapping)* Hey. Hey. Hey. Hey.

MISS OTIS For our kind, for our kind!

BENJI But what do I do?

MISS OTIS About what?

BENJI About my human being . . . sad.

MISS OTIS You do what you do . . . you keep jumping on him and licking him, and whatever else you do. I mean, isn't that why humans like dogs? You treat them like they're the greatest thing ever. Treat him like that.

LADY HALO What about me?

MISS OTIS Well, the same, duh!

[Pause, as LADY HALO thinks this through.]

LADY HALO If humans like dogs because we make them feel like they're the greatest, why do humans like cats?

MISS OTIS Because they realize that they must be special for *us* to have chosen *them*.

CATTLEYA She's happy to see me when she comes home, but . . . I don't know. She's not the same.

MISS OTIS Mine aren't the same either. And not just because one of them is home so much more. I think they used to laugh more. They used to go out more, and come home, happy.

They used to invite other humans over. Now, they just sit on the sofa and stare at the TV. They still talk to me, but they don't talk to each other so much. And . . . like Benji said—I can feel the things coming out of them. Not good things. They're still both there, but . . . something . . . something's different. Something changed.

[She shakes her head].

Humans.

CATTLEYA   *(sighing)* Humans.

LADY HALO   *(sad)* Humans.

BENJI   *(loving)* Humans.

[End of play.]

One-Act Plays

Role Play

Brendan Powers and Rachel Burttram

Production History

Role Play premiered on Facebook Live as part of the April 20, 2022 episode of tiny_Theatre with Brendan Powers as Fritz and Rachel Burttram as Margot

Characters

FRITZ
MARGOT

Time

The present

[MARGOT'S apartment. Evening. FRITZ and MARGOT are sitting on the couch drinking wine. Perhaps music plays softly.]

FRITZ   Your turn.

MARGOT   Let's see. Have you ever . . . played the banjo?

FRITZ   I've not. You?

MARGOT   Once. In a haunting play called *Forgotten Meadow*. I played a reclusive musician who could talk to field mice.

FRITZ   I bet you were heartbreaking.

MARGOT   The critics loved me but hated the play. They said it had no future.

FRITZ   What was it called again?

MARGOT   *Forgotten Meadow*. I hope you get to do it one day. You're perfect for the tormented Sheriff. Your turn.

FRITZ   Have you ever . . . bungee jumped?

MARGOT   It's number seven on my bucket list.

FRITZ   Number four on mine! We're so sympatico, Margot. How is it that a month ago neither of us knew the other existed and now we're inseparable?

MARGOT   Fate, pure and simple.

[They clink and kiss.]

FRITZ   God, I thought the show would never end tonight. I couldn't wait to take the bows and spirit away with you into the night.

MARGOT   I watched your death scene tonight from the wings. It turned me on.

FRITZ   I was being thrown into a volcano.

MARGOT   Yes, but it was that primitive scream you let forth as you fought with the tribal elders. You've never made that sound before.

FRITZ   That's because Dante caught me in the crotch with his blowpipe.

MARGOT   Point is, love: that scream aroused me tremendously.

FRITZ   I'll keep that in mind next performance.

MARGOT   Do.

FRITZ   What aroused me was your speech at the end of act one. I wanted to storm the stage and take you in my arms.

MARGOT   You have such admirable self-restraint. *(Margot studies the bottle.)* The label on this bottle has won my heart with its romantic yet melancholy font.

FRITZ   I knew it would speak to you.

MARGOT   You know me well.

FRITZ   Plus it was Buy One Get One. Shall we resume play?

MARGOT   Oh. Let's see. Have you ever . . . Have you ever role played? With a lover?

FRITZ   We're in a show right now, Margot.

MARGOT   No, no. I mean role played. With a lover?

FRITZ   Ah. I've not.

MARGOT   Neither have I.

FRITZ   Hmm.

MARGOT   I've read that it can be very thrilling.

FRITZ   A memorable way to celebrate one month together. Shall we?

MARGOT   Why not. The night is young.

FRITZ   And no matinee tomorrow.

MARGOT   Oh, Fritzee, a new adventure! *(picking up her phone)* Let's see . . .

FRITZ   Funny that neither of us have ever done this. I sat near a couple at the bar the other night who I think were doing it. She was saying she was a spy. He was telling her how he flew fighter jets. But I recognized him from the front desk at the YMCA.

MARGOT   Ooh, here we go. Twelve Erotic Role Plays to Heat Up Your Evening.

FRITZ   Twelve in one evening?

MARGOT   *(looking through them)* Let's see . . .

FRITZ   How many are we committing to? We're not doing twelve.

MARGOT   We do however many we want.

FRITZ   I don't have twelve in me, Margot. Not after a two-show day.

MARGOT   We'll just do one tonight to ease into it. How about . . . Librarian and Grad student.

FRITZ   Whispering's not good for the voice.

MARGOT   Smart. Ooh! Tarot Card Reader and Client. I like that. Lots of mystery. Let's do that one.

FRITZ   Okay, so you're the tarot card reader, I'm the client. I'm envisioning a dimly lit room. We need some props.

MARGOT   I have candles.

FRITZ   Battery powered?

MARGOT   Of course. *(She goes to a drawer and takes out several candles; they place them around the room and shut out a few lights.)*

FRITZ   What could we use for tarot cards?

MARGOT   I have Uno. *(She goes to another drawer and takes out Uno cards.)*

FRITZ   I feel like the place would smell of incense. Do you have incense?

MARGOT   No, but I have Febreeze. *(She goes to a third drawer, gets Febreeze and sprays.)*

[FRITZ clears the table and pulls a chair up to it opposite the couch.]

FRITZ   You sit on the couch, I'll enter from up left. Should we strike this table?

MARGOT   It's immensely heavy.

FRITZ   *(He tries to move it. It is immensely heavy)*. The table stays but I'll need glow tape for the legs. Do you have any glow?

MARGOT   Of course.

[A fourth drawer. She gives him a small roll of fluorescent yellow tape with a pair of scissors. FRITZ begins cutting small strips and sticking them on each table leg. Maybe he even has a small flashlight to activate the glow tape].

MARGOT   I'm thinking something flowing for her and lots of jewelry. Maybe a shawl.

FRITZ   I'm going to do a few warm-ups.

MARGOT   Okay. I'm going to put my hair up. *(She exits to the bedroom.)*

[As FRITZ applies the glow tape he does various vocal warm-ups.]

FRITZ   What about accents? Are we doing accents? *(FRITZ does a series of accents).* "Hello, how are you?"

[MARGOT enters in a flowing robe and shawl and a headscarf. Bangles and bracelets.]

MARGOT   I'm going Russian. *(with accent)* "Good evening, please step inside." Did you stretch?

FRITZ   Not yet.

[They both start to stretch.]

FRITZ   What's your backstory? I'm a drifter who has amnesia. My name is Chance.

MARGOT   I'm the great-great-granddaughter of a Russian mystic. I'm known as Madame Rachmaninoff.

FRITZ   I've been wandering the world, trying to figure out why a woman named Hazel comes to me in my dreams.

MARGOT   I stay hidden in the shadows of my dwelling with a ferret named Prospero. I've been expecting your arrival.

FRITZ   Should we rehearse a bit or just improvise?

MARGOT   We should practice your entrance, make sure it's not too dark.

FRITZ   Good idea.

MARGOT   Okay, from the top.

[They turn on the candles and set them around the room. All other lights are shut off. MARGOT sits on the couch. The table and MARGOT are pretty well lit; FRITZ is merely a silhouette on the other side of the room.]

MARGOT   Alright, so you'll knock on the door.

[FRITZ knocks.]

MARGOT   *(as Madame)* Please come in.

[FRITZ steps forward but still in shadow.]

FRITZ   *(as Chance, his accent an odd mix of several)* My name is Chance. I'm a drifter. I have amnesia. I'm told you are the best in the business.

MARGOT   *(as Madame)* Please, come forth. You are very handsome—

FRITZ   Hold!

MARGOT   Hold!

FRITZ   I'm sorry. I can't see a damn thing over here. I need more glow tape.

MARGOT   It's over there.

[FRITZ gets the glow tape and puts a few pieces in various places. As he's doing that MARGOT practices different takes.]

MARGOT   And now, I shall read your cards. And now, I shall read your cards. And now I shall read your cards.

FRITZ   Okay I'm set. Sorry. Let's take it from the top again. *(He knocks.)*

MARGOT   *(as Madame)* Please come in.

[FRITZ steps forward.]

FRITZ   *(as Chance)* My name is Chance. I'm a drifter. I have amnesia. I'm told you are the best in the business.

MARGOT   *(as Madame)* Please, come forth. *FRITZ emerges from the darkness and heads for the chair.* Let me gaze at your—

[BANG! Fritz's toes connect with the immensely heavy table leg. A loud primitive scream as he falls to the floor. MARGOT is aroused.]

MARGOT   *(rising, as Madame)* Ah! The primitive scream! You are the one who knows my secret desire!

FRITZ   *(in pain)* Oh, God, wait!

MARGOT   *(as Madame)* For years I've been waiting for you, amnesiac drifter!

FRITZ   No, please! I can't go on!

MARGOT   *(as Madame getting on top of FRITZ)* You can! You will! Touch me, drifter!

FRITZ   Cut! Cut!!

MARGOT   *(as Madame)* I shall quell your pain with my lips! *(She lunges in for a kiss.)*

FRITZ   Stop!! Stop with your role playing, Margot!

MARGOT   Stop?

FRITZ   I'm in agony!

MARGOT   . . . Is that what you really think of my acting?

FRITZ   What? No, no. My toe—

MARGOT   *(getting up off of FRITZ and turning on a light)* My performance is "agony" to you?

FRITZ   Just give me a minute, please, Margot. Oh, God . . .

MARGOT   I'll tell you what's agony, Fritz—that piece of shit accent! You sound like a song being played backwards. But *I* went along with it, Fritz. *I* stayed in the moment. *I* remained true to the scene. That's what a professional does.

FRITZ   Margot—

MARGOT   *(heading to her bedroom)* The evening is over, Fritz. The magic has been shattered. You're not the artist I thought you were. *(deep sigh)* God. *Actors! (She slams the door. FRITZ looks around, bewildered. Perhaps music still plays softly.)*

[END OF PLAY]

Stay Awhile

Dana Hall

Production History

Stay Awhile premiered with Prism Theatre Company's Spotlight On Women Festival. It was directed by Wendy Greenwood.

The cast was as follows:

SAMANTHA   Kelly Howe

JANICE   Carmen Garcia (carmenunscripted.com)

Stay Awhile was also featured in Craig Houk's Two Hander Slam Competition in 2021. It was awarded Best of Show.

Other performances of *Stay Awhile* include Palos Village Players (Chicago), Inkwell Theatre (California), Open Door Playhouse (LA), and Thornhill Theatre Space.

Resources

"Lazy" by Irving Berlin: This song is in the public domain; visit the Library of Congress to obtain a copy.

Characters

SAMANTHA   Daughter, Stage-age late 20s–40
JANICE   Mother, Stage-age 60–75+, Grief stricken

Time

The present, early evening

Place

This is a virtual production; each character appears in their home.

[SAMANTHA is alone on a virtual call talking to herself. She is checking her email and waiting for her mother to log on. It has been some time since SAMANTHA has seen JANICE. JANICE is not technologically inclined and enters the call a bit frazzled.]

SAMANTHA   *(to self)* Where is she? I sent very detailed instructions. Come on, mom—just click the link.

[JANICE enters the call first with her camera off.]

JANICE   Hello? *(to computer)* Call. Samantha.

SAMANTHA   Mom. I'm already here. You just have to turn the camera on . . . it's the button at the bottom/

[JANICE turns on the camera.]

JANICE   *(waves)* Well, hello, dear. I did it. *(looking longingly)* There's my little girl.

SAMANTHA   Mom, I'm married with a kid of my own.

JANICE   Don't care; you'll always be *my* baby. So, aren't you proud of me? Look at me using technology like a millennium.

SAMANTHA   *Millennial* Mom.

JANICE   Can you hear me, ok? Am I doing this right? Gosh—I'm afraid to touch anything on here! This is your Daddy's old computer, and all he used it for was solitaire.

SAMANTHA   I'm glad you finally agreed to try this!

JANICE   I've just been busy, dear.

SAMANTHA   Busy? Mom, how long has it been since you left the house?

JANICE   Awhile, I suppose/

SAMANTHA   Are you ok? You look terrible.

JANICE   Thanks.

SAMANTHA   I mean, it looks like you haven't been sleeping again. Are you eating?

JANICE   I'm fine/

SAMANTHA   I can pick you up tomorrow. Take you over to the salon/

JANICE   That's not necessary/

SAMANTHA   Oh—we could swing by the grocery store. I'll make you dinner/

JANICE   Samantha—no.

SAMANTHA   What? Why?

JANICE   You're a terrible cook, dear.

SAMANTHA   Thanks. *(smiles)* Well, consider it a consequence if you don't start taking better care of yourself. So—what've you been up to—I've been calling you for days, and all I get is a text here or there. If you didn't agree to this video call, I was heading over.

JANICE   I told you in the text thingy. I've just been going through some old paperwork. There's a lot to take care of in this big ol' house.

SAMANTHA   *(noticing)* Mom, your hands are shaking.

JANICE   Oh, it's nothing. Dr. Trapps prescribed something to take the "edge off." Guess it makes me a little shaky—good thing I'm not a surgeon.

[There's a pause. JANICE is going through some old mail. JANICE's hands are visibly trembling.]

SAMANTHA   It's been months. Don't you think it's time we talk about dad?

JANICE   *(gestures to letter)* Look—the electric bill is still in your father's mother's name. Boy, she was a terrible woman. *(a jab)* Well, I'm sure I can't forward this to where she's at/

SAMANTHA   Mom/

JANICE   I know, I know—we shouldn't speak ill of the dead.

[JANICE makes the sign of the cross over her heart and adds the bill to the garbage pile.]

SAMANTHA   The cemetery called. *(pause)* His headstone is done.

[Silence. JANICE is shuffling papers, anything to avoid SAMANTHA.]

JANICE   *(jovial)* How are the kids? Is Liam in school—is he doing half days again?/

SAMANTHA   Mom/

JANICE   Boy, he's sure growing up fast! A weed, that one./

SAMANTHA   I could take you to see it.

JANICE   See what?

SAMANTHA   The headstone. Maybe we should talk about Daddy, we haven't talked about his passing since the funeral.

JANICE   *(firm)* There's nothing to see and nothing to talk about.

SAMANTHA   Not talking about it doesn't make it any less real.

[Silence. JANICE switches gears again.]

JANICE   You know what's unreal? That my grandbaby is four. Gosh, it feels like yesterday you were being induced.

SAMANTHA   Don't remind me.

JANICE   You remember when Daddy first held Liam, he said, "He has my father's eyes and Sammy's stubbornness."

[SAMANTHA mouths the last part as her JANICE says it.]

SAMANTHA   He had a way with words, didn't he?

JANICE   Boy, was he right, though; that little guy gives you a run for your money. What's he into lately? Uhh, don't tell me what was it—oh, uh, the green guy—Hulk—right?

SAMANTHA   Yeah—this week it's the Hulk, last week it was Captain America.

JANICE   They grow up so fast, Sammy. You give him kisses from his grammy.

SAMANTHA   I always do. *(Beat. She refers to her cellphone.)* Uh—Mom? Did you talk to the lawyers about the estate yet? It's just they've been leaving me all kinds of messages. *(pause)* I can help you. Apparently, we have to put some things in your name and settle up some medical bills.

JANICE   Did you hear that?

SAMANTHA   What?

[JANICE is staring off and distracted.]

SAMANTHA   *(cont.)* Mom. You ok? Is there someone there with you? Is it the Millers? They text to say they were bringing you over some food this week.

JANICE   Oh—there you are . . .

[JANICE leaves the screen.]

SAMANTHA   Who? Where are you going?

[We see glimpses of JANICE walk away then walk back past the screen slowly.]

SAMANTHA   Mom.

JANICE   *(OS)* Don't go. Just stay awhile/

SAMANTHA   Mom. *(pause)* Answer me or I'm driving over there!

[After a long pause, JANICE returns to the camera jovial. She does not have a glass of water.]

JANICE   Hi Honey. Sorry. I just needed a glass of water.

SAMANTHA   Who were you talking to?

JANICE   Talking to? Oh, must've been the old record player. I took it out the other night.

SAMANTHA   *(concerned)* You shouldn't be moving heavy things, mom. Tomorrow after Dave gets home, I'll stop by. I can help you with stuff around the house, or we can just sit together—whatever you want.

JANICE   That's nice dear. No need though.

[JANICE starts coughing.]

SAMANTHA   Take a sip of your water.

[SAMANTHA looks worried.]

JANICE   I don't have any. Hold on, honey.

[JANICE leaves the screen again. She is singing Irving Berlin's "Lazy." This does not have to be performed by a vocalist—it can be a sing/song version we might sing when no one else is listening. OS we hear her singing and coughing a bit more.]

JANICE   *(contd.) Ev'ry time / I see a puppy upon a summer's day / A puppy dog at play / My heart is filled with envy / That's because / My heart is yearning to pass the time away*

[JANICE comes back with a glass of water.]

JANICE   There—all better.

[SAMANTHA is a bit emotional as she recognized the song.]

SAMANTHA   Have you been forgetting things, mom?

JANICE   *(smiling)* No more than usual honey.

[JANICE goes to take a sip of the water. Exposing her hand is bandaged in a towel. This is new.]

SAMANTHA   *(alarmed)* Mom! What's on your hand? Did you just cut yourself?

JANICE   Oh this? It's nothing. You know me—clumsy. Remember when Liam knocked grandma's antique plate off the wall? I picked a rogue piece off the floor.

[JANICE stares off in the same direction as before.]

SAMANTHA   Just now? Liam hasn't been to see you since Daddy died three months ago. Are things ok? Mom. Are you ok?

[JANICE, with a slight smile, continues singing. She closes her eyes for long stretches as she sings . . .]

JANICE   *Lazy / I want to be lazy / I want to be out in the sun / With no work to be done*

[SAMANTHA interrupts the last few lines as Janice sings.]

SAMANTHA   Mom. *(tearful)* I'm still here.

JANICE   *(contd.) Under that awning / Stretching and yawning / And let the world go drifting by*

SAMANTHA   I'm worried about you. Should I be?

JANICE   Oh no dear, things are fine. I meant to tell you the Fosters are moving. Saw a truck yesterday.

SAMANTHA   I'm concerned with you being all alone/

JANICE   *(aggressive)* I'm not alone.

SAMANTHA   I know—you have all our support, I just mean in the house.

JANICE   *(leans in and whispers)* Drop it, Samantha.

SAMANTHA   Mom?

JANICE   There were so many boxes.

SAMANTHA   *(confused)* Where?

JANICE   The Foster's honey—I was telling you they sold the house. Turned a little profit on it from what I hear/

SAMANTHA   Are *you* thinking of selling too?

JANICE   No, dear.

SAMANTHA   Well, it might not be a bad idea if the Foster's sold so fast. You could come and stay at our house/

JANICE *(tantrum)* I said NO! NO! NO! I'm not leaving him! You and your brother think you know what's best, but you don't. Leave it alone—Ok, Sammy?

SAMANTHA *(choking back emotions)* Ok. Hey—I understand, Mom. It's ok. No one is saying you have to. I know you have a lot of memories in that house. Daddy built that beautiful sunroom for you—and Tommy and I still have all of our stuff in the crawl space/

JANICE *(as if nothing happened)* How *is* your brother—he doesn't call much these days? So busy with work, I imagine.

SAMANTHA He's great Becky, and the kids were over the other day. He said he stopped by the house last weekend to see you, but no one answered.

JANICE Becky is so lovely, and the girls are precious.

SAMANTHA Mom, are you avoiding us? I thought maybe you were just taking some time to yourself, but as time goes on, I'm starting to think it's something more.

JANICE I think I'd know if someone came by, Sammy.

[JANICE is not paying attention as SAMANTHA speaks. She appears to be staring into a corner of the room, sort of smiling.]

SAMANTHA Mom, this isn't healthy. You have to talk to someone. If not me, maybe Aunt Linda or . . . *(tries a different angle)* ya know some people are trained to be able to help people through their grief. I could take you, or maybe we could find something online like a support group, you know?—Mom. Mom, are you listening to me?

JANICE Sure honey. I'm so glad we had a chance to catch up.

SAMANTHA You know we all miss Daddy. Just hearing his records take me back to five years old—remember how he'd let me dance on his feet? I'd make him twirl me around and around. *(pause)* You know, I went to his gravesite the other day. I brought some flowers Liam picked. Maybe we could go together sometime—now that the headstone is done.

JANICE *(cold)* Why would I want to go there?

SAMANTHA To say goodbye, mom. It might do you good to see he's at peace.

JANICE *(shaking/very upset)* You listen to me, daughter—I will not be told what to do by any of you. You hear me—I loved that man for 40 years, and I will love him until I take my last breath—no amount of time changes that. Peace? A piece of my heart—of who I am is gone—just like that—gone! This is all I have, Sammy—this is all that's left. After creating a life together, a house, two beautiful kids, grandbabies—I'm alone. I lay in bed, and there's his pillow. I can still feel him next to me. He's there. I feel him. I won't let you take that from me. You don't understand? No, you can't possibly. I'm not saying goodbye, Sammy—I won't lose more of him/

SAMANTHA Mom—please. You don't have to do this alone.

JANICE His memory is all I have—what happens when that's gone too? No, I won't let it go.

SAMANTHA *We* need you mom.

JANICE No. I said NO.

[JANICE hums to herself, ignoring Samantha.]

SAMANTHA I miss you—you've been shut away for months. What about us? Losing Daddy was devastating, and I don't want to lose you too. Mom. Mom, come on, just hear me out. Don't you think the grandbabies miss their Grammy?

[SAMANTHA tries to pull herself together.]

SAMANTHA *(defeated)* Fine.

[JANICE Stops humming.]

SAMANTHA Why don't you just let me pick up some dinner for you?

JANICE *(as if nothing happened)* Oh dear, that's so kind of you—but I'm making your Daddy's favorite dinner tonight.

SAMANTHA *(resigned)* Ok—Mom/

JANICE   *(happily)* You know how dinner has to be on the plate by 7:00 p.m. sharp.

SAMANTHA   Yes, no matter where we were, it was always—*(imitates father's strict rules)* Home by 6:45 p.m., wash up, set the table, then dinner. We would sit around that table for hours just chit-chatting. Those were great *memories*, Mom.

JANICE   Well, it has to be nearly dinner time over by you too.

SAMANTHA   We ate already, mom.

JANICE   *(hurt)* Oh—I see.

SAMANTHA   Liam is still little mom we have to eat earlier/

JANICE   No-no, it's fine honey. You're such a good mom. I don't tell you that enough.

SAMANTHA   Thanks, I try—I learned from the best. *(pause)* Well, I should get going. Nowadays, it's bath by 7:00 p.m., jammies, storytime, then off to bed.

JANICE   You've made your father and me very proud.

SAMANTHA   You know I love you *so* much right?

JANICE   Of course, my love. It was so nice seeing you—you should visit more often. Oh, and tell Tommy and the girls that I love them too.

SAMANTHA   They know. We all know mom. I'll stop by tomorrow and check in on you. You sure you're ok tonight?

JANICE   Oh yes—going to start prepping the ribs with Daddy's secret recipe—you know what Daddy's secret ingredient is?

SAMANTHA   Ha. Yah. Love—

JANICE   *(looks around, then whispers)* He also adds a pinch of sugar. Bye, darling.

SAMANTHA   Bye, Mom.

JANICE   *(waves)* Bye, dear.

[SAMANTHA logs off. JANICE remains.]

JANICE   Oh my—how does this fancy contraption work?

[JANICE sings the following as she tries to figure out how to leave the call.]

JANICE   *Lazy I want to be lazy / I want to be out in the sun / With no work to be done / Stretching and yawning in the sky*

[JANICE looks off in the direction of the kitchen.]

JANICE   *(yells off)* Coming, Dear!

[JANICE throws a small kitchen towel over the camera.]

JANICE   *(contd. singing) Stretching and yawning and letting the world go drifting by—*

[End Play]

Fish Tank

Aly Kantor

Production History

Fish Tank premiered as part of One House Productions' *One House, One Heart* Virtual Play Festival in October 2020. The piece was directed by Melissa Meyers.

The cast was as follows:
MADDY   Kiana Douglas
ELLISON   Noah VanderVeer-Harris

Characters

MADDY   23 years old, she/her, incredibly smart, incredibly dark, and incredibly lonely
ELLISON   Older than Maddy, he/him, conservative and a bit naive

Time

Approximately five years after the start of a pandemic. Maybe 2025. Maybe 2125.

Place

ELLISON is in a non-descript government office. MADDY is in her home. They are both in the United States. They communicate in a third space, over a two-way video relay platform.

MADDY *(wryly)* I really thought I killed all the bugs in here.

ELLISON Are you having a problem with bugs?

MADDY You could say that, yeah—government bugged it up real good before they turned it over. You know I found a camera in the refrigerator once? You never know when something cool's gonna happen to the milk, right? If big brother was watching, he definitely lost interest.

ELLISON Ah.

MADDY Yeah, *ah*. You say "ah," like you didn't know. Who do you work for, again? Did you say? CDC? Military?

ELLISON Neither. As I explained a moment ago, my name is Grant Ellison, and I'm a representative of the Department of Homeland Security.

MADDY Are you a shrink? Government shrink?

ELLISON No, ma'am. This is not any sort of psychiatric evaluation. It's a general welfare check. We want to be sure that you're sound of mind and body.

MADDY Yeah, alright. Was there any doubt, sir?

ELLISON There was some, yes. Can you tell me anything about the incident that took place last evening? Upon reviewing surveillance, it seemed like . . . you were attempting to take your life.

MADDY Was worth a shot.

ELLISON I've looked back at your records, ma'am. I've seen transcripts from your conversations with others. You've had psychological screenings, and for all intents and purposes, you've passed. You've had IQ tests. You're not a dumb girl and we—

MADDY I'm not a girl. According to the government, I'm a woman and have been since I came into custody five fucking years ago.

ELLISON Right. My apologies. What I meant to say was, you're an intelligent *woman*, and the evaluations suggest that you are completely sound of mind and understand your circumstances. In the eyes of the government, you can be held responsible for your actions. As you are under government protection, you've received all of the most up-to-date reports directly from the source. So . . .

MADDY So.

ELLISON So what were you trying to do last night?

MADDY I slit my wrists. For science.

ELLISON For science?

MADDY If you were me, wouldn't you be curious? It was science. I wanted to know.

ELLISON That's . . . that's fair. Though . . . you do recall, when you came under our protection, that you were offered remote occupational training in the sciences, gratis? Dr. Chambers from the CDC spoke to you on numerous occasions about using your situation to assist with the research. We could have built you a laboratory, supported any project you wanted to undertake. We still could, if it's really science you're interested in. Something tells me it isn't.

MADDY This body *is* a god damned laboratory. I'm not allowed to have questions about my own body without specialized training? I'm the one who has to exist in my skin. Everyday.

ELLISON I understand.

MADDY Do you? Do you really? Do I ever put up a fucking fight when they come in their hazmat suits to suck my blood? Ever? I contribute enough to science.

ELLISON We just thought, as an intelligent person, it might feel good to contribute solutions that could serve others.

MADDY I am *intelligent* enough to recognize that my antibodies are more valuable than my humanity. That's my contribution. I know. I know that. I am in this pre-furnished cage because one day a smear of my blood on a slide might be the thing that brings things "back to normal." Meanwhile, I haven't touched another human's flesh in five years. I'm not dumb. So how about you do your science, I'll do mine.

ELLISON From our end, your actions looked like a cry for help, and we have a responsibility to—

MADDY You know why I'm here, right?

ELLISON I do. Yes.

MADDY I mean *here*. Specifically here, this little government-supplied abode.

ELLISON Specifically, no.

MADDY I was "lucky."

ELLISON Why do you say that?

MADDY I was identified as an asymptomatic carrier a *week* after I turned 18. Not even a week—six days. If I'd been a kid . . .

ELLISON You would have been at the . . . the holding facility for minor carriers . . . during the . . .

MADDY Yeah. Eleven kids died in that fire. Do you know their names?

[ELLISON is silent.]

MADDY *(cont'd)* Really? Not even the six month old? I can see the gears turning. You're picturing their faces, aren't you? Bet you thought you'd blocked those out. Well? Their names?

[MADDY waits. ELLISON squirms.]

MADDY *(cont'd)* Didn't think so.

ELLISON Did you know one of them? The children?

MADDY No, but I didn't have to know them to feel guilty about being *six days too old* to have been the twelfth. I have enough dead kids on my conscience, believe me. Did you know I worked at an ice cream shop? It was my first job . . . and my last. God knows why it was allowed to reopen that first summer. Fucking idiots. How many ice cream cones did I hand to a dad, who handed it down to a kid, who shared it with their mom and the baby? It doesn't matter that it's not that horror movie bullshit. Dead is dead. I didn't know I was carrying it, but I still killed them.

ELLISON   The fire was an act of domestic terrorism. There is no reason for you to hold any guilt about those deaths, or any deaths you may have caused before we confirmed your status.

MADDY   Just because there's no reason doesn't mean it's not real.

ELLISON   Is that a source of your unhappiness? You could start regular counseling through the relay.

MADDY   Yeah, I'd say that's a source of unhappiness. Killing everyone I love? Yeah.

ELLISON   We'll have a professional—

MADDY   Wanna hear something sick? That fire was good for me, in a way. You couldn't let me wander after that, but you couldn't lock me in a facility without someone crying foul play after that shit show, either. Had to keep me comfortable enough that I'd give you access to my bodily fluids with a smile, right? I'm comfortable here. I'm not happy. I kill your bugs, and last night I tried some science. Good to have hobbies. Speaking of, I gotta feed the damned fish.

[MADDY gets up to feed the fish, off-screen.]

ELLISON   Right—the, uh, tropical fish. I have to say, you really haven't asked for much, all things considered. Is that something you care about? Pets, animals?

MADDY   *(from off-screen)* Fish can't catch it.

ELLISON   Right.

MADDY   Fish can't do much of anything but swim, eat, shit, and die. I can relate, with that one pesky exception.

ELLISON   Is that why you asked for fish? I'll admit, we assumed it was out of monotony, or boredom . . . or for company, maybe.

MADDY   *(returning to frame)* Fish are fantastic. When they die, they stay dead. Rare in this day and age, right? It's this little aquatic world that I can't fuck up. I feed them, I stare at them, and when they die, I bury them like in the old days, before we started passing this thing around. Flipper and Sparkles aren't going to wake up and try to infect Goldie.

ELLISON Do you get something out of that?

MADDY What?

ELLISON Burying the fish.

MADDY It's something to do. Not a lot of novelty under government quarantine. Frankly, that's mostly the reason I haven't lost interest in this conversation.

ELLISON Well, before you do, is there anything we can do to add some novelty to your life? Maybe something that doesn't involve death, burial, or exsanguination?

MADDY Jesus, when you put it that way . . .

ELLISON Was that the wrong way to put it?

MADDY Are you sure you're not a shrink? Maybe consider a career change.

ELLISON Tell me. What do you want? What can we provide that would help you until a cure is developed that also works on living carriers?

MADDY I don't know. A friend? A husband? Hell, an escort? I'd love a kitten, if being around me wouldn't give it an illness with a 96 percent mortality rate. Though . . . watching a kitten convulse would be novelty. Alright, why not? Send me a kitten.

ELLISON Unfortunately, I can't do that. You know that I can't do that.

MADDY Why? You like cats?

ELLISON It would defeat the purpose of your quarantine, not to mention it's cruel.

MADDY Send me a laboratory cat with a sad life. Pluck it from a cage where it's wasting away. If it lives, someone will love him. If it dies, it'll be a mercy.

ELLISON   Based on what we know about transmission in that weight class, it'll almost certainly die.

MADDY   And then wake up again. It won't have any brain function. It'll just be a host to this thing, drooling and emitting . . . spores, or whatever the scientists think it is now. It's hard to tell when every other word in the reports is "redacted."

ELLISON   Right. A lot of the latest is classified. But regardless, I couldn't get a cat approved. It would be cruel.

[A beat.]

MADDY   You believe in God, huh?

ELLISON   I do.

MADDY   You can just smell it on some people, you know? People who take home big bucks to do welfare checks on government prisoners, and then go home to their families and meditate on the cruelty of hypothetical zombie cats. How about heaven?

ELLISON   The two go together, typically.

MADDY   Hell?

ELLISON   Hell I'm a little bit more ambivalent about. I believe there's a lot of ambiguity in life. I think a lot about intention. I think most people do try to do good. I like to think that most people would make the cut in the end. I can't know, of course, but I'm hopeful. What about you?

MADDY   Doesn't matter.

ELLISON   No?

MADDY   You realize who you're talking to, right?

ELLISON   I'm pretty certain, yes.

MADDY   Then why doesn't it matter? You're not a "dumb boy," figure it out.

[ELLISON thinks for a time, then shakes his head, shrugs.]

MADDY *(cont'd)* I'm something of a god myself.

ELLISON Pardon?

MADDY I'm the asymptomatic carrier of a disease that regenerates damaged cells at an insane rate. It wakes the dead.

[MADDY holds up a pristine wrist, not a mark on it.]

MADDY *(cont'd)* I can do anything, short of burning to ash. I do read those CDC reports, you know. They think I could live indefinitely without intervention. And I'm trapped in a government box because I can pass judgment. I could smite you by putting a hand on your shoulder.

ELLISON It's . . . You are . . .

MADDY Maybe invincible. Possibly immortal.

ELLISON Yes.

MADDY I am the closest living thing to a sentient biological weapon, and the United States government has been containing me with an electric fence and a prayer.

ELLISON You realize your condition is dangerous?

MADDY *You* realize an electric fence can't kill me? Or a bullet? I'd do more harm to the shooter. I can leave whenever I want. I don't look like anyone special. I can populate this whole world with drooling, braindead meat creatures. I can find others like me and start it all again. I figured that out two years into this. I'm Not. A. Dumb. Girl.

ELLISON Can . . . can I ask . . . why do you stay?

MADDY Gotta feed the fish. Plus, I've got eternity to fuck shit up. And maybe you're right about people. I would disagree, but someone's got to be right—and the only thing I have to do to keep from ushering in the end of days is stay home? Cake.

ELLISON Well . . . thank you for . . . thank you for doing that. For staying. And if there is absolutely *anything* we can do to—

MADDY How about this, sir? Just practice what you preach.

ELLISON   Yeah. Yeah. I . . . yes.

MADDY   You still can't decide about Hell, though?

ELLISON   I, uh, think I've been persuaded. That it exists, anyway.

MADDY   Right.

[ELLISON logs off. His screen goes black. For a moment, we're alone with MADDY, a chapped-lipped, wild-haired god in pajamas. All we hear is the sound of the fish tank as she reaches forward and turns off the screen.]

[End of play.]

Together, Even When You're Not

Kitt Lavoie

Production History

Together, Even When You're Not was originally presented as part of the *Scene Study Emergency Pack*, a collection of short plays that take place between characters communicating via video chat that was made available for free for use in remote classrooms during the COVID-19 pandemic. Conceived and edited by Kitt Lavoie and including plays by twenty-eight playwrights, the collection was written, compiled, and shared for use in remote classrooms at universities around the United States and Europe within ten days of the first US university cancellation due to COVID-19.

Characters

> JAMES   male, twenties, in the flush of early love
> KATIE   female, twenties, similarly smitten
> MARK   male, twenties, trying hard to hold on

Time

> The present, late evening.

Place

> A corporate office and a suburban bedroom decorated by a teenaged girl.

[The desktop of a Macintosh computer. The cursor tracks to the bottom of the screen, bringing up the dock. The cursor scrolls over the application icons, magnifying each in turn, until it arrives on the Skype icon.

With the sound of a click, the Skype window opens. The cursor clicks on contacts and scrolls down the long list of names and avatars until it reaches "jameskeller."

With a click, a new window pops up. On one side of the window, a woman in her mid-twenties, KATIE, sits in her pajamas in the room of a teenage girl. Late night. She peers mischievously into the camera as the Skype ring tone chirps out.

After a moment, the other side of the window lights up with the image of JAMES, late-twenties, sitting in an office, the glass door to his back. By this time, KATIE's eye is almost pressed up against her camera.]

JAMES   Hey you!

KATIE   *(like a playful robot)* I am looking at you!

[JAMES holds up three fingers.]

JAMES   How many fingers am I holding up?

KATIE   *(still the playful robot)* Okay. I am looking at the camera.

[KATIE pulls her face back away from the camera. JAMES's three fingers turn into a playful wave.]

JAMES   Hey, you.

KATIE   Hey. You're not still there, are you?

JAMES   Things got complicated.

KATIE   I'm so sorry.

JAMES   It's not your fault.

KATIE   I mean, I'm sorry I'm not there to help.

JAMES   I know, and it's not your fault you're not here. It's your sister's fault. Her and her love.

KATIE   Yes, her damn'ned love.

JAMES   How was the rehearsal dinner?

KATIE   It was good. It was nice to see everybody.

JAMES   I wish I could have been there.

KATIE   I wish you could have been, too. And I wish I could have been *there*.

JAMES   No you don't.

KATIE   No. But I wish you didn't have to be, either.

JAMES   Me, too.

KATIE   What happened?

JAMES   Just Susan being Susan. What time is it there?

KATIE   Eleven.

JAMES   Kind of early to be in your pajamas, no?

KATIE   Big day tomorrow. Plus everyone's asleep. My aunt's on the couch, so I can't watch TV. So it's jammies and chatting with you.

JAMES   *(re: the jammies)* They're cute.

KATIE   *(modeling, with a grin)* Thank you.

[JAMES leans back. He scans the screen up and down.]

KATIE   *(cont'd)* What?

JAMES   I've just never seen you dressed for bed before.

[KATIE smiles and leans back away from the camera, spreading her arms "Here it is."]

JAMES   *(cont'd)* It's just weird. The number of times I've seen you "undressed for bed" . . .

KATIE   James—

JAMES   I know. Damn'ned love.

KATIE   Soon.

JAMES   I wish I was there with you tonight.

KATIE   You couldn't sleep in here with me, anyway. My parents would kill you.

JAMES   I wouldn't need to sleep. Just see you in those jammies in person. Slide you out of them. Climb into your childhood bed . . .

KATIE   James!

JAMES   What?

KATIE   That's sick.

JAMES   It's not sick. And I know you. You would like it.

KATIE   You're funny.

JAMES   Show me your room.

[KATIE grins.]

KATIE   Okay.

[KATIE picks up her computer and disappears from the frame, aiming the camera around the room.]

KATIE   *(cont'd)* There's my bed.

JAMES   Which we've discussed.

KATIE   *(off-camera, panning around the room)* Dresser . . . posters . . .

[She pushes in on a photo.]

KATIE   *(off-camera, cont'd)* That's me at graduation.

JAMES   Adorable.

[She pulls back to reveal . . .]

KATIE   My desk.

JAMES   I know what we could do on that, for sure.

KATIE   *(panning)* Shhhh! My Barbie collection.

JAMES   And with *those*—

[KATIE swings the camera towards her.]

KATIE   Quit it!

[KATIE's hand reaches towards the keyboard. The volume indicator appears on the screen, lowering.]

JAMES Who's going to hear?

KATIE They're going to hear me laughing. Shhhh!

[KATIE returns to the bed and sits. They look at each other a moment.]

KATIE *(cont'd)* I should let you go.

JAMES It's okay.

KATIE You've still got Susan's mess to clean up.

JAMES Yeah.

[A mischievous look crosses JAMES's face.]

JAMES *(cont'd)* Let me see them.

KATIE No.

JAMES Come on.

KATIE No.

JAMES Why?

KATIE You've already got Susan's mess to clean up. You don't need to make one of your own.

[JAMES shoots a look over his shoulder, then pivots himself around the table he is sitting at so that the glass door is no longer over his shoulder.]

JAMES Come on.

KATIE Nooo.

JAMES Just a little.

[KATIE perfunctorily slides the collar of her pajamas slightly to the side.]

JAMES *(cont'd)* That was a very little.

KATIE There's no lock on the door.

JAMES A holdover from your misspent youth?

KATIE   My youth was spent fine.

JAMES   What's the worst that could happen?

KATIE   Monday. I promise.

JAMES   *(joking, like it's forever from now)* Monday!

KATIE   Aaron has a conference call at eleven. Five after. In the supply closet. You can look at them all you want.

JAMES   It's a date.

KATIE   If that's what passes as a date.

JAMES   Wear the shirt with the . . .

[He points with some indistinguishable twirling motion at his chest.]

KATIE   Okay. Don't stay there too late.

JAMES   I'm gonna try. Have a good time at the wedding.

KATIE   I will.

JAMES   And—

[Suddenly, the sound of a door opening. KATIE's eyes shoot up away from the screen. Her hand reaches forward and pulls her laptop partway shut, so that just her stomach and legs are visible, along with some of the keyboard and a girlish bedspread.]

KATIE   *(off-camera, to someone off-screen)* Hey.

[From elsewhere in the room, an unseen young man responds.]

MARK   *(off-camera)* Hey.

[JAMES listens with interest.]

MARK   *(off-camera, cont'd)* What are you doing?

KATIE   *(off-camera)* Nothing. Surfing.

MARK   *(off-camera)* Anything interesting?

KATIE *(off-camera)* No. You shouldn't be up here. My mom is down the hall.

MARK *(off-camera)* I'm being quiet.

[*KATIE's hand subtly slides into frame and to the mouse pad. The cursor begins dancing around the screen.*]

MARK *(off-camera, cont'd)* Can I get in?

[*KATIE's hand reaches to the top of the keypad. The computer's volume indicator pops up again, now set to "mute."*]

KATIE *(off-camera)* You shouldn't be up here.

MARK *(off-camera)* You looked so beautiful tonight.

KATIE *(off-camera)* Thank you. You should go back downstairs.

MARK *(off-camera)* I will.

[*A silence.*]

KATIE *(off-camera)* Now.

MARK *(off-camera)* You really did look great tonight.

KATIE *(off-camera)* Thank you.

MARK *(off-camera)* And it was great to see your mom. And your dad. And Annie. *(a beat)* Thank you for letting me come.

KATIE *(off-camera)* Of course. You should go to bed.

MARK *(off-camera)* I know. Can I get in?

KATIE *(off-camera)* No.

MARK *(off-camera)* For a few minutes?

KATIE *(off-camera)* No.

MARK *(off-camera)* They won't come in.

KATIE *(off-camera)* Mark—

MARK   (*off-camera*) You said you wish I did the last time. When we were here.

KATIE   (*off-camera*) I know.

MARK   (*off-camera*) Well?

KATIE   (*off-camera*) It's different now.

MARK   (*off-camera*) I know. And I'm trying to make it different. You said I never try anymore. So I'm trying.

KATIE   (*off-camera*) Not here. Not tonight.

MARK   (*off-camera*) When?

KATIE   (*off-camera*) Go to bed.

MARK   (*off-camera*) I thought you'd want to.

KATE   (*off-camera*) Go to bed.

MARK   (*off-camera*) How about just a little something?

KATIE   (*off-camera*) No.

MARK   (*off-camera, assuring her*) I want to.

[A beat.]

KATIE   (*off-camera*) The door doesn't lock.

[The sound of footsteps.]

MARK   (*off-camera*) Look. I'm leaning against it.

KATIE   (*off-camera*) Mark—

MARK   (*off-camera*) Then I'll go to bed.

[A beat. The top of the laptop closes a bit more just before KATIE's hand reaches into the frame and grabs hold of the bottom of her pajama top. She lifts it out of the frame, exposing her bare stomach.]

KATIE   (*off-camera*) Now go to bed.

[The sound of footsteps. A shadow falls across KATIE and the part of the bed we can see. Her pajama top falls back into frame, covering her stomach again.

The legs of a man in pajama bottoms enter the frame, standing over KATIE.]

MARK   *(off-camera)* Goodnight.

[The sound of a kiss on the forehead.]

MARK   *(off-camera, cont'd)* You're so beautiful.

KATIE   *(off-camera)* Bed. I'll see you tomorrow.

[The legs of the man turn and exit the frame. The shadow passes away from KATIE. The sound of footsteps, then the door opening and closing. KATIE becomes visible again as her laptop hinges open. She reaches for the keyboard and the volume indicator pops up again, now up where it had been before. JAMES looks away from the camera.]

KATIE   *(cont'd)* I'm sorry about that.

JAMES   Yeah. Okay. I've got to go.

[JAMES reaches for his keyboard.]

KATIE   James—

[JAMES stops. He still can't quite look at the screen.]

KATIE   *(off-camera)* You knew he was coming with me.

JAMES   Yeah.

KATIE   Look, James. My family doesn't know. Okay? It's my sister's wedding and I was not going to ruin it by telling them that there's not going to be another wedding next year. And that means Mark comes. And— . . . You know that. We talked about this.

JAMES   Yes.

KATIE   So?

JAMES   I get that they don't know.

KATIE   So?

JAMES   So. It doesn't seem like he knows, either.

KATIE   He was drunk.

JAMES He didn't sound drunk. You said you told him.

KATIE I did.

JAMES About me.

KATIE I did.

JAMES What did you tell him.

KATIE I told him that there was someone else. That I cheated on him.

JAMES "Cheated?" Like, once?

KATIE "Cheating." That I was. Currently.

JAMES And?

KATIE And I told him.

JAMES You said it was over?

KATIE Yes.

JAMES And what did he say?

KATIE He said he wanted to work it out.

JAMES Really?

KATIE Yes.

JAMES Is that what you want?

KATIE No.

JAMES So what did you tell him?

KATIE I told him I don't know.

JAMES But you *do*.

KATIE Yes.

JAMES So why didn't you tell him that?

KATIE *(bursting out) Because I don't know.*

[*KATIE shoots a look to the door, then settles back down, quieting.*]

KATIE *(cont'd)* I don't know how to do this. I have been with him since I was nineteen years old and I don't know how to just stop. I don't know how to just cut him out of my life, okay? It's not just asking him to sleep on the couch. It is not asking him to move out. He is *everywhere* in my life. And I don't know how to just make that go away. Even if I want him to. I've been with him for *five years*.

JAMES *(throwing down the gauntlet)* And you've been happy for how many of those?

[A beat.]

KATIE *(picking it up)* Five. Some of the time.

JAMES Then what are we about?

KATIE The rest of the time.

[A beat.]

JAMES I can't do this anymore.

KATIE James—

JAMES I can't make another date with you in the storage closet. Or to slip off for lunch between meetings so we have twenty minutes to talk. I want to take you to *dinner*. After work. I want to take you to a movie. Or to a concert. And I want to take you home to my house. I want those pajamas to be in my house.

KATIE They will be.

JAMES When?

KATIE I don't know.

JAMES *(getting loud)* You can't just keep fucking me and expect me to wait.

[KATIE reaches for the keyboard. The volume indicator pops up again, lowering.]

KATIE Why not?

JAMES Because you can't.

KATIE   Why not?

JAMES   Because that's not the way it works.

KATIE   Why can't it be?

JAMES   *(bursting out) Because it isn't!*

[JAMES looks away from the screen and around. KATIE reaches for the keyboard and the volume indicator pops up, lowering some more.]

KATIE   I was with him the first time we were together. At the Christmas party. You had met him *that night*. He was *downstairs*. So *please*.

JAMES   That was six months ago.

KATIE   I am not going back to him.

JAMES   "Going back to him?" He was just in the room with you. And I'm here.

KATIE   And I'm not going back to him. And you know that because I am still, as you put it, "fucking" you. And that's all I can do for now.

JAMES   Well, if that's "all you can do."

KATIE   It's been enough up until now.

JAMES   It really hasn't, though. Is I think what I'm saying.

[A beat. They stare at each other through the screen.]

JAMES   *(cont'd, a threat)* I could tell him.

KATIE   I already told him.

JAMES   It would sound different coming from me.

KATIE   I know.

[A beat.]

JAMES   Well, isn't this romantic.

KATIE   I'm just saying, you don't get to sleep with an engaged woman, then get upset when it takes her some time to disentangle herself.

JAMES   I can wait for you to disentangle yourself. But I can't wait for you to decide if you want to.

KATIE   I want to.

JAMES   You told me you hadn't had sex with him in eight months. That he didn't even seem to want to anymore.

KATIE   Yeah.

JAMES   And how *unattractive* that made you feel.

KATIE   Yeah.

JAMES   Well, he sure seemed to want to tonight. Is what I'm saying.

KATIE   Yeah.

JAMES   So? Which is it?

KATIE   We hadn't. Until I told him about you.

[They sit for a moment.]

KATIE   *(cont'd)* It's complicated, James.

JAMES   It's easy.

KATIE   It isn't.

JAMES   You could make it easy.

KATIE   I really can't. It's hard to leave. When he's trying. But it won't last. It's just time. Here . . .

[She reaches for the top button of her pajamas. She looks up and away towards the door. She begins unbuttoning her pajama top.]

KATIE   *(cont'd, eyes still on the door)* I promise, it's just a matter of time.

[As KATIE continues to unbutton—eyes still towards the door—JAMES watches closely as the hand dances down the front of her pajama top—and at the diamond ring sparkling on it.

Just as KATIE undoes the last button and reaches to open the top, JAMES reaches forward to the keyboard on his laptop. His image disappears as the metallic Skype "Clunk" pulls KATIE's eyes back to the screen.

She watches the empty box that JAMES once inhabited for a moment, then buttons up her pajama top, and closes the laptop into black.]

[*END OF PLAY.*]

Guru of Touch

Jenny Lyn Bader

Production History

Guru of Touch premiered in the virtual Edinburgh Festival Fringe in August of 2020, in a digital production presented by Flying Solo! Presents Productions (producing artistic director, Penny Cole), hosted by theSpaceUK, and produced by This Is Not a Theatre Company (artistic director, Erin B. Mee). The site-specific zoom play was directed by Erin B. Mee. The stage manager was Caroline Ragland. The production assistant was Madeleine Berkowitz, who also served as designer of the closing credits.

The cast was as follows:

GURU   James Kiberd
TECH   Kara Green
ZOEY   Lipica Shah
ANN   Lynnette R. Freeman
CARA   Juliette Bennett
ISABEL   Mariana Cardenas
EMILY   Amy Stiller

Characters

GURU   A charismatic healer, well established in the field of energy work over some years

TECH   A young woman who works in technology

ZOEY   An introvert who wants to believe and have hope

ANN   A highly rational person

CARA   A woman who imagines herself as a seeker

ISABEL   A skeptic not sold on the idea of tele-healing

EMILY   An observer with her own reasons for dropping by virtually, about the same age as the Guru

Author's Note: There are a few lines written in the Zoom "chat" rather than spoken, but the play can also be performed without them.

Time

Spring 2020, early in the COVID-19 pandemic—or anytime there is an effort to "shelter in place" and stay home.

Place

The online platform Zoom.

[A Zoom session. The GURU, a charismatic man in midlife, is in a box labeled "Healing" where his name should be. His video is pinned so he is the only person we see.]

GURU   I'd like to thank everyone for coming today to do the work. Energy work. It's so powerful. I was looking forward to being with all of you in a room. That's what I do, what I'm known for doing. I teach healing, in a room. I teach aliveness. I help you reach a more realized level of consciousness through simple exercises. Learning to hold light, to pass light itself to the person next to you. To help a roomful of people overcome what ails their bodies and minds and souls by engaging in a circle of meditation. Holding each other's hands. In a room. Not in a "zoom"! They call me the "Guru of Touch." But how can I be the guru of touch when I can't touch? That question keeps arising now that we can't meet in person. I was going to tell the institute to refund all of your tickets. Actually, I did tell them to refund all of your tickets. But then I started to wonder. . . . Maybe, just maybe, I can send you that same healing energy through space and through time and over videoconference. With the right intention and the right vibration, it can work. If I have a sense of where you are and can see you. It's known as distance healing. Remote healing. And it seems to be increasingly popular among certain gurus. But it's one thing to be popular. The question is not whether you can be popular but whether you can be powerful. How powerful is it? And if it works well enough, can this work become even more powerful than we knew before? Are you willing to try? To take a leap of faith for the sake of healing, improving, and transforming yourselves? How can you best open yourself to receive the light? Are you with me?

[A second box appears, belonging to the TECH, a young woman. Her caption says "Tech."]

TECH   Yeah, I got all that. The level sounds good.

GURU   But are you with me in spirit?

TECH   I'm the technical liaison from the institute. I don't have a spirit.

GURU   I'm sure that's not true.

TECH   No, it is.

GURU   Everyone else—are you with me?

TECH   They're not here yet.

GURU   What? But it says they're in the zoom room.

TECH   They're in the waiting room. We've got a security barrier on the main chamber to prevent hacking. We always do a soundcheck before letting people in. That was your sound check.

GURU   Soundcheck? That was my innermost outpouring of my soul's deepest wanderings in the forest of faith and doubt and affirmation!

TECH   Maybe so, but it was also a soundcheck.

GURU   No one heard me.

TECH   I heard you.

GURU   Without spirit.

TECH   Without trying to engage the spirit. I was focused on checking the levels. Now it's almost start time—the system has messaged the guests that they'll be let in the room momentarily. So, quickly: I'm in control of the hosting tools. If you want to mute anyone or unmute anyone or make anyone's video appear or disappear, just send me a message in the chat.

GURU   The "chat"?

TECH   Click chat on the bottom, then it should come up on your right. You see it?

GURU   Yes! No. It went away! Oh, there it is.

TECH   Try to send me a private message.

GURU   Okay. It just says your name is "tech"?

TECH   That's just our handle for the tech department. My name is Emily.

GURU   Nice to meet you, Emily. You share a name but hopefully not a world view with my ex-wife.

TECH   Ha!

GURU   Okay. *(speaking out loud while typing)* "Hi, Emily." *(looks up)* Did you get it?

TECH   Yes. Got it. Wrote back. Did you get it?

GURU   It says "hi—just testing." Actually, "just testing" is something she would do. The other Emily, I mean.

TECH   So that's how you send me a message. If you want to pin the video of you so they only see you, or share your screen, just let me know by private chat message. If you want to know someone's name, they're written below them.

GURU   Oh good. I'm terrible with names.

TECH   Do you have any questions?

GURU   Do you think this whole thing can work?

TECH   You mean, transmitting energy virtually? Or making people think you did?

GURU   Either.

TECH   Nah, it can't be either. It can only be both or none.

GURU   What the hell are you talking about, Emily?

TECH   I mean, if you do one, then you've done the other. Either one leads to the other one, right? If you do transmit energy, they'll think you did it. If they think you did it, you might as well have transmitted it.

GURU   No, there are other possibilities. I could do it without it being recognized. Or: they could imagine I did it when nothing had actually happened.

TECH   I wouldn't focus on those other possibilities if I were you.

GURU   Oh! So you're a believer in the power of positive thinking!

TECH   Definitely not. But I do believe in not giving up before you've started.

GURU   *(takes this in)* You're right. I shouldn't be so defeatist. I should have a better attitude in my introduction. Thank you! Let's let them in.

[EMILY's box goes black, so we no longer see her; we only see the caption "TECH." More squares are added as more people enter the meeting: ZOEY, who sometimes puts her face especially close to the camera; ANN, who has a bookshelf or pile of books in the background; ISABEL, sitting at her desk and looking skeptical; CARA, smiling serenely with a lit candle in the background. There is also a black box labeled "MEDITATION SESSION"—and possibly others labeled "LURKER" and "PERSEPHONE'S iPAD."]

GURU   Welcome, everyone, to our Zoom room of distance healing. It sounds strange but there's a long history of distance healing. Of powerful seers able to impact the life and health of those thousands of miles away. Of masses of people with a shared hope that impossibly found its way into reality. Of the power of prayer, which is of course the original remote healing. If we were sitting next to each other, I'd tell you about the medieval kings who practiced laying on of hands. I'd tell you stories about physical touch, to introduce this lesson. But I think the lesson here and now is: you don't have to touch, to touch. Does that make sense to everyone?

ZOEY   It absolutely makes sense. That's why I'm here.

ANN   But you do have to touch, to touch.

ISABEL   If it doesn't work, can we still get our money back? I emailed about that but . . .

GURU   Great. Why don't we go around the room and—

CARA   I know it works.

GURU   How do you know that?

CARA   Because I was at your energy circle in Woodstock last year. And I asked you to do a laying on of hands for my grandmother who was in the cancer ward, but she couldn't leave the cancer ward, so I just asked you to lay your hands on my head while I thought about my grandmother, and about an hour later her T-cell numbers went way up. And they released her from the hospital later that night. So I know you can do remote healing.

GURU   Holy shit. I mean, that's great. Of course I can do remote healing. I just need everyone else to understand that touch doesn't always mean touch.

ISABEL   See, that's where I'm losing you.

CARA   How do you not get that? Don't you ever find something "touching"? Aren't you ever touched by an emotional event?

ISABEL   Different kind of touching.

CARA   Hey, why don't we stop arguing about whether he can do it and just let him do it?

GURU   Thank you. Why don't we start with you . . . *(mispronouncing her name as "Car-ah")* Cara.

CARA   *(correcting his pronunciation to "Care-ah")* Care-ah.

GURU   *(gets it right this time)* Care-ah. Please begin.

CARA   Great. I'm here today because I've been having stress migraines.

GURU   Do you have one now?

CARA   Yes, I've been having it all morning.

GURU   Can you tell me exactly where?

CARA   My left temple.

GURU   *(mispronouncing her name again)* Where are you in the world, Car-ah?

CARA   *Care*-ah. I'm in Croton-on-Hudson.

GURU   Great. Thank you. *(types into his phone and looks at the map)* I'm seeing your location. Can you place two fingers gently against your left temple? And close your eyes.

CARA   Yes.

GURU   Thank you. Now get a little closer to the camera, so I can see the affected area. Keep your fingers there. And envision the pain. What color is it?

CARA   It's blue.

GURU   And how big is it?

CARA   The size of a small orange? Or a large mandarin orange.

GURU   A large blue mandarin orange. Okay. Thank you.

CARA   Now what?

GURU   Now I do the rest.

[He closes his eyes and concentrates on transmitting energy. The others look on, reacting with various degrees of acceptance and incredulity.]

CARA   Wow.

GURU   How do you feel?

CARA   Just like I wanted to feel.

GURU   By which you mean . . . ?

CARA   Better. I wanted to feel better.

ZOEY   Oh my god this is so beautiful!

ISABEL   This feels a little like a set-up.

ZOEY   A set-up? She feels better!

ISABEL   Sure she does. But she went first.

ANN   She sure got that ball rolling, didn't she?

ISABEL   *(agreeing)* As if she's not real.

CARA   I'm real!

ANN   She doesn't mean you're not an actual person. She means you're not a real participant. You're someone planted here.

ISABEL   Exactly. An audience plant. To get things off on the right foot.

GURU   Are you kidding me? I've never met her before.

CARA   Yes you have.

GURU   I mean, yes, I healed your grandmother remotely in Woodstock.

CARA   While she was in Teaneck.

GURU   While she was in Teaneck. But we didn't arrange anything for today. I don't know Care-ah. I didn't even pronounce her name correctly!

CARA   It's true. That was hurtful.

GURU   Tell them.

CARA   He doesn't remember meeting me before. I haven't spoken to him since. He can't get my name right. He's not good with names. He's just good with sending the energy, that's what he's good with. Believe it. Try it. You wanna feel better? I feel better.

ISABEL   I'm sorry, she sounds a little like a commercial right now.

ANN   You know what? I'm starting to believe her. She's too insulted about the Car-ah/Care-ah thing to be a commercial.

CARA   Don't you hate it when people get your name wrong?

ANN   My name is Ann. No one gets it wrong.

GURU   Great. If no one else is having a particular pain right now, I'd like to move on to doing a general exercise for everyone to increase our power to heal ourselves. Put both of your hands on the sides of your faces, palms facing forward. Good. Now we're each going to imagine holding the person's hand that's next to you on the screen. That means that Isabel, you'll hold Zoey's hand, and Zoey will hold . . .

ISABEL   But on my screen, I'm not next to her. Do you not know how this works? We all have a different order on our screens.

GURU   Oh. I didn't realize that. In that case . . . everyone look at your own screen. And imagine you're holding the hands of the person next to you . . .

ZOEY   I'm sorry, I really want to do this but I can't. Oh god I hate Zoom so much! There are so many things I would go to if it weren't for my hate of Zoom. I came here today because I love this work even more than I hate Zoom but now . . . ooooh.

GURU   Hey. Relax. Why can't you do it? Are you resisting picturing it?

ZOEY   No, no, I'm in a very open place. It's that I can't see the person next to me. I'm on the side, and the only person next to me is a black box. They have their video off.

GURU   Can you picture holding hands with someone with their name?

ZOEY   But they don't have a name. Their box just says, "meditation session."

GURU   Oh, I see. Meditation Session, can you turn your video on? Hello? Can you unmute? Or maybe I can do this . . . no, it has to be . . . where is that damn chat window? It's gone. *(calling out to the TECH)* Emily!

[The TECH turns her video on.]

GURU   Emily! Can you unmute . . . ?

[EMILY, the GURU's ex-wife, is revealed in the formerly black box labeled "MEDITATION SESSION."]

EMILY   How did you know it was me?!

[TECH realizes what's happening and reacts, turning her video back off.]

GURU   I . . . uh . . . I don't know! I sensed it! What are you doing here?

EMILY   I've been curious about your energy work for a while now. I thought I could come see it today without you seeing me, so I kept my video off.

GURU   You called yourself "Meditation Session."

EMILY   Yeah, so you wouldn't notice me.

GURU   But you hate meditation!

EMILY   I know, I do! I thought it would help me blend in here.

ISABEL   Wow.

EMILY   But you saw me anyway, and you did good with the tele-healing. Is it called tele-healing? I'm glad I was here to see it for myself.

GURU   Really?

EMILY   Yeah, yeah. I was skeptical but I guess . . . you have developed some powers since I last saw you.

GURU   Maybe I have.

ZOEY   When did you last see him?

EMILY   In divorce court. During our divorce.

ISABEL   You married him?

CARA   Can we get back to the healing circle of hands?

ISABEL   You guys, I think the ex-wife is a plant too!

ZOEY   You think everyone's a plant.

ISABEL   C'mon. What are the chances that someone you last saw in divorce court comes into your online video healing conference and tells you that you have powers she didn't realize you had during your marriage?

[ISABEL is now typing into the chat]

GURU   I know, it's incredible isn't it?

[As he takes a beat to consider this, ISABEL's chat comment appears in the comments field:]

> Hey um, "Persephone's iPad"—what about you? Are you a plant? Or are you for real??

GURU   . . . It feels like I'm dreaming, only awake.

[In the chat, an answer comes from "PERSEPHONE's iPAD":]

> @Isabel: you're very suspicious

EMILY   I can promise you this is not a set-up. And he didn't have any powers when we were married. I'm not sure what powers he has now. But he does seem . . . just a little more powerful.

GURU   Thank you, Emily.

EMILY   You're welcome. Fred.

GURU   That means a lot to me.

ANN   His name is Fred?

[A beat . . . and one more answer arrives from "PERSEPHONE's iPAD":]

> I'm real. For six months of the year

ZOEY   Oh my god this is definitely happening. Can you all see it's happening?

CARA   I see it.

ANN   It both can't be happening and is.

GURU   Now that we have rendered you visible, Emily, do you want to join the healing circle of hands?

EMILY   Um. Sure. I will.

ISABEL   Hey Fred, are you okay?

CARA   Are you kidding? Of course he's okay. He's healed us and he's touched us, and himself, without even being in the same room.

ANN   . . . And: without having any idea of what he's doing.

GURU   Just think of the light.

[They all hold their palms facing forward, to the sides of their faces, filling each square. On the screen, it seems as if their hands might be touching—a healing circle within a grid of squares.]

GURU   Even if your video is off, even if this isn't what you were planning to do today, try to reach out. Just reach out to the next person. Reach out in your mind.

[He allows the moment to land. Then, about 10 seconds later, a breath. And:]

Great work today. If you come back, this is where we'll start next time.

[A note appears in the chat from "PERSEPHONE's iPAD" to Everybody:]

Gotta run! Thank you!!!

["PERSEPHONE's iPAD" leaves the room. Isabel leaves the room. Ad lib as the others leave one by one, waving and saying their goodbyes or expressing thanks.]

[END PLAY]

Toshanisha—
The New Normals

Ivam Cabral and Rodolfo García Vázquez

Production History

The show *The New Normals*, a theatrical text in a single act and 12 scenes, by Ivam Cabral and Rodolfo García Vázquez, premiered on September 13, 2020, on the Zoom platform. On June 12, 2021—also on Zoom and in coproduction with the Bold Theatre group from Kenya—the premiere of a new version of *Toshanisha—The New Normals* took place. The following text is the one used in the Kenyan-Brazilian coproduction.

Brazilian Production Cast

Alessandra Nassi, Alex de Felix, Alex de Jesus, Anna Kuller, André Lu, Beatriz Medina, Bruno de Paula, Dominique, Elisa Barboza, Felipe Estevão, Guilherme Andrade, Heyde Sayama, Ícaro Gimenes, Ingrid Soares, Júlia Francez, Karina Bastos, Luís Holiver, Marcelo Vinci, Roberto Francisco, and Vitor Lins

Kenyan/Brazilian Cast

Aroji Otieno, Awuor Onyango, Calvin Kinyua, Cindy Nyambura, Idris leem, Mariana França, Martina Ayoro, Nungari Kiore, and Rey Bulambo
Direction: Rodolfo García Vázquez
Visual design: Adriana Vaz
Visual design assistant: Rogério Romualdo (Brazilian production) and Letícia Gomide (Kenyan-Brazilian production)
Soundtrack: Ivam Cabral
Assistant director (Brazil): Gustavo Ferreira

Graphic design: Henrique Mello
Executive producers: Diego Ribeiro and Janna Julian
Artistic director, Bold Theatre: Aroji Otieno
Produced by: Cia de Teatro Os Satyros (Brazil) and Bold Theatre (Kenya)

SCENE 1: INTRO

AROJI   Fifteen months, fifteen months. . . . In Kenya more than 170,000 people have been infected. More than 3,400 died. So far we have had three waves, but we are still not out of the woods yet. So we still have a curfew. The lockdowns brought our country on its knees. For fifteen months, thespians have been out of work. After all, who are artists to the government? Who are thespians to the public? It is not us alone. Many industries have been destroyed and people are changing businesses or careers. But Kenyans are used to this. We are as tough as diamonds.

  We, the working class, are the backbone of our nation. Everyone does what little they can do to keep the nation alive. For me it's this . . . the nyatiti. This is an eight-stringed instrument that my ancestors carried with them all the way from Sudan, a Place called Barl El Gazr. They then followed the Nile as they settled in different parts of East Africa. It is made up of eight strings which are inspired by voices of cattle: The ones on top are the cows and these ones at the bottom are the bulls. And they discuss among themselves. The player then joins the conversation. . . .

[He begins to pluck.]

[As he plucks he talks about what he misses, then calls the others to do the same.]

MARTINA   I miss going to the beach without wearing a mask. I miss hanging out with my friends without having to social distance.

CALVIN   I miss hanging out with my big brother. I miss the talks, the small arguments and fights. I just miss every moment of life we spend together. I just miss him.

MARIANA   I miss the unexpected invitations from my friends, the stories and the affection. I miss the unexpected life.

IDRIS   I miss night life. I miss going for shawarma late at night. I miss Taraweeh. I miss seeing the crowded streets late at night.

CINDY   I miss hanging out with my friends and family. Drinking, eating . . . just the good vibes.

KIORE   I miss travelling. The beaches. I miss girl time with the girls. The sleepovers, crying over boys. I miss my friends, the ones I've lost and the last ones I gained. I miss everything.

DAISY   I miss hugging my friends and family. That warm embrace that tells you everything will be fine. I miss the human touch.

REY   I miss my colleagues who got the chance to go away. We had a good time and beautiful memories and friends who visited us in the camp to bring their love and smile with us in order to have hope of life.

SCENE 2: CAMP

REY   This is the Kakuma refugee camp. Kakuma is divided into four sections and I'm here in section one, known as Kakuma 1. The gate you see here separates the refugee camp and the host community, which is under the second community, the Congolese and Ethiopian community. Let me take you through the street of Kakuma 1.* The water tanks you are seeing here . . . these are the ones supplying water for refugees twice a day, morning hours and afternoon. Since the beginning of COVID and the closure of the camp, both refugee and host community are being affected, particularly in my case, as I have been working for UNHCR for the last five years as a driver, I'm really hurting because even we citizens depend on refugees. UNHCR gave us jobs. Take a look at this tailoring shop owned by a refugee. It is empty. No customers come to make the clothes due to this closure of the camp. The people you see here wearing traditional clothes, they are from the host community. They used to work in their own businesses and afterwards would help the refugees in some domestic tasks. Then, late in the evening, they could go back to their own homes. But nowadays there is no work anymore. That's why they leave earlier. These goats belong to the host. This is a place where people take trash and burn it; the kids you see there on top are from the host. They usually come here to look for something to eat every

* There are two refugees communities. The second community has Congolese and Ethiopian refugees. Rey has lived in the first community since 2013.

day; sometimes they get it; sometimes they miss it. Life here is very tricky in the camp from both sides, the refugees and the host community. And the worst thing: we will be losing even our jobs one day. UNHCH is going to close the camp. There is a boy here close to me. Let's talk to him. He is crying since he has been here for a long time and he has not got anything to eat yet. And the time remaining for the camp grows short. Let's pray to God that the government of Kenya and UNHCR will have more negotiations so that the issue of closing the camp might be cancelled, *because, without the camp, life is going to be twice as hard as it was.*

SCENE 3: MOTHER AND CALVIN

MOTHER   Calvin, Calvin, Calvin.

CALVIN   YEESSS!!!!!!!!

MOTHER   Wake up!! You are going to be late for school. Don't be lazy like your father!!!

CALVIN   Nakuja, wacha nivae!* Mum I can't go to school tomorrow.

MOTHER   Why can't you go to school tomorrow?

CALVIN   Mom, I don't want to be caned by teacher Omondi. He told us to bring 500 shillings for a mask, and you know very well the strokes of teacher Omondi's cane are very hot.

MOTHER   Ooh wow! So you are now buying masks. I thought the government purchased that for every student.

[Picks the phone to call teacher. Second attempt.]

CALVIN   Mom who are you calling, MOM, MOM! Please mom don't call teacher Omondi. Mom I beg you please!

MOTHER   *[Insulting him]* Funga mkebe wewe kasuku. Kazi ni kupayuka hapa kama mam wa kifaranga. Hallo mwalimu.† Yes, I am sending him today. He will bring 500 shillings for a mask . . . *(Ends call)* What!!! CALVIN!!! CALVIN!!!!!!!

---

* I'm coming, let me dress up.

† Teacher

SCENE 4: TABLE SCENE

CINDY   As you can all see, this is a table, and we know tables come in different shapes and are made of different materials. Here with me you can see toothpicks, dental floss, and a salt shaker. Towards my right we can see newspapers, a notebook, a pen and tape. With me is the Sunday edition, and the front page is filled with a bunch of politicians and our very dear own Mr. President, who is one of the most intelligent men in Africa. Don't come for me guys; that's my opinion. This is how the Kenyan newspaper looks. Here in Kenya newspapers are not only used for reading but also for packing meat, covering books, cleaning windows, construction. "AFRICAN GIRL SINGS HER WAY TO FAME IN AMERICA." Good for her. So basically that's what it entails, and then we have sports on the back page. Back to the table. This table has just been a rollercoaster of emotions. We've had birthdays, shared meals, hosted guests, I've been scolded A LOT, done my assignment, drooled, cried, laughed, but there's this incident that occurred to me that will still remain fresh in my heart. On this table that you're all looking at, this very table. This is where I became a woman.

SCENE 5: SENSUAL DANCE

[A sensual dance with the female artists of the ensemble. They show part of their bodies to the audience.]

SCENE 6: CINDY'S MONOLOGUE

CINDY   I know what you're thinking. I became a woman? How, and why? Well, long story short, when I was 10, I was touched. Touched by my teacher. I remember at that time I was so naïve, innocent, and pretty much didn't have a voice. I was touched. I remember his lips brushing all over my neck, his right hand grabbing my waist and the other one grabbing my bum. I mean . . . I was small; did I really deserve all this? To make matters worse, the same thing happened when I was 13. This time round I was in boarding school. You could imagine the trauma that was going on in my head. Every day I was caned and touched. Lashes after lashes after lashes. At some point I felt like committing suicide, but still at the same time I was telling myself better days are coming. To be honest, till today I regret that I never said anything. To every girl, every lady, every woman who's watching this or listening to this, I urge you to find your voice.

SCENE 7: GIRLS

MARIANA   The majority of sexual violence victims are shockingly young. 81.8 percent are female, with cases most common for girls between 11 and 15 years old. In my case it was when I was 13. I was walking down the street when a man in a car stopped next to me asking for information. He rolled down his window and that's when I saw that he was masturbating. This is not exactly a new phenomenon, but it's a problem that has traditionally been made invisible in Brazil.

KIORE   I lack words. I was just a kid. Just a small kid.

MARTINA   A man once called me a slut. I don't know if I walked like one, talked like one, or looked like one. This same man wanted to rape me. Today, I choose not to be touched, I choose not to be afraid, and I choose not to be raped.

DAISY   A man once touched my boob and put the blame on me. He said it was my fault for allowing it. Oh God! He just sat there like he did nothing and even after I confronted him, I didn't feel the same. I was disgusted. I still am. I couldn't say anything. I couldn't process what I wanted to feel or do. I cleaned myself twenty times, but I couldn't wash away that feeling. How do you just permit yourself to touch me? I didn't do anything. Maybe I could've done something to stop it. The trend didn't stop with me. Many others were touched but remained silent.

CINDY   I was a girl, just a girl, just a teenage girl.

SCENE 8: TRIBUTE TO DEAD PEOPLE

AROJI   *(wail)* Wuololo I am the waterfall that flows. *(repeat)* I am the one flowing for the late Small Ogutu, my fellow artist. We loved each other, we supported each other, and we could visit each other here in Nairobi city.

MARTINA My friend lost his dad during the pandemic. I haven't been able to go and see him and properly give my condolences. I miss him. Time will heal the wounds, but the memories last with us forever.

CALVIN It's hard to believe that ten years from now I won't see you anymore. To see your smile, to hear your jokes. But I know you're waiting for us on the other end. Mom and Dad will be happy to see you once again. I am just waiting for the day to tell you how much I have missed spending my life with you. . . . May we meet again, my dear brother, may we meet again.

MARIANA Eneas Carvalho, known as MC Enezimo, a great representative of Sao Paulo's hip hop scene. He was a great coworker these last four years in Santo Andre. Four months ago in Santo Andre, he died at 46, leaving a legacy and thousands of young people who were inspired by his career.

IDRIS Perfect journalist you were. Seeing you reporting news motivated me to pursue journalism. Sad I never met you. COVID took you, but what do we say? Rest in peace, tutaonana baadaye.*

CINDY To all the doctors, nurses, health workers. Thank you for your sacrifice and brave hearts even during these hard times. We love you and we miss you.

KIORE Not long since you've left us. You are still fresh in our memories. We miss you dearly friend. May you rest in peace Kym.

DAISY A kind soul you were. Always working diligently even when you were not paid for a long time. You took care of others with so much love and care. When your turn came, the system failed you and it didn't care. Rest.

REY Since the breakout of this COVID-19 we lost our beloved ones, as well as the most important person, pan-Africanist and patriot, the late Tanzania president, Pombe Joseph Magufuli. Rest in internal peace.

AROJI *(singing)* I beseech you to remember the soil.

---

* We will meet soon.

The soil is resilient.
What you partake of is yours,
but do not desire what is not yours.
What begun as a passing cloud,
has gone with our loved ones.
Some of them were family,
some friends,
some leaders of our communities.
But we want you to know
that they shall not be forgotten.
Tonight we salute you.
To God nothing is a coincidence.
So we decide to keep
your memories alive
deep in our hearts
and spirits.
Salute!
Salute!
Salute!
Salute!
Salute!

SCENE 9: WEED

[Idris finds Calvin in the toilet.]

IDRIS Bazuu bazenga.

CALVIN Aren't you a form one?

IDRIS Don't mind that, take it slow.

CALVIN Go away, I do not want to be involved in your stories.

IDRIS Listen, during the pandemic, I started trafficking this stuff. I even have some at home. I can bring some for you. I am even thinking of quitting school and running a business, and within no time I will be owning a huge mansion and a convertible car.

CALVIN For real!! Stop joking.

IDRIS I am not joking! Eeiiiish! Do faster; we are running out of time.

[Calvin gives Idris the weed. Idris smokes, three puffs and then coughs. He gives the weed back to Calvin.]

IDRIS This one smells bad!

[After some minutes, he starts hallucinating and shouting claiming that he's blind and he is seeing seven other Idrises.]

CALVIN Idris, shut up, you will sell us out. Drink some water.

[IDRIS can't swallow the water.]

CALVIN What have I done now!

IDRIS Calvin, what have you done to me, what have you done to me, Calvin? Calvin, the sun has been switched off! I Can't see! Oh my God, I have lost sight.

CALVIN Let me check it for you.

IDRIS I can see now . . . But . . . But there is a lion. Calvin, there is a lion!

CALVIN Lion? Where?

IDRIS Somebody help! I need help! There is a lion, Calvin let's run!

CALVIN Idris!

IDRIS I need help!

SCENE 10: UN

AROJI Ladies and gentlemen, welcome to the 47th UNICEF annual Black Caucus global conference. As you can all attest to, we are meeting under very different circumstances. However, I must congratulate you for being part of the 3,300 people joining us via Zoom. The topic of this session is stated in a question form, "Are vaccines the final solution?" The panel is made up of a panel of highly qualified ladies. I will not go through their bios because we might need another hour of additional time. So, I'll head straight away to introduce the team, beginning with, all the way from Burkina Faso, Dr. Awuor Onyango . . .

DAISY   Merci beaucoup. Je suis très heureuse d'être ici. J'espère que nous allons avoir une très bonne discussion.

AROJI   All the way from Sao Paulo, Brazil, Dr. Mariana Franca.

MARIANA   Hello. Meu nome é Mariana.

AROJI   And last but not least, Miss Cindy Nyambara.

CINDY   Hallo Sir!! First of all do not butcher my name like that. If you cannot pronounce it, just shut up.

AROJI   Apologies. . . . Straight to the topic at hand. Dr. Awuor, are vaccinations the final solution?

DAISY   Le vaccin est une bonne idée. Il nous protégera contre le COVID. Tout le monde doit le prendre. COVID est une maladie terrible. Tout le monde doit être prudent.

AROJI   Dr. Mariana, should we look for a cure or should we develop the vaccination structures?

MARIANA   I don't have anything to say.

AROJI   I thought this chloroquine idea ended with Trump. . . . Madam Cindy, do you agree that vaccines won't work especially considering Kenya has had only 1 percent vaccinated so far?

CINDY   What do you mean. First can you stop listening to these idle youths who are bashing all over social media saying vaccines are expensive. Saying vaccines go for 5,000 shillings.
What is the meaning of this!!

AROJI   Okay. Dr. Awuor, what's your say on this 1 percent vaccination situation.

DAISY   Malheureusement notre situation c'est terrible. Le vaccin . . .

AROJI   Sorry, one moment please. Madam Cindy, your video is not off. . . . Someone switch off her video!

[Mariana and Daisy complain about the situation.]

AROJI   Ladies and Gentlemen. Sorry about those technical challenges. . . . I'll be back after ten minutes.

SCENE 11: HALVES

MARIANA I have two halves inside of me. They struggle. They fight. They take me over during the days and nights.

DAISY *[Singing. Jatugo koro awuotho . . .]*

KIORE—???

MARTINA *And the other half of me is anxious for the future*
Organizing trips
Planning parties
Dreaming of sex with the one I love.

KIORE *Half of me is afraid of the future*
Its hiding in its shell
Full of resentment and pain
And the other half of me is proud
Of being resilient
Of having survived
During this horrible war.
Half of me will never love again
And the other half of me wants so many babies
And create a new future
Half of me is missing the past
The people I loved to hug
And the bars
And friends chattering through the nights
And the other half of me is anxious for the future
Organizing trips. Planning parties
Dreaming of sex with the one I love.

SCENE 12: HOPE FOR THE FUTURE

AROJI This is a photo of me and my sisters. It was taken during my niece's first birthday celebration. I hope that when this craziness ends, we will have more family parties and enjoy some time with the ones we love.

CINDY This was me during my aunt's wedding. My hope is that by next year we get to attend more parties, weddings, and concerts.

Children deserve to play as much as they want. I hope in the near future, children will play happily and freely.

CALVIN   My mom told me this is her favorite photo. Back in the day we could hang out with my brother and mom. I know in the future it will be much better than this, because these are the unfaded memories, these are the dreams.

IDRIS   Which country are you in? Yes, next year, I will be coming to your country because I will be moving around the world without any restrictions. I will also do a grand royal wedding, throw a huge party, and invite y'all. How is that??

MARTINA   I hope, I can celebrate life again with the people I love, like in this picture. I was celebrating my birthday with my friends. May we soon be able to gather without fear.

KIORE   I hope children in the future will be able to play katii as I did. With their parents not having to worry they'll get sick. They will be able to play without social distancing. I hope they'll have a free childhood as mine.

DAISY   In the future, I hope we will be able to go to the theatres again and I will be able to enjoy time with my family, friends, and the audience after a performance like I did here: without having to worry about social distance, a pandemic, COVID. Just be carefree and live in the moment.

REY   The party boy has changed into a broken gentleman, this wallet before COVID, it was heavy with a lot of money, but since the breakout of this pandemic it is now full of paper. I hope next year it will be full of cash.

[THE END]

The Cure

Michael Hagins

Production History

The Cure was developed and produced by C.A.G.E. Theatre Company on Zoom.

The cast was as follows:

DR. MOIRA SCOTT   Eliko Aharon
MARTIN JEFFREY   Ellie Raab
ALEX   Colleen Nugent
KELLY   Jonathan G. Galvez
STEVIE   Kristen Keim

Characters (in order of appearance)

DR. MOIRA SCOTT   any adult age, researcher of infectious diseases

MARTIN JEFFREY   any adult age, test subject for a drug trial

ALEX   any adult age, partner of Martin

KELLY   any adult age, friend of Martin

STEVIE   any adult age, friend of Martin

Setting

Present Day, during the times of a pandemic, on multiple Zoom video calls

Scene 1: Day 1—5/15/2020, 11:59 a.m.

[Scene opens on a Zoom call. The prevalent picture is of DR. MOIRA SCOTT, a researcher of viral infections. She is in her lab.]

DR. SCOTT This is Doctor Moira Scott. The date is May 15th, 2020. We are beginning clinical trials for the cure and vaccine to viral strain PRUMTIDE-16. The test cure we are using is labeled RE-2216. Our patient is numbered 1260. His name is Martin Jeffrey. Along with Patient 1260 documenting any physical changes to his body, we will be conducting a series of cognitive tests via Zoom to cover the results of the cure on the subject. A mild strain of the virus has been administered to Patient 1260 and today is Day 1 of the curing process.

[MARTIN appears on the Zoom call in his home.]

Martin, hello. How are you feeling?

MARTIN Dr. Scott, hello! I'm feeling fine.

DR. SCOTT Excellent. I see connections are working OK. Now . . . you can feel free to use the laptop for any and all communications you need to do while you're in quarantine. Do know that all of your content on here will be recorded, so I'd use your phone if you wish to do any of your more personal communication. However, should you feel any emergency is coming on, do not dial 911. Call us directly through your phone or on here and we will send our medical team to you much more quickly. We have a dedicated medical staff to handle any of your needs, and we don't want 911 to be called and affect any results that we are tracking. Understood?

MARTIN Yeah, no problem. Should I be worried about anything?

DR. SCOTT As you know, all medicine has side effects, but I wouldn't bet on anything too severe.

MARTIN Gotcha.

DR. SCOTT I'd expect some nausea, shortness of breath, fatigue, and fevers, but nothing more severe than that.

MARTIN Great.

DR. SCOTT Have you received your packet?

MARTIN Uh . . . *(finding an envelope)* Yeah . . . I have it here.

DR. SCOTT   Good. In there should be a vial labeled RE-2216. Make sure all of that is confirmed, then administer one syringe full of that to yourself now. Tomorrow when we're on, you'll tell me about how you're feeling and any effects you're experiencing.

MARTIN   Got it.

[MARTIN opens the envelope. Inside is a medicine vial and a syringe. MARTIN takes it, uses the syringe to capture the medicine and uses it on his left arm. He moves his arm to allow the medicine to flow.]

DR. SCOTT   Any issues?

MARTIN   None. No problem injecting.

DR. SCOTT   Excellent. Keep track and chart everything you can. Nothing is too small. You know how to find us if you have any issues.

MARTIN   Wonderful. Thank you.

DR. SCOTT   No, Martin . . . thank you. You're doing a brave thing.

MARTIN   I'm happy to be of service.

DR. SCOTT   I'll be signing off now. Have a nice day.

MARTIN   Talk to you later!

[DR. SCOTT exits. MARTIN looks at his arm, then exits the meeting.]

Scene 2: Day 2—5/16/2020, 11:34 a.m.

[MARTIN comes onto the call. He moves his arm around to get circulation. There is a small black spot where the injection went. Entering the call is ALEX.)

MARTIN   Hey there!

ALEX   Hi! How are you feeling?

MARTIN   Oh, I'm good, I'm good. No real side effects so far.

ALEX   None? Well, it's only been a day.

MARTIN   True. But that's still a good thing.

ALEX   What's wrong with your arm?

MARTIN   Oh, just getting circulation. Keeping the blood flowing.

ALEX   You sure you're OK?

MARTIN   I'm sure. I'm doing pretty good. I gotta talk with the doctor in about 20 minutes and update my progress . . . ah, shit.

ALEX   What?

MARTIN   I just realized . . . this is recorded. I'm using their account to talk to you. Everything we say they'll have it recorded.

ALEX   So what?

MARTIN   Well . . . I had some ideas but . . . *(hinting toward something sexual . . .)*

ALEX   We are NOT doing that.

MARTIN   What? A man has needs.

ALEX   Well . . . a man shouldn't have volunteered for a drug trial and quarantined himself for 28 days.

MARTIN   I am doing my part to help the world. Come on . . . that's gotta be a little bit sexy to you.

ALEX   You got courage . . . I'll give you that.

MARTIN   I'm just saying . . . every now and then . . . I'd love a little bit of encouragement for my service.

ALEX   Encouragement for your service? Oh, come on. You've barely started. Who knows if you'll even—

MARTIN   Oh, here we go.

ALEX   What?

MARTIN   I'm gonna finish this.

ALEX   Marty—

MARTIN   No, I get it. "Martin's gonna get bored of this and drop out before it gets to be too much . . . like he always does."

ALEX   Don't do this now.

MARTIN   I swear I'm doing everything correctly.

ALEX   I know you are! I believe in you!

MARTIN   . . . You do?

ALEX   Marty . . . You're a hero. You're gonna save the world.

MARTIN   Well . . . I won't go that far.

ALEX   Marty . . . I'm proud of you.

MARTIN   *(a bit surprised)* You're proud of me?

ALEX   I am.

MARTIN   Well . . . I'm only doing what any good hero would do.

ALEX   You are my hero, you know that?

MARTIN   Oh, yeah. Want to see me in my cape . . . just my cape?

ALEX   Later on. NOT when we're being recorded.

MARTIN   I'll use my phone. What time will you be free?

ALEX   I'm not working so whenever.

MARTIN   After my call with the doc I'll get a nap and call you later. Sound good?

ALEX   Sounds good. I love you!

MARTIN   I love you too. Talk later on!

ALEX   See you later!

[The call ends.]

Scene 3: Day 4—5/18/2020 at 11:59 a.m.

[DR. SCOTT is on the call.]

DR. SCOTT   This is Doctor Moira Scott. The date is May 18th, 2020. We are continuing clinical trials for the cure and vaccine to viral strain PRUMTIDE-16. The test cure we are using is labeled

RE-2216. Patient 1260, Martin Jeffrey, will be coming onto Zoom to document any physical changes to his body. In addition we will be conducting a series of cognitive tests via Zoom to cover the results of the cure on the subject.

[MARTIN appears on the call. He looks much the same as he did before, except that the black mark on his left arm from the injection is a bit larger, he's a little warm and he has noticeable bags under his eyes.]

Hello, Martin.

MARTIN   Hello, Dr. Scott! Hope you're doing well today!

DR. SCOTT   Thank you. You, too. This is Day 4 of our tests. Martin, can you tell me how you're feeling?

MARTIN   Sure. Um . . . I feel fine overall. I feel warm, but I don't think it's a fever. I have not experienced any nausea or shortness of breath, or really any other side effects. The only thing I notice is that the spot where I injected the cure hasn't left. It looks like it's a bruise, maybe?

[MARTIN holds up his left arm, showing it to DR. SCOTT. She documents it.]

DR. SCOTT   It could be a nick on the artery where you inserted the medicine. Bruising can happen to patients with sensitive skin.

MARTIN   Hey now. I have some tough skin. Tough like bull!

DR. SCOTT   *(unamused)* Does it hurt?

MARTIN   Um . . . no. It doesn't hurt. I just noticed it.

DR. SCOTT   Well, that's good. *(She documents it.)* Um . . . have you been sleeping well?

MARTIN   Yeah, pretty good I'd say. Why?

DR. SCOTT   I was just noticing you have circles under your eyes. That's usually a by-product of insomnia.

MARTIN   Really? *(He looks closer at his face on the computer screen.)* I didn't notice. Um . . . no . . . I think I'm sleeping OK. I certainly don't feel tired. Maybe I'm watching too much TV in the dark?

DR. SCOTT   Well . . . if you're not feeling any side effects and as long as you don't feel any severe insomnia, I guess it's nothing to be concerned about. Are you ready for me to ask you some cognitive tests?

MARTIN   Yeah, sure. Go ahead.

DR. SCOTT   I am starting the cognitive test now on Patient 1260. Jeffrey, Martin.

MARTIN   Blame my parents.

DR. SCOTT   I'm sorry, what?

MARTIN   Blame my parents for the two first names. Sorry that it's confusing.

DR. SCOTT   No problem. It's why we give you a number.

MARTIN   True. I guess it also can—

DR. SCOTT   I'm sorry, Martin, but I need to finish the cognitive tests. If you don't mind . . .

MARTIN   Oh! Right. Sorry. I'm rambling on. Go ahead. I do that sometimes. Just run my mouth when it's not necessary. My mother used to say—

DR. SCOTT   *(sternly)* Martin.

MARTIN   Right. Shutting up.

DR. SCOTT   I am now starting the cognitive test on Patient 1260. Jeffrey, Martin. First question: what is today's date?

MARTIN   May 18th, 2020.

[DR. SCOTT documents everything and writes quick notes as needed.]

DR. SCOTT   And can you quickly tell me without looking approximately what time it is?

MARTIN   Around 12:05 p.m. I'd say.

DR. SCOTT   Please raise your right hand. *(MARTIN does so.)* Now your left. *(MARTIN does so.)* Lower your right hand. *(MARTIN does so.)* Now wiggle two of your fingers on your left hand. *(MARTIN does so.)* Now put your left hand on top of your head. *(MARTIN does so.)* Now, touch your nose with your right hand. *(MARTIN does so.)* While holding your hands in place, tell me the capital of New York state.

MARTIN   Well, the official state capital is Albany, but the economical center of the state and really the world would be—

DR. SCOTT   Albany is all I need, Martin.

MARTIN   Right. Sorry.

DR. SCOTT   You can take your hands down now. *(MARTIN does so.)* No issues standing or bending, right?

MARTIN   No, nothing.

DR. SCOTT   OK. Excellent progress. I'll be back tomorrow at the same time to record any progress. Do you have any plans tonight?

MARTIN   Well, I was going to use Zoom to host a poker game if that's all right?

DR. SCOTT   What time?

MARTIN   Around 7 p.m.

DR. SCOTT   That should be fine. But I wouldn't make any real money bets on the call. You could be arrested.

MARTIN   Oh, I know. My friends suck. I'll rob them blind.

DR. SCOTT   No, I'm serious. It'll be recorded and can be used as evidence.

MARTIN   Oh, shit.

DR. SCOTT   I'd recommend pausing the recording on your end when you're hosting.

MARTIN   I can do that?

DR. SCOTT   You can. But do know that tech support will still have access to your camera and microphone, even if you do pause.

MARTIN   Wow. Scary. OK. I'll figure it out.

DR. SCOTT   So, if there's nothing else . . .

MARTIN   Nope, nothing. Talk to you tomorrow!

DR. SCOTT   Have a good night. And Martin?

MARTIN   Yeah, doctor?

DR. SCOTT   Have fun with your friends.

[DR. SCOTT exits the call.]

MARTIN   *(nervously)* I'll try.

[MARTIN looks at the call suspiciously. He then exits.]

Scene 4: Day 4—5/18/2020 continued at 6:59 p.m.

[The ZOOM call comes on. It is blank until MARTIN enters. He puts on a nicer shirt and looks at the screen. He begins clicking at the buttons.]

MARTIN   How do I turn off—

[The Zoom call abruptly ends.]

Scene 5: Day 4—5/18/2020 continued at 8:34 p.m.

[The Zoom call comes on mid-call. On the screen is MARTIN, ALEX, STEVIE, and KELLY. They are playing poker on their phones with each other.]

ALEX   What did you touch?

MARTIN   What?

ALEX   Oh, never mind.

MARTIN   I adjusted my video. I swear to God Kelly is cheating.

KELLY   Don't hate because I'm winning.

MARTIN   I'm not hating because you're winning. I'm saying no one wins 4 hands in a row.

STEVIE   Especially video game poker.

KELLY   You're just mad because I'm winning all your money. Actually . . . Martin . . . how are you gonna pay me when you're quarantined in the death house?

MARTIN   I ain't paying you shit. But *you* can mail *me* a check when we're done.

STEVIE   Mail? What is this, the '80s?

[Everyone laughs.]

ALEX   Alright, come on guys. New hand. Reload.

[They all push buttons on their phones. After a beat, MARTIN's eyes perk up.]

KELLY   Opening bet.

MARTIN   Check.

ALEX   Check.

STEVIE   Check.

KELLY   I bid 20 bucks!

ALEX   Someone is starting big!

MARTIN   Your hand can't be that good.

KELLY   It'll cost you $20 to find out.

[MARTIN looks at his phone, then the screen. He thinks, then decides . . .]

MARTIN   Raise it $10.

ALEX   Oh hell no.

STEVIE   You two fight this out.

KELLY   Call.

[They push buttons on their phones. After a beat . . .]

KELLY   It's on you.

MARTIN $50.

ALEX   Martin, you're kidding!

MARTIN   Don't doubt my amazing powers.

KELLY   Oh, please. You definitely got a pair of Jacks. Maybe higher. But it's a pair regardless. Raise it $50.

[MARTIN's eyes shift downward.]

MARTIN   Um . . .

STEVIE   No way . . .

[MARTIN thinks deeply. After a few beats . . .]

MARTIN   I call!

[They push buttons on their phones. KELLY wins.]

KELLY   Gotcha!

[MARTIN lowers his head in frustration.]

MARTIN   How in the hell did you know?

KELLY   Martin . . . I can read you like a Dr. Seuss book. I will beat you on a boat. / I will beat you on a goat. / I will take your money on a Friday. / I will take your money on a Saturday. / I will—

[MARTIN looks up and sees the recording sign is on.]

MARTIN   Wait, wait . . . stop.

KELLY   Can't take it? It's just some harmless—

MARTIN   No, chill a minute. *(He realizes what's happening.)* Ah, shit.

ALEX   What—

[MARTIN pauses the recording, which turns the Zoom call off from view.]

Scene 6: Day 7—5/21/2020 at 11:57 a.m.

[DR. SCOTT is on the call.]

DR. SCOTT   This is Doctor Moira Scott. The date is May 21st, 2020. We are continuing clinical trials for the cure and vaccine to viral strain PRUMTIDE-16. The test cure we are using is labeled

RE-2216. This is the continual monitoring of Patient 1260, Martin Jeffrey, who will be coming onto Zoom to document any physical changes to his body. Also, we will be conducting further cognitive tests via Zoom to cover the results of the cure on the subject. Being this is Day 7, I am documenting that Patient 1260 has not experienced any of the usual side effects of RE-2216. I find this strange, as other patients using the same medicine, and are of a similar build and health have experienced at least 2–3 of the common side effects. While this may be encouraging in some cases, I feel that further monitoring and documentation is necessary, as there are some irregular side effects happening.

[MARTIN enters the call. The black mark on his left arm is bigger now, and every now and then it itches. The circles under his eyes are a bit deeper. He is sweating, and his teeth show a slight discoloration.]

Hello, Martin.

MARTIN Hello, doctor! How are you?

DR. SCOTT I'm fine. Thank you for asking. How are you feeling?

[She documents everything he says.]

MARTIN Well, I'm noticeably warmer I admit. I don't usually run hot like this, but I've had to run a fan because I get hot.

DR. SCOTT You may have a fever. Has it caused any fatigue or shortness of breath?

MARTIN No, nothing like that. Just sweaty. Also . . . the bruise on my arm is bigger. It's not going away.

DR. SCOTT Let me see.

[MARTIN holds up his left arm.]

MARTIN There. It wasn't that big a week ago.

DR. SCOTT Does it hurt?

MARTIN No. Still doesn't hurt.

DR. SCOTT Can you touch that spot for me? Tell me how it feels?

[MARTIN touches the spot. He checks it a few times. He instinctively scratches it as if there were an itch there.]

MARTIN   No, I don't feel anything.

DR. SCOTT   No pain?

MARTIN   More than that. I don't feel *anything*. It's like when I go to the dentist and my teeth are numb.

DR. SCOTT   Interesting. I notice you scratch there sometimes. Does it itch?

MARTIN   I guess. Every now and then. But I figured it was just an itch, you know?

DR. SCOTT   Interesting.

MARTIN   What does that mean?

DR. SCOTT   My best guess is you nicked something in your arm and it's bleeding out.

MARTIN   Isn't that bad?

DR. SCOTT   Not really. You'd experience more pain if it was. Still . . . I'm going to send the medical team and have them check it out.

MARTIN   No, it's OK. I don't want to bother them.

DR. SCOTT   Actually I'd like to schedule it for tomorrow. I'd like them to give you a physical.

MARTIN   I thought that came around Day 14?

DR. SCOTT   It is, but I'd like a checkup now. It's very routine.

MARTIN   Something wrong?

DR. SCOTT   To be honest, you're not showing any of the common side effects and other patients are. I'd like to see how RE-2216 is reacting to you and make sure the medicine is working properly.

MARTIN   You're the doctor.

DR. SCOTT   Any other physical issues? I'm seeing you're still not sleeping well.

MARTIN   Just TV. Plus it's hard to sleep when I'm sweating, but I feel rested.

DR. SCOTT   Well . . . I'll have them check you out, but tonight I recommend getting some sleep for sure.

MARTIN   OK. I'll definitely turn in early.

DR. SCOTT   What about your teeth?

MARTIN   What about them?

DR. SCOTT   They seem a little discolored.

MARTIN   Oh . . . I haven't brushed my teeth yet. I had steak and eggs this morning from a cafe, and I like medium rare. Might have been too much blood.

DR. SCOTT   OK then. Are you ready for cognitive tests?

MARTIN   I am ready.

DR. SCOTT   I am now starting the cognitive test on Patient 1260. Jeffrey, Martin. First question: what is today's date?

MARTIN   May 21st, 2020.

DR. SCOTT   And without looking, can you approximately tell me what time it is?

MARTIN   Roughly 12:04 p.m.

DR. SCOTT   OK. And raise your left hand please. *(MARTIN does so but slower than last time.)* Raise your right hand. *(MARTIN does so.)* Make a circle with your right hand. *(MARTIN does so.)* Lower your right hand. *(MARTIN does so.)* Make a circle with your left hand. *(MARTIN does so slowly.)* Touch your nose with your left hand. *(MARTIN does so slowly.)* Put your right hand on your head. *(MARTIN does so.)* Can you tell me the capital of the United States of America?

MARTIN Washington, D.C. It . . . *(He stops himself from going into a long diatribe.)*

DR. SCOTT Did you want to say anything else?

MARTIN I didn't want to ramble.

DR. SCOTT Oh. Good. *(MARTIN makes a face.)* Got it. You can put your hands down.

[MARTIN lowers his hand.]

MARTIN Did I pass my test? Easier than the SATs.

DR. SCOTT I have it all documented here.

MARTIN That's encouraging.

DR. SCOTT Everything is fine, Martin. You're doing very well.

MARTIN Thank you. I appreciate that.

DR. SCOTT I've scheduled a medical visit for you at 3 p.m. tomorrow. Until then, please get some sleep, and try to fast at least 12 hours before you see them.

MARTIN Got it.

DR. SCOTT Anything else you'd like to share with me?

MARTIN No, nothing else. Thanks, Dr. Scott.

DR. SCOTT Thank you, Martin. Have a nice day.

[DR. SCOTT exits the call. MARTIN looks at his arm, then the camera. He shows his teeth and is surprised at what he sees. He turns off the call.]

Scene 7: Day 8—5/22/2020 at 5:42 p.m.

[ALEX enters the Zoom room. She is waiting for MARTIN. After a few beats, she picks up her phone and texts him. She impatiently waits.]

ALEX Come on, Martin.

[After a few beats, MARTIN comes on the call. He looks the same as the previous scene: circles under his eyes; sweating; and discoloration on his teeth. The black mark is now covered by a large bandage, but still itches underneath.]

MARTIN   Sorry I'm late. I'm still a little drained.

ALEX   Are you OK? What happened?

MARTIN   I told you . . . I'm drained. Literally. They took blood from me. *(showing off his left arm with the bandage)* Plus I had to fast starting last night and I'm starving.

ALEX   You haven't eaten yet?

MARTIN   I haven't had time. The medical team came by right at 3 p.m. and ran all these tests on me. They took some blood. I had to give them a stool sample AND pee in a cup. They even took some skin.

ALEX   A skin sample? That doesn't seem normal.

MARTIN   I was more worried about the piss test. That wasn't something they said they'd do.

ALEX   You know you're not supposed to be smoking—

[MARTIN cuts her off from saying any more.]

MARTIN   No, no. Don't say anything.

ALEX   What?

MARTIN   Remember . . . we're on the Zoom call. They record everything.

ALEX   Oh, right. Why didn't you call me on the phone?

MARTIN   Huh?

ALEX   Normally you'd call me on the phone and not here.

MARTIN   Oh. I . . . I guess I forgot. Plus . . . it's easier to see your lovely face on HD.

ALEX   Good save.

MARTIN   Thank you.

ALEX   Hey . . . why don't you get some food and call me back on your phone? I'm worried that you haven't eaten.

MARTIN   No, I don't wanna cut off our time together.

ALEX   Baby, it's fine. Eat. Rest. Then call me later . . . on your phone this time.

MARTIN   OK. I'll order some food and talk to you around . . . *(He thinks and looks at the screen.)* What time is it? Ah . . . I should be done by 8 p.m. Sound good?

ALEX   Sounds good.

MARTIN   Talk to you later on!

ALEX   Oh . . . Martin?

MARTIN   Yeah?

ALEX   Can you . . . um . . . can you brush your teeth?

MARTIN   What?!

ALEX   I'm sorry . . . it's just . . . your teeth look so red and dirty on here.

MARTIN   Oh, shit. Yeah, sure. Sorry.

ALEX   It's OK. I know you've been fasting and sleeping a lot.

MARTIN   I'll get right on that. I will look presentable for you.

ALEX   Thank you. Have a nice dinner!

MARTIN   Thank you. Love you!

ALEX   Love you too!

[ALEX exits the call. MARTIN looks at his teeth on screen.]

MARTIN   That does look disgusting.

[He goes to wipe them with his finger and turns the call off.]

Scene 8: Day 10—5/24/2020 at 11:57 a.m.

> *[DR. SCOTT enters the Zoom room]*

DR. SCOTT   This is Doctor Moira Scott. The date is May 24th, 2020. We are continuing clinical trials for the cure and vaccine to viral strain PRUMTIDE-16. The test cure we are using is labeled RE-2216. This is the continual monitoring of Patient 1260, Martin Jeffrey. Due to a bruising in his left arm, I had our traveling medical team administer a routine physical 7 days earlier than scheduled. Some of the results have come back . . . and it's concerning. I see a lowered heart rate, skin deterioration at an accelerated pace, and some foreign substances were discovered in his blood and stool. In addition, the bruising on his left arm has not subsided, and the on-site examination showed no signs of any internal damage. Because of the timetable, we are still at least 6 days from comparing his test results. I will discuss with Martin his options for the drug trial, but I fear he is having an unexpected and adverse side effect to RE-2216. Therefore, we may have to consider—

[MARTIN enters the room. He is much more ragged now. The dark circles under his eyes are very apparent, his teeth are shaded very black now, and the spot on his left arm has made most of his forearm and bicep black as well. He itches a lot more now, and the skin on his face and right arm has blotches of red and black. He looks like he hasn't slept in weeks, and he leans his head to the left. His disposition is less positive than usual.]

MARTIN   Hello, doctor.

DR. SCOTT   Hello, Martin. You look very tired. Are you OK?

MARTIN   I am fine. No side effects.

DR. SCOTT   Are you sure? You're leaning your head to the left.

MARTIN   I must have slept on it funny.

DR. SCOTT   I see. *(documenting in her notes)*

MARTIN   What?

DR. SCOTT   Just taking notes. Anything you want to document today?

MARTIN   I don't feel any pain. My skin looks and feels musty. I'm itching a lot. My head feels hot. This black mark is growing. I ran out of toothpaste. I can't go and buy anymore. Alex won't talk to me if my teeth look bad.

DR. SCOTT   We can send you some.

MARTIN   Good. Thank you.

DR. SCOTT   Anything else you want to report? None of the other possible side effects?

MARTIN   Nothing. Not a single one that you mentioned. But what are these blotches on my skin? Why do I look like this? Is it normal? You're not telling me anything.

DR. SCOTT   It's definitely strange, I'll admit.

MARTIN   When will the doctors come back?

DR. SCOTT   They'll be back in 3 days. Are you concerned about something?

MARTIN   Look at me! Doctor, I peeled some skin off of my left arm this morning. I peeled my skin off! What the fuck?

DR. SCOTT   Martin . . . it'll be OK. If you're not feeling any pain then you're not in any danger. Everything happening to you is cosmetic at best. Now, sadly, this is the danger of testing drugs like this. I'm still waiting on the results of your remaining tests, but I don't believe anything will threaten your life. Now . . . is there anything else you want to tell me before we begin cognitive tests?

MARTIN   Um . . . *(He thinks. It hurts to think. Finally, he responds.)* No.

DR. SCOTT   OK. I am now starting the cognitive test on Patient 1260. Jeffrey, Martin. First question: what is today's date?

MARTIN   *(thinking)* May 24th, 2020.

DR. SCOTT   And without looking, can you approximately tell me what time it is?

MARTIN   *(thinking)* 12 noon time.

DR. SCOTT   OK, Martin . . . raise your left hand please. *(MARTIN does so very slowly.)* Raise your right hand. *(MARTIN does so very slowly.)* Make a circle with your left hand. *(MARTIN turns his head and looks at his left hand. He slowly makes a circle with it.)* Now, touch your nose with your right hand. *(MARTIN thinks. He moves his right hand to his nose very slowly, which affects making a circle with his left hand. He looks confused but is able to figure it out. DR. SCOTT is not happy with the result. It's almost scary to her.)* Martin . . . what is one hundred minus ten?

[MARTIN thinks hard. It hurts to think. He stops moving his hands to think. He finally responds . . .]

MARTIN Ninety.

DR. SCOTT OK. You can put your hands down now. *(MARTIN does so very slowly.)* You're set.

MARTIN That's all?

DR. SCOTT Yes.

MARTIN OK.

DR. SCOTT Have you eaten today?

MARTIN No. Too tired.

DR. SCOTT Eat something and we'll talk tomorrow.

MARTIN OK. Talk . . . to . . . goodbye, doctor.

DR. SCOTT Goodbye, Martin.

[MARTIN exits the call. DR. SCOTT writes down more notes, then rubs her head in exasperation. She takes out her phone and types. She realizes she's on Zoom and exits the call.]

Scene 9: Day 11—5/25/2020 at 7:06 p.m.

[The Zoom call comes on. MARTIN, ALEX, STEVIE, and KELLY are on screen. MARTIN looks worse than in the previous scene and much more irritable.]

KELLY It's about time you got here! My bank account was getting worried!

ALEX Martin, you look awful.

STEVIE   Are they letting you sleep, or are you running on a hamster wheel there?

MARTIN   I'm fine.

KELLY   You ready to lose more money?

MARTIN   I'll kill you tonight.

ALEX   I don't know. Martin, you look like you need to get some sleep.

MARTIN   I'm sleeping fine.

ALEX   Are you sure? You look like you—

MARTIN   *(snapping)* I'm fine! Lay off me!

ALEX   Wow. Fine. No need to be a dick about it.

STEVIE   Yeah, dude. Chill. Let's play some poker and calm down.

ALEX   Yeah. I'm sorry.

[They all pull out their phones and log in to play. MARTIN is having noticeable trouble working his phone.]

KELLY   You OK there, guinea pig?

MARTIN   Fine.

KELLY   Well, log in so we can get started.

MARTIN   I . . . I . . . um . . .

KELLY   Just go to the app and hit the button. That's it.

ALEX   Martin? You OK?

MARTIN   Go to the app . . . push the . . . *(MARTIN looks confused as he stares at his phone.)* Push the . . .

KELLY   Instead of curing PRUMTIDE, they must have given him low blood sugar.

ALEX   Martin? Baby, we don't need to play poker, OK? You really should get some rest.

MARTIN   Goddamn it! *(He throws his phone off-screen in frustration, scaring the others.)* Dumb thing.

ALEX   Martin, really?

STEVIE   Good luck replacing that phone!

KELLY   Let's . . . um . . . *(realizing how awkward this is)* . . . I'm gonna go. I'm still in the mood to play something and I'll see if anyone else is on.

STEVIE   Yeah, we're gonna go. Feel better, Martin.

MARTIN   Ah . . . fuck off.

STEVIE   Jesus Christ.

[KELLY and STEVIE exit the call.]

ALEX   Martin? I'm really worried. You're not acting like yourself.

MARTIN   I'm fine.

ALEX   And your teeth are still all black. Are you brushing your teeth?

MARTIN   I ran out of toothpaste! Doctor said she'd send me more. She lied!

ALEX   OK.

MARTIN   I try! I try to make you happy and you . . . you . . . damn it!

ALEX   Martin, it's OK. I was just asking.

MARTIN   I'm hungry. I'm . . . itchy! I'm . . . going.

[MARTIN looks at the computer to exit. He can't figure out how to exit. He thinks about it.]

ALEX   Martin, there's no reason to go, all right? We can just talk. We haven't had a good conversation in a while. Just tell me how you're feeling. What has the doctor been saying? We don't need—

[MARTIN exits the call.]

Damn it. *(ALEX takes out her phone and dials.)* That's it.

[She realizes she's on Zoom and exits the call.]

Scene 10: Day 12—5/26/2020 at 11:58 a.m.

[DR. SCOTT enters the Zoom room.]

DR. SCOTT   This is Doctor Moira Scott. The date is May 26th, 2020.
We are continuing clinical trials for the cure and vaccine to viral
strain PRUMTIDE-16. The test cure we are using is labeled
RE-2216. This is the continual monitoring of Patient 1260, Martin
Jeffrey. Unfortunately, some outside troubles may affect the test.
The patient's girlfriend, Alex Reynolds, called 911 and reported
Martin Jeffrey as ill. Luckily we were able to intercept them before
they took him away. Then I received a call that she arrived at the site
to visit, which is not allowed due to the nature of the testing. While
I can understand her concern for the patient, the nature of his side
effects are still undetermined, and we simply cannot allow anyone
from outside to contaminate the patients any further. It is now 12:00
p.m., and Patient 1260 has not come onto the call yet. He has never
been late up until now. *(She pushes some buttons on the computer.)* I
have found his phone number and will call him to see if he'll answer.
(She dials a number. It goes right to voicemail.) It's going right to
voicemail. He may be on another call. *(She looks at her notes and
thinks for a beat.)* This is important. I'm gonna contact tech support
and hack into the laptop to turn his camera on. *(She dials tech support.
It rings and connects.)* Hello? I need a B27 hack to laptop 1260.
Emergency. *(pause)* Yes. Turn on the Zoom account. *(pause)* Thank
you. *(DR. SCOTT hangs up the phone. She writes in her notes.)* I had to
initiate a B27 hack to open the Zoom account of Patient 1260. I hate
to do such a thing but I need to make sure there are no further
issues. Therefore I—

*[MARTIN's laptop comes on the call. MARTIN is in the background. On the
floor is a bloody sheet covering what appears to be a body. If possible, the body
would be of ALEX, but it need not be seen. He is kneeling in front of it. DR.
SCOTT looks horrified at the scene.]*

   Martin? Martin?

[MARTIN looks up and sees the screen. His face now almost resembles a skull: his eyes darkened out; his teeth black, sunken lines all over. He now also has blood on his mouth from eating the body on the floor. He stands up and drags his left foot as he walks towards the screen. He sits down and stares at it, lost of nearly all humanity.]

Martin? What happened? Tell me what you did!

MARTIN I no feel hot any more. Arm is itchy. Hungry so want food. Alex come see me. She hate my ugly face. Itchy. Itchy. Kill pretty face. Hungry for food. Alex. Tasty.

DR. SCOTT *(horrified)* Oh my God.

MARTIN Alex. Hungry. Alex. Ugly. Alex.

DR. SCOTT Jesus Christ. *(MARTIN continues to chant as DR. SCOTT calls on her phone.)* Hello. Emergency extraction at Patient 1260. We need secure e-vac and containment immediately! *(DR. SCOTT hangs up the phone.)* Martin, stay right there. Don't go anywhere.

MARTIN Ugly. Hungry. Alex.

[DR. SCOTT turns off the Zoom call.]

Scene 11: Day 12—5/26/2020, continued at 1:02 p.m.

[A video appears. MARTIN is killed by unseen soldiers. The camera turns off. This can be via any device you choose.]

Scene 12: Day 12—5/27/2020, continued at 2:13 p.m.

[DR. SCOTT is on the Zoom call. MARTIN's screen is up but he isn't there.]

DR. SCOTT Patient 1260 has been extracted from the residence. He did not go peacefully, and as a result he had to be terminated. Unfortunately we found blood that did not seem to be his at the residence, and we will have a clean-up team do any further examinations. This seems to be caused by unforeseen side effects in RE-2216 that changed the chemical makeup of the patient. I now have the vial that was administered to Patient 1260, and as it turns out, this is a bad mix of the agents. This happens in our field, as it very much is trial and error. However, we will notify Patient 1260's loved ones and tell of his bravery in this trying time, and we seek to— *(DR. SCOTT's phone rings)* Hello? *(pause)* Yes . . . Ah, yes. Thank you. We need to do a full recall on vial RE-2216. How much more has been administered? *(pause)* Oh. Oh, no. How much globally? *(A pause. She hears the news. It's distressing.)* Oh. Oh my god. We need to do full physical workups right now on any of the patients that have been administered RE-2216. *(pause)* No. No. We need to work past the paperwork and get this done. I will send you all I have on Patient 1260 so you can see for yourself. *(pause)* Yes. Thank you. *(She hangs up. She receives an email.)* Ah, Patient 1260 has arrived. I will be going to conduct an autopsy on him and see what has happened. Hopefully we can continue to pursue a cure of PRUMTIDE-16 and prevent what happened to Patient 1260 from any other vict . . . volunteers.

[DR. SCOTT gets up to grab her tools. In the background of MARTIN's place, ALEX walks into the shot and slowly stalks towards the camera. She is covered in blood and moving like a zombie. DR. SCOTT walks by her computer, and as ALEX stares at the camera, she turns off the Zoom call, not seeing the screen.]

[The end.]

Killjoy, Ohio

Trey Tatum, with additional monologues by Jordan Trovillion

Production History

Killjoy, Ohio was performed and recorded on Zoom, in a single take, on May 27, 2020. It premiered at the 2020 Cincinnati Fringe Festival. The Production was directed by Bridget Leak and featured performances by Jordan Trovillion and Trey Tatum. Additionally, the voice of TAYLOR was provided by Taylor Hauter and the voice of SOME DUDE AT A TIKI PUTT-PUTT COURSE was provided by Rory Sheridan.

Killjoy, Ohio was presented at the 2020 Saskatoon "This Is NOT That" Festival, August 4–5, 2020.

Killjoy, Ohio can be streamed at treytatum.com. Captions and Audio Description available.

Characters

Two roles. Actors play themselves, with changes to the script as necessary.

Time

The present

Place

Killjoy, Ohio—in places real and remembered

[Credits and Tour Sequence: MUSIC. A cell phone camera moves around a room, stopping momentarily at printed sheets of paper, a virtual program: "Queen City Flash presents—Killjoy, Ohio—Bridget Leak, Director—Trey Tatum,

Playwright/Composer/Performer—Jordan Trovillion, Performer." A hand is visible turning off the lights in the room as the camera turns, revealing a closet door. Behind the door, a cramped performance space awaits: A computer on top of a dresser surrounded by black curtains, a microphone, lights, a lighting console, a QLab remote—as well as an assortment of props hidden just out of camera sight.]

[Two other cameras unmute and, the preshow tour concluded, TREY mutes the camera on his cell phone. TREY, left, and JORDAN, right, are side by side in Zoom windows. Both performers stand in empty, brightly lit, white rooms.]

TREY   Hey Jordan.

JORDAN   Hi Trey.

TREY   Wanna tell a story?

JORDAN   Yeah.

[The play begins. Two actors on Zoom, wearing bland T-shirts, talking in front of a boring white background, absolutely nothing of note.]

TREY   *(out)* Heading north out of Zanesville, traveling along the Muskingum River on—and this is real—Ohio State Route 666, you eventually turn a wide corner and are greeted by a large, painted, wooden sign:

JORDAN   *(out)* Welcome to Killjoy, Ohio—Population: 720. State Route 666 pulls away from the Muskingum River and passes thru the center of town.

TREY   The corner of Alasdair Ave. and 666

JORDAN   2nd Lives Consignment

TREY   An Ace Hardware Store

JORDAN   Hell Freezes Over Ice Cream Parlor

TREY   And Alvin's Pump and Pantry: gas station, convenience store

JORDAN   The power is out at the only red light in town. A woman stands at the intersection with a small child, staring up at the singular, darkened light hanging above the middle of the road.

TREY The woman is wearing a beautiful blue dress with white flowers. The child is eating an ice cream cone. Strawberry. Dipped in blue. It leaves a wide ring around the child's lips. It is late Spring but hot days are coming.

JORDAN The small child squeezes the woman's hand—

TREY "Are we going?"

JORDAN "Yes."

TREY They look both ways—

JORDAN and with nothing coming in either direction, woman and child move diagonally across the intersection.

TREY You wouldn't know it—if you were fixated on an ice cream cone slowly dribbling down your wrist.

JORDAN You wouldn't know it—if you were staring into the window of the consignment store—at the smartly dressed mannequin.

TREY You wouldn't know it, but—

JORDAN But above them, as they move thru the unlit intersection . . . a dark set of clouds briefly rove across the mounting sun.

TREY Clouds that seem to . . . bobble.

JORDAN A cool wind rushes down Alasdair Avenue. The air has shifted. The woman stops at the storefront window. The reflection of her face almost perfectly aligns with the head of the mannequin and—as if staring into an alternate reality—she sees the mannequin's dress on her body. The mannequin fades as the window catches a reflection and heats up in a fevered purple, glow.

[MUSIC. The rooms around TREY and JORDAN swell up in a brilliant purple and then fade back.]

TREY There is a tearing screech—

JORDAN And the woman whips around.

TREY   A pickup truck, skid marks trailing behind its tires. A solid red light. Power restored.

JORDAN   Clouds pass. The sun shines, bright and hot. Behind her, a mannequin feigns boredom at all the bustle.

TREY   A man in a light-colored suit walks up to the woman.

JORDAN   Hi.

TREY   Hey.

JORDAN   They kiss.

TREY   They take hands.

JORDAN   The light turns green.

TREY   The truck pulls away.

JORDAN   The couple—

TREY   And only the couple—

JORDAN   The couple walks down Alasdair Avenue towards the park that runs the river. It is a beautiful day in late Spring.

TREY   Meanwhile, in front of 2nd Lives Consignment, a rising tide of strawberry breaks thru a blue dike and runs wild down the sidewalk.

JORDAN   North, out of Zanesville, along Ohio State Route number 666, you will find a sign on the outskirts of a small town. Welcome to Killjoy, Ohio—Population: 719

[MUSIC. Lights shift. TREY and JORDAN are silhouetted in dark blue. Nighttime.]

TREY   The air has shifted, that's how it feels. Lying awake, staring up at the darkened ceiling. The clock on the dresser.

JORDAN   4:38

TREY   He listens.

[They listen.]

JORDAN   Downstairs. The shifting of weight on an old wood floor.

TREY   Peeling back covers, toes reaching for the floor.

JORDAN   And now a drawer being slid open—the scratchy breath of wood pulling across wood.

[Out of sight, JORDAN pulls WOOD across her DESKTOP, replicating the sound.]

TREY   Shit—why couldn't I be one of those people who sleep with a bat next to their bed? Oh right, those people suck.

JORDAN   A bag being set on the floor, slowly placing things inside.

[TREY finds a FLASHLIGHT, cuts it on, scans the room.]

TREY   A flashlight in a bedside table.

[TREY shines the light into TREY'S CAMERA. With an unseen hand, JORDAN lights herself, casting her shadow on the back wall.]

Hey!

JORDAN   Shit.

TREY   Okay. Uh. Just. Stay right there.

JORDAN   Aww fuck, I'm sorry.

TREY   Don't move.

[They just stare at each other.]

JORDAN   Okay, now what?

TREY   I don't know. I kinda expected you to run.

JORDAN   You said don't move.

TREY   I'm really just working thru this one moment at a time.

JORDAN   Look—my bad. Honest, I had no idea anyone was home.

TREY   What difference does that make?

JORDAN   Do you think this was how I wanted this to go?
Hey. Can you—

[JORDAN motions TREY to put down the flashlight.]

    I get headaches. And if I start to get one, I'm pretty much out of commission.

[TREY lowers his flashlight. JORDAN is no longer lit. TREY reaches for an off-screen light switch. Lights shift. Soft front light.]

TREY   'the fuck are you doing in my living room?

JORDAN   Oh. I mean. I want your things to be my things.

TREY   Well sure.

JORDAN   I mean that seems super obvious.

TREY   Okay. I don't have a lot of experience with this.

JORDAN   Well how do you think it makes me feel? I'm the one who got caught. So. Now I guess I'm going to have to kill you. I'm kidding. Serious. I mean, what would I even do? Saw your head off? Put it in a bag? Take it with me?

TREY   Why would you take the head?

JORDAN   So the police couldn't identify you.

TREY   My body would be in my house.

JORDAN   That. That's smart. You would be good at this. *(looking off)* You should be breaking into my house.

TREY   Are you the girl from next door?

JORDAN   No.

[TREY looks off.]

TREY   Your backdoor's open.

JORDAN   Shit, is it?

TREY   Like a screen door.

JORDAN   It has trouble latching. Crap. I'll be right back.

TREY   Uh, no.

JORDAN   My cat mighta got out. I'm just gonna check.

TREY   You can't leave.

JORDAN   That's a dick move.

TREY   You were robbing me.

JORDAN   I already apologized.

TREY   No you didn't.

JORDAN   Uh yeah. You were like "freeze, motherfucker" and I said "aww shit, I'm sorry."

TREY   That was your apology?

JORDAN   Well I don't hear you doing any better?

TREY   What did I do?

JORDAN   I'm a bad pet owner. I'm not good at breaking into houses. You have made me feel this big ever since I've been a guest in your home.

TREY   You weren't invited.

JORDAN   She has feline aids so if she gets out I hope you feel like a giant dog dick.

TREY   . . . Okay. Go check.

JORDAN   Thank you.

[JORDAN picks up her BAG OF STOLEN ITEMS.]

TREY   Uh. Leave the bag.

JORDAN   Oh. Shit. Yeah. I didn't mean to, it's just habit.

[JORDAN exits stage left, climbing out of an unseen window.]

TREY   Do you want to use the door?

JORDAN   no-I-do noooot.

[JORDAN'S gone. TREY watches JORDAN leave.]

Quit checking me out, creep!

[*TREY turns back. A moment. TREY finds JORDAN'S BAG, opens it, pulls out . . . HANDMADE CERAMIC MUGS.*]

[*JORDAN comes back in thru the window.*]

She's fine. Literally did not move. Where's your car?

TREY (*re: the mugs*) What are you doing with these?

JORDAN D'you like get in a wreck?

TREY I walked home.

JORDAN Too much to drink.

TREY What the fuck are we doing?

JORDAN I dunno. Let's trash the place!!

TREY Look, I gotta call the cops.

JORDAN Why? I mean . . . I know why. I mean . . . don't.

TREY Do you see my phone?

[*JORDAN holds up a CELL PHONE.*]

JORDAN Oh—it's right here. Why don't you sleep with your phone?

TREY I have to keep it in the other room. I wake easy.

JORDAN Oh my god, you walked home, you're a light sleeper. I was like, "why am I so bad at this?" That makes me feel so much better.

TREY Give it to me.

JORDAN Who you callin'?

TREY 911, obviously.

JORDAN This isn't an emergency.

TREY You have my things in a bag.

JORDAN When you woke up, sure, someone's downstairs, that's an emergency. Talking with your neighbor??

TREY Why would you rob your own neighbor?

JORDAN Because. Eventually I'm going to rob everybody. That's my thing. I'm a cunt burglar.

TREY I'm sorry wut?

JORDAN A cunt burglar.

TREY . . . A cat burglar?

JORDAN Oh, I like that so much better.

TREY Can I have my phone, please?

JORDAN I don't trust you. Do you have the number for the police station? The non-emergency number.

TREY I just call 911.

JORDAN And overtax an already stressed and fragile system? That's tacky.

TREY It is not.

JORDAN *(schoolyard taunts)* Gauche! Sorry—I can't let this go. Did you get in a wreck? Did it get towed?

TREY I went into town, got a little lost, couldn't find it.

JORDAN So, drunk.

TREY I'm new in town.

JORDAN Bullshit. You're not new.

TREY I just moved in.

JORDAN You're a local. No. You used to be.

TREY How do you know that?

JORDAN Look. I'm going to bed. It's late. I'm definitely getting a headache. Let's just pick this up in the morning.

TREY I'm not gonna let you just leave with my phone.

JORDAN What's your name?

TREY   Trey.

JORDAN   Hi Trey. Jordan.

[JORDAN holds up the PHONE.]

> I'll hold on to this. I'll be back around breakfast time. *(Starts to leave, stops.)* I don't do savory. French toast, pop tarts, waffles, something fun. We can sort all this out then.

[JORDAN exits thru the window.]

> See ya tomorrow neighbor. Trey.

TREY   The door?

JORDAN   Nope.

[JORDAN pops her head back in, pointing:]

> Oh. Hey. Your postcards—I fixed them for you. 'Night!

[JORDAN leaves. TREY is dumbfounded.]

TREY   *(out)* The only thing the burglar had left behind was questions. She had settled one thing though. In the morning, if he got his phone back, he wouldn't be calling the police.

[TREY grabs the two MUGS.]

[JORDAN walks onscreen.]

JORDAN   *(out)* A little lopsided—a little ugly. Hand-made mugs in earth tones with "Killjoy River Days" printed on the side.

TREY   He put them back on his mantle. He sat at his kitchen table, looking down at a panorama of vintage postcards, laid out in stacks and rows and columns, recently shuffled.

[MUSIC. TREY examines a pair of postcards, grabs a sticky note and a sharpie, makes a note, places it. During:]

JORDAN   People collect things. Organize them. Put them in goofy stacks bound by a logic only they understand. The wonder was in all the post-it notes: roads of Post-it notes that traversed the table, labeled Front Street, Center Street, River Road, Alasdair Ave. They were the roads of Killjoy.

[JORDAN blacks out her room but does not mute her camera.]

TREY He'd been piecing the town back together with weathered images of the past, making little headway. That is . . . until the break-in. The third time a person sneaks into your house thru an open window . . .

[Lights shift. Morning. TREY's house is a pleasant KitchenAid-mixer green. JORDAN climbs back in, PHONE in hand.]

JORDAN Your mother keeps calling.

TREY . . . it ceases to be news.

[JORDAN sets the PHONE on an unseen kitchen table. TREY picks it up.]

JORDAN I told her you'd call.

TREY You talked to Mom?

JORDAN What am I gonna do, have her worry?

TREY What did you say?

JORDAN I broke into your house—you caught me—I stole your phone—meeting for breakfast—the whole thing, really.

TREY You didn't.

[JORDAN finds a toaster strudel.]

JORDAN *(gasps)* Is this for me?

TREY Jordan?

[JORDAN is busy, squeezing the icing packet into her mouth.]

JORDAN I'm not going to lie to your mom. It's fine. We talked for like an hour—very sweet woman—she was going to call the police but she didn't have your new address.

[JORDAN starts in on the STRUDEL.]

So, postcards. How'd I do? I think I did a pretty great job. You're welcome.

TREY How'd you do this?

JORDAN Why are you making a postcard map of Killjoy? . . . Hey! Best friends tell each other everything.

TREY We are not best friends.

JORDAN Because we just met—because I'm secretly still planning on robbing you?

TREY I don't want you to rob me!

JORDAN Best friends come in all shapes. Here. Put your hands in my hands.

[JORDAN puts out her hands. TREY reluctantly places his hands on hers.]

Now. Repeat after me. Jordan. Jordan . . .

TREY Jordan

JORDAN You're my best friend

TREY You're my best friend

JORDAN And best friends trust each other

TREY And best friends trust each other?

JORDAN And don't keep secrets

TREY You're really squeezing my *(JORDAN tightens her grip)*— OWWWWWW—

JORDAN And don't keep secrets

TREY Anddontkeepsecrets!

JORDAN And so I'm going to tell you all about my creepy-as-fuck postcard collection.

[TREY doesn't respond.]

I can't help you if I don't know what you want.

TREY It's a hobby.

JORDAN Oh, shit. And I fucked with it.

TREY It's fine.

JORDAN No—I hate people who do shit like that.

There is nothing worse than someone coming in behind you and saying "black ten on red jack." Here—I'll undo it.

[JORDAN starts grabbing POSTCARDS off the table, throwing them behind her:]

TREY NoNoNoNo—

JORDAN Tell me.

TREY You're messing it up.

JORDAN I'm fixing it!

TREY Please stop!

JORDAN Who am I?

TREY You're my best friend.

JORDAN And best friends don't have secrets.

[JORDAN hands TREY back his POSTCARD.]

TREY We lived here when I was little. Moved away when I was in middle school. Honestly, I barely remember the place. There's this hole-in-the-wall shop in Birmingham—less an antique store and more a time capsule to the bizarre—sells these vintage postcards, like hundreds of thousands of them. This sweeping vista of the river is now a condo with an overpriced steakhouse in the lobby. This cute motel attached to a kitschy Tiki Putt-Putt course is now a Jimmy Johns. This German-style biergarten, this greyhound racetrack, both gone. Thing is—other than this postcard—I can't find any proof that the little tiki putt-putt course ever existed. Same with the greyhound track. I've got 53 postcards—more than half of them form a picture of a Killjoy that nobody seems to know ever existed. I have spent the last two weeks pacing these streets, trying to stitch this map together. Last night I got a little turned around and lost my car.

[JORDAN scans the table, picks up one or two POSTCARDS, holding them like a puzzle piece and searching for the right gap to plug.]

JORDAN   Your car is at the corner of Highpointe and Center. Your mom actually kinda led me to it. You were looking for where you grew up and got turned around. Totally can happen there—all those homes look alike.

[JORDAN picks up a card:]

This is where that one goes by the way.

[placing it:]

Right there on the corner of Highpointe and Center. It's not the house you grew up in—would have been torn down long before you were here—but that's where it would have been. And this one says Alasdair Ave. and Front Street in the caption, but you've got the corner wrong—see?

TREY   You're just fucking with me.

JORDAN   I'm not. And ordinarily, I wouldn't be sharing any of this with you. Except.

[JORDAN picks up a postcard of a small amusement park that reads, "Riverland Adventure Park—Killjoy, Ohio"]

Except you placed this one right. And there's no way you could know about this one.

TREY   You recognize that?

JORDAN   That sounds like the sort of question a best friend would have to answer.

[JORDAN gets up.]

Bring your car keys.

[JORDAN leaves thru the window.]

TREY   Can I at least take the door?

JORDAN   You do you!

[MUSIC. TREY follows JORDAN out of the window, awkwardly, falling out of screen. Lights shift. A beautiful morning in late spring.]

TREY Hold up. We're not going to take your car?

JORDAN It's not that far a walk. Just the other side of town.

TREY That sounds like a long walk.

JORDAN It is. That first part was a lie.

TREY *(out)* And she took off walking.

JORDAN *(out)* Early mornings were still brisk in Killjoy.

TREY Like who-are-you-trying-to-impress power walking.

JORDAN A shaded bike trail that wound alongside 666.

TREY Woods. It was just woods. A metal guardrail alongside the sidewalk, next to a—

[TREY and JORDAN stand behind a CHAIN LINK FENCE. Note: this next prop was assembled using cardboard, EVA foam and screen-door screen. It's a small frame that sits on top of the computer and can be slid in front of the computer's built-in camera, placing a piece of screen between the camera and the performer.]

—chain link fence, topped with barbed wire. A bird sanctuary sign. Tires. Old televisions. It was that out-of-the-way place where the locals come to dump their shit.

[MUSIC. TREY pulls out his POSTCARD of Riverland Adventure Park, studies it.]

JORDAN It was a glorious and vibrant '60s postcard of what he remembered as a shitty '90s amusement park: A large wooden roller coaster rising above the rest of the surrounding area. A giant concourse full of rides and games. It was (because the '60s . . . I guess) a postcard that heavily featured the parking lot.

TREY When did they tear it down?

JORDAN You're going to have to be more specific.

TREY   Riverland Adventure Park. When did the town tear it down?

JORDAN   Do you remember it?

TREY   I think . . . I know I've been here. But god, the size of these trees. They seem like they'd have to be so much older.

[TREY points off, away from the woods.]

>   That used to be a Big Bee Drugs Store.

JORDAN   Yeah. I haven't heard anyone say Big Bee Drugs . . .

TREY   We must be in the wrong—what are you doing!

JORDAN   Lift up on this. I think I can squeeze thru.

TREY   I feel like the fence is probably the first clue that we shouldn't be over there.

[JORDAN feigns snoring.]

>   Actually kinda hurt my feelings.

JORDAN   Right? Simple but effective. Come on, I'll hold it for you.

[TREY looks both ways, ducks under. TREY and JORDAN remove their sections of fencing.]

JORDAN   Town must have really left its mark if all you remember is the drug store.

TREY   It was the first time I ever stole anything.

JORDAN   Oh ho ho!

TREY   Okay.

JORDAN   I didn't realize I was in the presence of a fellow thief.

TREY   I was in second grade. Does it smell like . . . I think I crawled thru a diaper?

[JORDAN smells.]

JORDAN   Hm . . . maybe.

TREY *(out)* She led him into the woods, not following naturally forming trails but pushing thru deep brambles, like she knew exactly where she wanted to go.

JORDAN *(out)* I'll own it, we went like . . . murderer-leading-prey deep into these woods.

TREY Oh god . . . maybe she was telling the truth about sawing my head off . . . *(the realization)* And I told her not to do it in the house!

JORDAN So tell me—

TREY *(terrified)* What.

JORDAN So you were like, stealing cigarettes to sell to kids on the bus?

TREY I wanted a piece of candy and a spiral-bound pocket notebook. Mom made me pick, so I chose the immediate gratification one and, while I was pretending to take it back, put the notebook in my pocket.

JORDAN And now you're with me, sneaking under fences. We got a real Bonnie and Clyde thing going.

[They've stopped. JORDAN and TREY take in their surroundings.]

TREY There's nothing here. Like, you hear about how quickly nature can reclaim something but. There's no paved ground, no crumbling ring toss stands, no rusted infrastructure from the sky buckets. I remember . . . this giant concrete dome—like a big igloo. And in front of it this huge, blue . . .

[TREY strikes a pose, makes a face.]

Like abominable snowman guarding it. And you walked under his legs to get to the ride, which I think was just like a tilt-a-whirl, but also. Snow. Snow and fog. And cold. And loud.

JORDAN Why do you give a shit about this place?

TREY I had this dream where—

JORDAN   BOOOO. Nobody cares. Nobody. And like truly, nobody wants to hear about your dream.

TREY   It was more than a dream tho.

JORDAN   Oh, sure. You're at the amusement park on a school field trip. And you're there with Alicia Silverstone, who's in your grade, and you, like, have a crush on her but she's never really taken any notice of you. But now you're sitting next to her on the Ferris wheel. Well, it was like a Ferris wheel but also a lake because then Alicia Silverstone is all, "we should totally make out on my Jet Ski."

[Erotic Jet Ski Object Work.]

Dreams only sound cool to the person talking: life lesson.

TREY   Okay. I shouldn't have called it a dream.

JORDAN   Here *(pointing)* the Big Bee was that direction. Where was the everything?

TREY   Umm . . . There was. A giant red baron airplane swing in one corner. And the Ferris wheel was like—centered there. And the uh—there was a figure eight go-cart track set up over there. And a big indoor section—I remember, the log flume was inside somehow.

JORDAN   Cool cool. This was a waste of my time.

TREY   Are you leaving?

JORDAN   Sho thang.

TREY   You're the one who drug me out to the middle of the woods?

JORDAN   Looking for your amusement park.

TREY   Well then where is it? Because you had me crawl thru a fucking baby diaper to get here. I thought you knew something. You're acting like I'm supposed to see a fucking broken branch and like Last-of-the-Mohican my way back to the Viking Boat.

JORDAN   I guess I read this wrong. I don't know that I can help you.

TREY   Um okay. Except for like. Me not calling the cops on you is pretty much predicated on you helping me.

[JORDAN slow claps.]

JORDAN   Oh. Bravo, asshole.

[JORDAN starts to leave.]

TREY   Jordan! Did it ever exist?

JORDAN   That's such an impossible question. No.

[TREY holds up his postcard.]

I don't know.

TREY   It was real. You said as much this morning.

JORDAN   I might take a walk along the river, if I were you.

TREY   *(out)* And then. Boom. Gone. Power walk. Shit . . . Hey!

JORDAN   *(out)* It took him twenty minutes to find his way back to the fence.

TREY   Oh. Good. Baby diaper. Just like in Last of the Mohicans.

[MUSIC. The Riverwalk. Sun. A breeze.]

(out) Whether it be a fur trading post, a bustling river town, a lawless mining town, or a utopian cult—there is never a dull day in Killjoy.

JORDAN   The riverwalk was a mile-long park along the Muskingum River, weaving between sculptures and swings, wild flower gardens and rustic playgrounds. The park was dotted with dozens of bronze plaques and signs.

[JORDAN dims her room.]

TREY   The first town of Kilroy. Settled in 1816 by Scottish immigrant Alasdair Kilroy, this fur trading post grew to include a grist mill and sawmill by the 1820s.

[JORDAN lights up, via a lighter held under the chin, like all good spooky stories.]

JORDAN   But was discovered mysteriously abandoned a decade later. Little is known of what became of the nearly 50 inhabitants.

[JORDAN is back in darkness.]

TREY   The second town of Kilroy. With the completion of a system of locks and dams along the Muskingum River, increased river travel led to Kilroy—as it was then known—being resettled by a Utopian Socialist Commune.

[JORDAN appears, under the glow of her lighter.]

JORDAN   But building their communal meeting hall along the banks of the river turned fatal when the inhabitants were all but wiped out by a massive flood in 1847.

[JORDAN is back in darkness.]

TREY   The third town of Kilroy. A third town is founded on the same site and quickly flourishes thanks to a new commerce route between Zanesville and the recently finished Erie-Ohio Canal.

[JORDAN appears.]

JORDAN   But river travel and unsafe drinking water would lead to a cholera epidemic in the 1870s.

[JORDAN is back in darkness.]

TREY   The fourth town of Kilroy. After being bought by the Muskingum Coal Company, Kilroy exploded, with a hospital, saloons, a theater, even its own baseball team. It developed a reputation as "the Appalachian Wild West," with frequent gunfights in the saloons and streets, eventually earning the town the nickname Killjoy.

[JORDAN appears.]

JORDAN   But, on September 25, 1924, Kilroy was burnt to the ground after disgruntled miners set fire to the mines with coal carts full of burning railroad ties.

[JORDAN is back in darkness.]

TREY   The fifth town of Kilroy. Beginning in 1925, the remains of the town were revitalized as a series of summer cottages brought new families to the area. In 1931, the town officially changed its name with the opening of the Killjoy, Ohio Post Office.

JORDAN   *(to TREY)* Losing stuff isn't what's bizarre—that's the first thing you have to understand.

TREY   She found him in late afternoon, sitting by himself in a quiet spot alongside the river.

JORDAN   For instance—in less than 24 hours you lost both your car and your car keys.

[JORDAN holds up a set of KEYS.]

   I found them in the hole under the chain link fence.

[JORDAN tosses the KEYS to TREY. In his screen, TREY catches them.]

   What's amazing in this world is when we find something again.

TREY   I'm not sure why you wanted me to come here.

JORDAN   It's a Bermuda Triangle. You know what a Bermuda Triangle is?

TREY   I know what "The" Bermuda Triangle is. Bermuda being fairly central to the whole thing.

JORDAN   I'm talking about the phenomenon, not the place, like the "Alaskan Bermuda Triangle," the "Pacific Bermuda Triangle?"

TREY   Sorry—that's not really something I knew to give a fuck about.

JORDAN   A fixed place where objects large and small routinely go missing.

TREY   Yeah, I don't think so.

JORDAN   Oh, thank god—I was so worried you would just believe me.

TREY   Really?

JORDAN   In the time that I've known you, I've found you to be easily persuadable. Here—you're going to love this.

[JORDAN hands TREY a PAIR OF YEARBOOKS, "1995" and "1996" emblazoned on the cover in some hilarious '90s font.]

TREY   Are these yearbooks?

JORDAN   First page, table of contents.

[TREY opens the 1995 YEARBOOK.]

> Out loud, please.

TREY   "Student Life. Organizations. Sports." There's no Junior Class.

JORDAN   Whooooaaaa . . .

TREY   Alright. It's a small town.

JORDAN   Not that small.

TREY   Or a printing error.

JORDAN   Look at the next one.

[TREY opens the 1996 YEARBOOK.]

> Killjoy High School had no class of 1996. You can go back all twelve years—I have—nothing. They got Bermuda Triangled. Come on, that's cool. *(whispering)* Bermuda Triangle . . .

TREY   It's ridiculous is what it is.

JORDAN   I've got more. This is from last year in the *Killjoy Onlooker*—local paper, silly name, move on.

[JORDAN hands over and TREY holds up a NEWSPAPER CLIPPING.]

> The Culletons had their boat stolen out of their driveway last summer. The boat, not the trailer.
> The Bermuda Triangle bermuda triangled it—noun and verb.

TREY   Fine—weird things go missing—ya got me.

JORDAN   When I was fifteen, I babysat this kid, Avery, down the street. When she turned six, she started losing her baby teeth. There were no adult teeth coming in behind them.

TREY   And you think her adult teeth sent out a mayday but by the time Search and Rescue got there there was no trace of them.

JORDAN   Precisely. The upright piano at the Adult Activity Center has no middle C. Goes from B to C Sharp and nobody knows what became of it. Mother fucker, I could show you.

TREY   So your grand theory is that somewhere out there, there is a nether plane full of teeth and Tiki Putt-Putt courses.

JORDAN   And an old mining town, and a fur trading post, and a weird sex cult.

TREY   The signs along the river made no mention of it being a sex cult.

JORDAN   Aww, all cults are sex cults. Read a book. I think that's what happened to your phantom amusement park. Okay. Thank you for humoring me. You may be convinced now.

TREY   Jordan, I appreciate that you're trying to help.

JORDAN   I said you could be convinced now.

TREY   Okay, I can't believe I have to explain this: Bermuda Triangles aren't a thing.

JORDAN   Oh, okay—thanks, Dr. Dad.

TREY   People have at least heard of the other Bermuda Triangle. Where are the parents of the class of '96—searching for their sons and daughters? Where are all the employees wondering where the fuck their Putt-Putt course went?

JORDAN   I have a theory . . .

TREY   I'm sure you do.

JORDAN   You're not even going to consider this?

TREY I'm not looking for boats and baby teeth, I'm not interested in Middle C. I'm sorry.

[JORDAN pulls out TREY'S POSTCARDS.]

JORDAN I went back to your house. What? Watching you read things was boring. You are a very slow walker. What's this one?

TREY That's the Palisades Drive-In Movie Theater.

JORDAN And you think what—they tore it down—forgot it was there.

TREY If it's been gone long enough. Yeah, I think they forgot about it.

JORDAN I don't. I think it got Bermuda Triangled. I think your postcard proves it.

[JORDAN hands over the POSTCARD. TREY scrutinizes it.]

That large concrete square in the middle of the parking lot. See it?

[TREY does.]

All those people walking around. All those cars. And somehow, no one seems to have noticed that the concession stand is gone. I can't help you if I don't know what you want.

[Lights shift. JORDAN is lit in a soft purple silhouette. The Past:]

TREY "Mom, take a look at this postcard—you remember this place?"

[JORDAN assumes the role.]

JORDAN "That an amusement park?"

TREY "Look look—Killjoy."

JORDAN "Isn't that something. Where did this come from?"

TREY "I bought it in a shop downtown. We went to an amusement park when we lived there."

JORDAN "I took you to the County Fairgrounds in Zanesville once."

TREY "I'm talking about this place."

JORDAN   "The Church there used to do a carnival."

TREY   "I'm not talking dunking booths and face painting. I'm talking something permanent. The abominable snowman, you remember that."

JORDAN   "That postcard looks like it's from the '60s. You must have seen a picture of it before."

TREY   "I'm telling ya, I've got a memory that's just nagging at me. We went to an amusement park. And we took this girl with us."

[MUSIC.]

JORDAN   "Friend from school."

TREY   "I don't think so."

JORDAN   "Well Trey, I didn't make a habit of carting around random children we found."

TREY   "You don't remember any of this?"

JORDAN   "It's a pretty postcard." *(flipping it over)* I wouldn't have paid six dollars.

[TREY shifts back to the boardwalk. JORDAN stays in silhouette.]

TREY   I went back and bought every postcard I could find. There are amusement park fanatics out there—they can tell you about every ride in every park, who made it, who bought it when the park shut its doors? Where is it now? This place wasn't torn down. It was never there. And yet. I've been there. I don't know how. It's not a dream. But I don't think it was a memory either. But I've been there. They're pulling people off the Ferris wheel because a storm is coming. I'm staring up because if it's gonna get struck by lightning—Ima goddam see that. And then I hear my name and there's this girl—younger than me—long brown hair, a too-big, hand-me-down Hard Rock Cafe shirt and jeans cut off just under the knee. She's walking back from the funnel cake stand with this mountain of powdered sugar and this lump of cherry compote on top. The two of us dig into this funnel cake when it starts to rain. So we run over to the Abominable Snowman, because that ride was indoors, inside this giant concrete igloo. And we're standing in line, trying to finish this funnel cake before the rain gets it. She keeps making me laugh. That's what I remember. And we get inside—and it's snowing—it's thick with snow and fog and I lose sight of her.

JORDAN *(as HERSELF)* You aren't looking for an amusement park. You're looking for her.

[MUSIC. TREY shifts back. The Past.]

TREY "Mom?"

JORDAN Who was she?

TREY "Mom."

JORDAN Who do you think she was?

TREY "Did you ever want another kid?"

JORDAN *(as TREY'S MOM)* "Where did that come from? No. We're pretty happy with you."

TREY "But did you ever think about having another?"

JORDAN "We tried but . . . I guess it just wasn't meant to be."

[Shift. The Boardwalk.]

TREY That's my dream. Well, and then Cameron Diaz showed up—

JORDAN And you had jetpack sex. That your mother forgot isn't really that interesting. No one mourns the Class of '96. That you remembered . . . that's what gets me.

[JORDAN holds up another POSTCARD.]

This place. I think you would like it. It still exists.

[JORDAN hands TREY the POSTCARD.]

TREY "Little Killjoy: An aerial view of Killjoy in a 1/64th-scale replica." Yeah. I already looked into this place. They boarded it up a decade ago.

JORDAN   Gosh. If only you knew a kitten burglar.

[JORDAN meows.]

TREY   I can't believe you've never heard this phrase.

[MUSIC. Shift. TREY and JORDAN exit. Little Killjoy. Night. A blue silhouette.]

TREY   *(whispering, off)* How far down is it?

JORDAN   *(whispering, off)* Just drop.

TREY   I can't feel the ground.

JORDAN   You don't think it's down there? You think I brought you to the one place in the world without ground? Drop.

[TREY drops, falling onscreen. JORDAN laughs.]

TREY   *(standing up)* Ow—shit. I banged my shin.

JORDAN   Yeah—you are not a graceful person.

TREY   I don't normally climb thru windows. Do you want me to help you?

[JORDAN drops gracefully.]

      Okay. You're much better at this.

JORDAN   Why are you whispering? We're the only ones here.

TREY   You're whispering.

JORDAN   To keep you from feeling like an idiot. *(talking)* 'Cause you kinda sound like an idiot.

[JORDAN shines her FLASHLIGHT at TREY, casting his shadow behind him.]

      What? It's how friends talk. It's a sign of affection.

TREY   Do you have other friends? Like, do you have a framework you're basing this on?

JORDAN   Alright—we wanna keep moving.

[TREY and JORDAN shine their FLASHLIGHTS around, scanning:]

This is like the historical section: fur-trading post, mining town, sex cult—don't bother, I've already looked, there's nothing raunchy. You want to be in that room.

TREY What am I looking for?

JORDAN You'll see. Go check it out. I'm gonna take a lap, see if there's anything I want.

[TREY blinds JORDAN with his FLASHLIGHT.]

TREY We're not here to rob the place.

[JORDAN blinds TREY as well.]

JORDAN One half of us is definitely here to rob the place.

TREY *(whispering again)* My fucking fingerprints are all over the window.

JORDAN Do you think you'll leave less trace evidence if you whisper?

TREY I don't know—you started mentioning crimes and it just sort of happened.

JORDAN The breaking and entering is already a crime, dummy.

TREY Well that's our one. No stealing.

JORDAN A little stealing.

TREY No.

JORDAN Three things.

TREY No things.

JORDAN Four.

TREY Stop.

JORDAN Okay—I'll meet you halfway. Five things. Four for me, one for you.

TREY Do not include me.

JORDAN   Well if you don't steal something, how can I trust you not to go to the cops?

TREY   We Are Not Tak-ing A-ny-thing.

[Ha-rumph! Ditto. TREY and JORDAN snap off their lights. Blue silhouette.]

JORDAN   Fine. I guess I'll just pass the time with all these fireworks.

[JORDAN holds up a giant silhouetted firework.]

TREY   What are you doing with fireworks?

JORDAN   They were in my backpack.

TREY   I'm not falling for this.

[JORDAN flicks her lighter, lighting up her face. Off-screen, TREY flicks a second lighter, casting him in a soft glow.]

JORDAN   This one looks loud.

TREY   Okay—you've made your point. Four things.

JORDAN   . . . we'll see. Quit being so paranoid.

TREY   *(out)* And she sprinted off to another room without the smallest sound.

JORDAN   *(out)* In the opposite direction, in a much larger room, Trey found modern-day Killjoy, spared the homogenous backwash of the 21st century—frozen in a time before every town had to have a P.F. Changs and a Dunkin Donuts. A monument to an era when small-town America was larger-than-life.

TREY   *(to HIMSELF)* The Pump & Pantry, Hell Freezes Over, Big Bee Drugs.

JORDAN   But no Palisades Drive-In, no greyhound racetrack, and in place of Riverland Adventure Park . . .

TREY   *(out)* Woods. It was just woods.

JORDAN   He stared at the map, defeated, his eyes wandering, his gaze softening.

TREY   Further down 666, towards the start to town.

JORDAN   A large parking lot in front of a strip mall.

TREY   Ordinary, but not quite right. Inside that gray rectangle of the parking lot was a mismatched, blob-like shape in the middle.

JORDAN   Was it a repair to the model? A hasty patch job?

[TREY begins ripping CLOTH off-screen.]

He pulled up on it, revealing underneath:

[TREY shines his light on something below the screen. His face glows a soft, reflected green.]

TREY   Eighteen small islands of grass surrounded by sand. A Tiki-themed Putt-Putt course.

JORDAN   His eyes followed the road back to the woods alongside the drug store.

[TREY starts to pull up the top layer of the model, more offscreen ripping.]

Pulling up on the woods like he was ripping up old carpet.

[TREY shines his FLASHLIGHT on the offscreen model, his face glowing a soft, reflected pink.]

A paved concourse. An unpainted section in the shape of . . . an igloo.

[TREY holds up a small model of an ABOMINABLE SNOWMAN, examining it with his flashlight, casting its SHADOW on the back wall.]

A pair of footsteps guarding the entrance to the igloo.

[TREY pockets the ABOMINABLE SNOWMAN.]

And for the second time in his life, he became a thief.

[TREY and JORDAN find each other. Lights shift.]

TREY   How does something this big just disappear?

JORDAN   The universe repairs itself. A Bermuda Triangle takes something and the Universe preserves itself, wipes memories, smooths over the edges.

TREY   Then why do I remember it?

JORDAN   Maybe its reach only extends so far. If you've moved away—if you mailed a postcard halfway across the country, traces remain. That's my theory anyway. You know how in *Back to the Future* they're always worried about time paradoxes unraveling the fabric of the space-time continuum and destroying the universe? Seems a bit much. Consider how small you are compared to this town. And now imagine how tiny you are compared to the planet, the galaxy. You're telling me the whole universe has to destroy itself just because one horned-up teenager decided to go back in time and fuck Lea Thompson?

TREY   That's his mom.

JORDAN   Billions of years in an infinite universe and you think there isn't one Marty McFly who took his mom to pound town? No thank you, I don't want to live there. E = mc2. If Lea Thompson wants to fuck, you fuck. Quod Erat Demonstrandum. The Universe preserves. You can be convinced now.

TREY   Fine. You are very clever. And gross . . .

JORDAN   Thank you

TREY   But it's unprovable.

JORDAN   I've seen it.

[MUSIC. Lights shift. A pair of kids on a neighborhood street, lit largely by street lamps.]

TREY   *(out)* It was 1:00 a.m. but the pavement still radiated heat from the day. It had taken an hour to walk the two and a half miles from Little Killjoy. God, he missed his car. Stars shone in a cloudless sky while two best stranger-friends stared at a wooded lot in a crowded neighborhood.

JORDAN   It was the perfect neighborhood—full of kids. The Hooks had a pair of street hockey nets that practically lived in the street. We would play capture the flag from stop sign to stop sign and behind the houses, down to the river. My bedroom was up there, top floor, facing the street.

TREY   When was it taken?

JORDAN   I was at summer camp. My grandmother came to pick me up at the end of July—which I thought was weird—Mom and Dad hadn't been able to take off work. It had taken everything: the family business, my childhood home, my friends.

TREY   You didn't see them at school?

JORDAN   It had taken all the spend-the-night parties, the morning bus rides, the summer cookouts. There was hardly any friendship left. That's what's so insidious. The Bermuda Triangle didn't take my childhood home. It wanted my childhood. The Universe preserves. See that tree closest to the sidewalk, the lowest branch on the left? And then out—that big knot. Stare at it, let your gaze soften, like those magic eye posters from when we were kids.

TREY   *(out)* Below the knot in the tree, a dark shadow in the shape of a keyhole. And then there was no knot at all but a perfectly smooth, brass doorknob. Out and out, branches melding into the woodgrain of a paint-split red door, weeds and grass giving way to steps. A faint house sitting just underneath, like double exposures in old photographs.

JORDAN   Take a step.

TREY   Can I?

JORDAN   Just keep your eyes on the door.

TREY   *(out)* A foot reaching out, hovering, uncertain.

JORDAN   You think I brought you to the one place in the world without ground?

TREY   Steps. Up to the door. Turning the knob. Peering in.

[Shift. JORDAN'S childhood home:]

> And now—no longer a double exposure, no longer a vacant lot. . . . They were standing inside a house, moonlight pouring in thru windows.

JORDAN *(out)* It took a moment to decipher why the house looked so foreign to him.

TREY It was half decorated, chairs around a void where a dining room table should have been. Records sat stacked in milk crates next to an empty entertainment center. Every room was half-full—painting, mirrors, rugs, chairs, but the spacing between them made it evident: this was a home decor cut off at the knees.

[JORDAN unzips her bag and pulls out TREY'S two lop-sided MUGS.]

> What are you doing with those?

JORDAN I told you I was going to rob you.

TREY Is that what you've been doing? Robbing the town so that you can—

JORDAN It's not stealing if it was mine to begin with.

TREY I used to dunk Oreos in those mugs.

JORDAN I'm sure. But they were mine first. The Bermuda Triangle took the house, and the universe was stuck to make sense of the aftermath. The Universe preserves. It redistributed my whole childhood, divvied it up, spread it around.

TREY *(out)* It was a lateral movement—from my mantle to hers, perfectly placed between a pair of candlesticks and an empty, cut-glass picture frame.

JORDAN We measure the passage of time in loss. When did you first lose a family pet? How many grandparents did you have at your graduation—at your wedding? When did you start losing your hair? How old were you when your first high school friend got a divorce? We experience loss so often that we cease to be blindsided by it. We get so accustomed to loss we never anticipate the notion that things can be found again.

TREY   Have you always been able to see it?

JORDAN   I found it by accident. Too many nights staring at a vacant lot. But once you know to search for it—it gets easier to see.

[MUSIC.]

TREY   *(out)* She gave him a tour of the house. Her childhood bedroom felt the most empty.

JORDAN   Not everything can be recovered.

TREY   An hour later, they made their way back out to the street.

[Shift. Back outside.]

Jordan, I'm so sorry.

JORDAN   You didn't do it.

TREY   Does it help? Having a bit of it back?

JORDAN   I've been holding on to this house for so long, I don't know if it eases or magnifies.

TREY   *(out)* They were two souls, united in loss. The air shifted. A cool breeze rushed past. Jordan pointed off at the end of Alasdair Avenue, where it crossed with State Route 666, where a red light was out.

JORDAN   Come on.

TREY   She took off, not courtesy power walking, but fell into an outright sprint. The only red light in town was dormant, so too were the streetlights. Gone even were the stars, covered over by fast-moving clouds that bobbled.

JORDAN   *(out)* As they ran, Trey saw Killjoy for the first time as it had always been, transfixed by—

TREY   The wooden-trestled specter of the Sidewinder Roller Coaster.

JORDAN   They came to a dead halt in the parking lot of the Ace Hardware Store.

TREY   There's no real reason why I should have, but secretly, I was kind of expecting a triangle. A glimmering portal. A bank of fog. Ball lightning. Anything. What we got was—

[MUSIC. Lights shift to a dark, unnatural purple.]

JORDAN   A purple glowing mass in the form of one of those rent-by-the-hour cement mixers.

TREY   Do you think it sees us?

JORDAN   Do you think it has eyes?

TREY   *(out)* She took a step towards it. *(to JORDAN)* That feels close enough.

JORDAN   I just want to look a little closer.

TREY   No no—that's crazy behavior. *(out)* She took a step.

JORDAN   The cement mixer shuddered, shrunk a little.

[Lights begin pulsing around them.]

TREY   Jordan.

JORDAN   It's okay.

TREY   They took a step.

JORDAN   The Bermuda Triangle's form shifted a little more.

TREY   Step after step.

JORDAN   Rearranging until it took the form of a pair of human bodies, joined at the hands.

(to TREY) Trey.

TREY   I know. But I don't think that I can.

JORDAN   We have to. We get so accustomed to loss we never anticipate the notion that things can be found again.

TREY   *(out)* Neither one of them had the power to step forward.

JORDAN *(out)* It was like they were kids with their hands on a Ouija board, guided by greater powers.

TREY They were just standing outside a Bermuda Triangle. And then they weren't.

JORDAN Hey Trey.

[The play stops. TREY and JORDAN stand in neutral rooms.]

TREY Yeah, Jordan, what's up?

JORDAN So I know we're in the middle of a play

TREY Yeah, I think we're getting close to the good bits.

JORDAN What's something that you've lost?

[At this point, both PERFORMERS share a story of something that they have lost. This "lost item" should be something physical, and not a clever answer to "what is something you've lost," i.e.—not "I lost myself, my mind, my virginity," etc.]

TREY My Dad gave me this sterling silver bracelet. He bought it on a mission trip to the Navajo Nation in New Mexico when he was a teenager in the mid-seventies. Now I don't know what the fuck a bunch of Southern Baptists from Alabama can do for the Navajo Indians so "mission trip" might just be seventies talk for "I wanna see some Indians." This bracelet was handcrafted and inlaid with turquoise. But as Dad got older, it didn't fit him anymore, so he gave it to me. Whenever Dad would see me wearing it, he would always launch into the same story. He was so excited about going on that mission trip. Not because he was a good Christian and not because he had never been out west, not because he was eager to meet American Indians. He was excited because he would finally get to try Coors Light. You see, if you were a high school student in the 1970s, there was no cooler status symbol than drinking a Coors Light— because, at the time, it was the only beer delivered in refrigerated trucks. And you couldn't get it in Alabama. Well Dad found somebody out there willing to buy it for him, only he got caught trying to smuggle it back on the church bus. The preacher made him walk up and down the aisle, apologizing one by one to all the women on the bus for trying to sneak pre-cooled beer onto God's party wagon. I don't know when I lost it. Maybe it slipped off on public transit. Maybe it was pickpocketed. I remember letting a friend wear it at a bar around the time that I last saw it but . . . I don't know. When we moved away from New York, I was hoping it would turn up behind a bedside table. Thing is—I lost more than the bracelet. I lost my connection with that story. Once a week, someone would comment on the bracelet and I would get to tell the story of the Coors Light. What I lost was the story.

JORDAN   I grew up in the middle of nowhere. Like you had to have a quarter tank if you passed the last gas station on the way home or else you wouldn't make it back to the gas station. It was a wonderful place to grow up, and I learned a lot about how to be with myself, but it meant that if I didn't want to be with just myself, I had to drive a ways. And much of the time "a ways" meant the ninety-minute trek to the suburbs of Detroit. This distance meant that I crashed on a lot of couches, and practically lived out of my car, with several changes of clothes and shoes in the trunk at any given time. You can imagine that this super robust organization system meant that I only had a tenuous grasp on the clothes I had and the clothes I had lost. Things I thought were definitely in the backseat turned out to be missing altogether when I went looking for them, and pieces I was certain I had lost would turn up when I did a deep clean—or had to change a tire. This was all fine; the sorrow of realizing a favorite skirt was gone was inevitably balanced by the happiness of not having lost that top after all, but years of living like that meant that I no longer have a sense of permanence about anything I've really lost. There was a forest green knit duster that I wore everywhere, and I lost and found it again and again. I'm pretty sure it has been truly gone for like, ten years, but I still find myself hoping to find it during spring cleaning, or a move. And even though I know better, even though I don't even drive the same car anymore, every so often I catch myself thinking "I bet it's just in the trunk."

TREY   I like that.

JORDAN   Thanks.

TREY   Do you want to finish a story?

JORDAN   Sure.

*[MUSIC. Lights shift. Killjoy. A Nether Plane. The world glitters and bobbles. *Note: We used a pair of cheap, outdoor LED Christmas lights that project a watery pattern in white light.]*

TREY   At 2:00 a.m. the clamor of Killjoy was startling.

JORDAN   Motorcycles and horse-drawn carriages jostled for rank as children and couples crowded the sidewalks.

TREY   Fur traders stood selling pelts while miners pushed an overburdened coal car down a rail-lined street.

JORDAN   A harsh wind kicked up dust. It felt as if Killjoy were poised on the edge of a squall.

[A FLASH of LIGHTNING and THUNDER.]

TREY   Lilac storm clouds jumped with lightning. In each flash could be seen the silhouettes of jagged, black wings hovering just inside the cloud cover.

JORDAN   The very air vibrated its warning: "do not stay long."

TREY   The Bermuda Triangle was shifting again, purple forms recombining into the shape of a park bench as the Triangle continued down Front Street.

JORDAN   They didn't need to check in, each knew instinctively what the other had to do.

[The BERMUDA TRIANGLE moves on, the watery glow fading and lights shifting back to a cool night.]

TREY   Don't leave without me.

JORDAN   Never. You're my best friend.

TREY   . . . You're my best friend.

JORDAN Just come get me when you're ready.

TREY How will I find you?

JORDAN You won't be able to miss me. I'm a cat burglar.

TREY Let's just agree we're gonna keep working on it.

[TREY darkens his screen.]

JORDAN The ground was a carpet of incidentals: loose change and books, individual socks and single earrings, leather wallets and pen caps. A thousand lifetimes of lost shit just piled up in the street. On a bench in front of Hell Freezes Over a small child, too young to be left alone, was contentedly eating an ice cream cone dipped in blue.

[JORDAN is startled.]

     The doors to the ice cream parlor opened as two men dragged out a body and stacked it neatly on the side of the road. Cholera, she supposed. Busy night in Killjoy. She moved on, down Alasdair Avenue.

[JORDAN darkens her screen. TREY reappears at Riverland Adventure Park. The sounds of screaming kids and rushing roller coasters.]

TREY The entrance to Riverland Adventure Park! A postcard, come to life: screaming children and spinning rides, the smell of deep-fried twinkies in molten sugar. "Every game a winner!" a barker called out from the balloon pop. They were unmistakable, all eighty of them palling around in their caps and gowns. The graduating class of 1996, eternally waiting to hear their names called. They were sitting in a grassy picnic area, petting a pack of greyhound race dogs. One of the seniors had a tape deck hoisted up on their shoulders. They were blasting "I Love You Always Forever" by Donna Lewis. At the end of the long concourse was an unmistakable blue form, guarding an igloo.

[TREY darkens his screen. JORDAN reappears on the front steps to her childhood home. MUSIC.]

JORDAN   A brass doorknob in a red door, it was there—no longer a double exposure.

[JORDAN pulls out a single KEY on a lone KEY RING.]

> She hadn't needed it since summer camp so long ago. Into the door, turning it slowly, feeling the tumbler click into place. She was home.

[JORDAN darkens her screen. TREY reappears. The inside of the igloo. The sound of an industrial AC unit along with a giant fan and blown snow.]

TREY   *(out)* Snow and Fog and Cold and Loud. It was meant to be a respite from the July heat. It was meant to feel like an Arctic Adventure. I quickly lose my bearings, it feels like I've walked further than the tilt-a-whirl-sized igloo would allow.

[JORDAN appears in silhouette.]

JORDAN   Trey?

TREY   Taylor!

[TREY darkens his screen. JORDAN reappears inside her childhood home. MUSIC.]

JORDAN   *(out)* The cut-glass picture frame on the mantle is whole again: a photo of mom and me with our backs to the Muskingum as the sun sets. The dining room table holding chairs in its orbit once more. The Fridge—the glorious fridge—choked with memories clinging to tacky magnets from forgotten vacations.

> Up the stairs to the second floor, turning the knob to my child-hood bedroom . . .

[JORDAN dims back to silhouette. TREY reappears, in a loud and cold igloo.]

TREY   Taylor.

JORDAN   You didn't sit with me!

TREY   I didn't mean to lose you.

JORDAN   I had to sit next to this kid that I totally thought was gonna blow chunks.

[TREY laughs.]

> It's not funny.

TREY   Yes it is.

JORDAN   Wanna go again? You have to stay with me next time.

TREY   We need to go.

JORDAN   We've got time for one more. Mom won't care.

TREY   Taylor, it's so much later than you think.

[TREY reaches out for her.]

> Come on. Let's go home.

[TREY darkens his screen. JORDAN appears in her childhood bedroom. MUSIC. JORDAN picks up a wonderfully '90s PHOTO ALBUM.]

JORDAN   *(out)* The one thing she could never steal back: the public pool and birthday parties, goofy, pig-nosed faces and gap-toothed smiles.

[JORDAN shows an old photo of childhood friends half-posing, half-goofing off.]

> Her desk, cluttered with books and notes and hair ties and—and the cordless phone I begged for all winter, with speed dial!

[JORDAN picks up the PHONE.]

> One touch dialing for Katie and Desiree and Brooke and—

[JORDAN sees a name she didn't expect.]

> Well isn't that something.

[TREY reappears with JORDAN, playing TAYLOR, by the turnstile at Riverland Adventure Park. Lights from carnival rides pulse different colors.]

TREY   *(out)* A long line on either side of them. Greyhound dogs and High School Seniors. They were staring. And . . . still listening to Donna Lewis. It was a weird combination.

JORDAN   *(pointing up)* Trey, look.

TREY   Above them, the clouds writhed, black wings beating faster. The Universe preserves. But how? What does it use as its enforcers?

JORDAN   I want to go home.

TREY   We will. Taylor, you have to promise me—until we get there, you will do whatever I do. If I run, you run, if I hide . . . do you understand?

JORDAN   Okay, spazz.

TREY   Taylor.

JORDAN   Okay. Promise.

TREY   Alright. Let's go.

JORDAN   *(out)* The greyhounds lowered into a crouch.

TREY   Just focus on the exit.

JORDAN   The Class of '96 took a step forward.

TREY   Keep walking—don't panic.

JORDAN   Tightening the tunnel.

TREY   Taylor, get ready.

JORDAN   Closing in on prey.

TREY   Run.

JORDAN   The rows collapsed behind them like surfers in the barrel of a wave.

TREY   *(out)* They hopped the turnstile. Ran back to the Ace Hardware.

JORDAN   Overhead, black wings beat in anger.

TREY   They stood in the vacant parking lot, next to the rent-by-the-hour cement mixer. Where is she?

JORDAN   Trey, I want to go home.

TREY   Come on, Jordan—where are you?

JORDAN   Behind them, they could hear the barking of dogs. And then.

[Both rooms pulse in bright flashes of green and red and blue.]

TREY   Green! *(smiling)* Green and red and blue. Fireworks.

JORDAN   They took off running again.

TREY   Wait!

[TREY pulls a KEYFOB out of his pocket, presses a button. BRP! BRP!]

JORDAN   When did you learn how to drive?

TREY   *(out)* Jordan was setting off the last of the fireworks when the car pulled up.

JORDAN   I don't know about you, but I kinda feel like getting the ever-loving fuck out of here.

TREY   The Bermuda Triangle is gone

JORDAN   *(scanning)* There—that purple beacon in the distance.

TREY   Okay—then I suggest—

[JORDAN is taken aback.]

          What is it?

[JORDAN points around them.]

          They had been gathering in ones and twos, resting on car hoods, perched in low branches, waiting on telephone lines.

JORDAN   They had come down from the clouds: the black-winged creatures.

TREY   I don't think they want us to leave.

JORDAN   Oh, you picked up on that?

TREY   What the fuck do we do now?

JORDAN   Okay, hey hey HEY! Listen to me.

[Donna Lewis's "I Love You Always Forever" begins playing.]

We are getting out of here. You and me . . . and this small child—sorry, it's just gonna take some getting used to—WE ARE GETTING OUT OF HERE. We're gonna thread this needle. We're gonna shoot the moon. We are going to fuck Lea Thompson!

TREY   Alright, yeah . . . Let's fuck our moms!

[TREY pulls out his CAR KEYS.]

JORDAN   Leave it. I know a faster way.

TREY   Are you serious? I just got it back. Damn.

[TREY throws his keys over his head.]

(*out*) They were off and running now—the three of them. Where others might have been disoriented by the overlapping of two centuries of Killjoy, Jordan was unfazed—thirteen again, running along backyards. It was a game of capture the flag. "We've taken something of yours. Come and find it."

JORDAN   (*out*) They cut over a street and froze midstride. Turning the corner was the pack of greyhounds.

TREY   But before the dogs could reach them a pistol fired nearby as a fight poured out of a saloon and into the street, blocking the dogs' path.

JORDAN   They turned the other way, towards the Muskingum.

TREY   A riverboat sat at anchor, black-winged hoards dotting the railings. They never moved, but it was obvious. It had to have been them that had turned the city against the trio.

JORDAN   The river began to boil as skinless horrors emerged. Reanimated creatures from the long-dead fur trade clawed their way onto the banks, water rolling off their pelt-less bodies.

TREY   Jordan grabbed the two and pulled them into a squat brick building along the banks.

[Blackout. In the darkness, the music is replaced with some fucking rad '70s porn soundtrack. Uh . . . just the music.]

[TREY and JORDAN have their FLASHLIGHTS. They shout, freeze, wide-eyed:]

> *(to JORDAN)* sex cult. Look away. Look away. *(to the cult)* Oh. No, thank you—we were just leaving.

JORDAN *(to the cult)* I'm open-minded, but y'all nasty.

[Lights resume. More Donna Lewis. The escape attempt continues.]

TREY *(out)* The trio was sprinting now, up Center Street, back towards 666. From up ahead, they could hear the growls and stampeding pads of the greyhound pack.

JORDAN They ducked behind a pile of dead cholera victims, praying the stench would mask them. The dogs raced along without a second glance.

[TREY sees something.]

TREY Hey—you think we could blend in over there?

JORDAN Oh . . . Okay.

[Lights shift.]

> Just walk casually. There are no undead animals trying to kill us. We're just three people on our way to the concession stand.

TREY *(out)* There were hundreds of them, in graphic tees and denim jackets, transfixed by the hypnotic glow of the towering monolith that was Palisades Drive-In Movie Theater.

[Lights flicker as dark shadows fly around the projection booth of the drive-in theater.]

JORDAN The black-winged creatures huddled like moths around the projection booth, casting fluttering demonic shadows a hundred feet high.

TREY And now more running towards a purple beacon hovering beneath a black thunderhead.

[Back at the Bermuda Triangle. The world pulses, threatening to fall apart.]

They could see it now—the short-circuiting, shape-shifting mess that was the Bermuda Triangle: a car, a body, a house, a billboard.

JORDAN   Before it—blocking the path stood the lost legion that was the graduating class of 1996.

TREY   Guarding the portal, flying in a tight circle, were the black-winged creatures: the inter-dimensional turkey vultures of the universe.

JORDAN   Behind them, they could hear the growl of hungry, lean bodies as the Greyhounds caught up.

TREY   They're not going to let us pass.

JORDAN   They will.

TREY   Jordan, we're trapped.

JORDAN   We're not.

[JORDAN picks something up off the ground.]

TREY   *(out)* She crouched down, her fingers searching, and chose her weapon off the litter-strewn ground. I'll never know how I lost it. I'll never know where I last had it. All I know is that it turned back up when I needed it most. Jordan stood, pulled back her arm, and threw.

[JORDAN winds up and throws. MUSIC climaxes. Sing it, Donna.]

JORDAN   The silver bracelet,* inlaid with turquoise, spun thru the air, glinting lilac against a black sky.

TREY   The Bermuda Triangle coughed and sputtered: a newspaper stand, an ice cream truck, a water tower.

JORDAN   The bracelet shot into the swirling pack of black-winged creatures, knocking one out of formation.

TREY   A high school senior caught the movement out of the corner of their eye and—mistaking the black wing for an airborne cap, pulled off his own tasseled headgear and let fly.

---

* This should be one of the items from the previous monologues.

JORDAN The poor senior class of 1996, deprived of so much, couldn't stand to let yet another milestone pass them by. One by one, they pulled off their caps, looked heavenward and threw.

TREY The Bermuda Triangle spasmed: a weeping willow tree, a little league baseball team. The trio ran.

JORDAN The greyhounds leapt.

TREY The black-winged creatures dove.

JORDAN But it didn't matter. They were all lost in the flailing of gowns and a bevy of caps.

[They enter the BERMUDA TRIANGLE. Shit gets real. Blackout. Silence. The Universe holds its breath.]

[From the darkness can be heard: "Hey asshole. You made me miss my shot."]

[Lights up. The soft sound of exotica music. TREY holds a PUTT-PUTT CLUB while JORDAN drinks from a TIKI MUG.]

JORDAN Sorry.

TREY You alright?

JORDAN Yeah. You okay?

TREY Fine. I think.

[The two stare at each other. TREY'S PHONE rings. JORDAN shrugs. He answers. Speakerphone:]

Hello?

TAYLOR *(prerecorded)* Did you lose your car again?

TREY Taylor? Where are you?

TAYLOR I'm at home. Starving. Mom told me to call and see if you're on your way.

TREY Uh . . . yeah, we're on our way.

TAYLOR Good. Jordan's parents have been here for like half an hour and Dad wants to know if he can start the grill.

Oh. Mom says pick up more buns.

[TREY hangs up.]

JORDAN   Don't look at me, you wanted a kid sister.

TREY   I did.

JORDAN   Well come on. You think you know how to get there?

TREY   Hold on. You think everything is back?

JORDAN   Maybe it was the easiest patch job . . . why are you staring at me?

TREY   I remember.

JORDAN   Remember what?

TREY   The mugs. We used to sit at your dining room table.

JORDAN   And dunk Oreos. Yeah. That's right. *(out)* We measure time in loss.

TREY   *(out)* Sometimes its ticking secondhand is the only thing we hear.

JORDAN   But not all lost things stay that way.

TREY   Because even as the world takes—

JORDAN   The Universe preserves.

[TREY and JORDAN hold up POSTCARDS from Riverland Adventure Park with the words "The" and "End." The POSTCARDS move closer, eventually covering a pair of webcams. Blackout.]

[End.]

Ravening

Colette Mazunik

Production History

Ravening was developed with the Red Rocks Community College Department of Theatre and Dance with the collective creativity of the cast. It premiered at Red Rocks Community Theatre as an online production and was directed by El Armstrong, Penny Benson, Colette Mazunik, and Leigh Miller.

The cast was as follows:

AMMON   Ammon Underhill
REVA   Reva Williams
PAXTON   Paxton Woodcook
BILL   Bill Thompson
STONE   Liam Lieren
RACHAEL   Rachael Hogan
BEN   Ben Clark

Characters

AMMON   A facilitator of a psychological study. A college student.
REVA   Another facilitator. A college student.
PAXTON   Subject #1-196. A college student.
BILL   Subject #2-197. A retired teacher.
STONE   Subject #3-198. A college student.
RACHAEL   Subject #4-199. A college student.
BEN   Subject #5-200. A college student.

Pronouns may be adjusted as needed. Character names may be changed to the names of the actors. References to a sister or brother may be changed as needed but should reference a sibling relationship.

Time

The present

Place

A research lab at a university

[*We are witnessing a psychological study. Two facilitators, REVA and AMMON, are in a control room. They are monitoring five video feeds, one for each of the five subjects in the study.*

The video feeds show extreme close-ups of subjects' faces. Subjects are already in place in feeds 1, 3, and 5. Feeds 2 and 4 are unoccupied.]

AMMON   Welcome. We'll be getting started in a few minutes. If you haven't already done so, please go ahead and place your face in the machine and get comfortable. You should be seeing a black-and-white image.

BILL   (SUBJECT #2-197, FEED 2) *(not yet on camera)* I don't know how to turn this thing on. I don't see an image.

AMMON   Okay, that's okay. There isn't anything for you to turn on, you just come to the machine, buckle in, and place your face . . .

BILL   I don't see anything.

STONE   (SUBJECT #3-198, FEED 3) I have a question.

AMMON   *(to STONE)* Okay, just a second. *(to REVA)* Can you help with Subject 3?

REVA   *(taking a bite of her hastily eaten meal)* Yep. Just a sec.

BILL   Hello?

AMMON   Subject #2-197, you'll need to come to the machine.

STONE   I just have a question.

AMMON   *(to REVA)* Number 3!

REVA   Calm down! Everything's fine.

AMMON   I can't help everyone at the same time.

REVA   They can wait fifteen seconds.

BILL Hello?

AMMON Yes, sorry about that sir.

BILL You said I was supposed to see something, but I can't see anything.

AMMON You have to put your face in the machine.

BILL I am.

AMMON No?

BILL Then what do I have my face in?

AMMON I don't know. Okay. Look around. There should be a black machine in front of you, it has an opening. Yes. I can see you. Yes. No. Turn to the . . . yes.

BILL Oh, this?

AMMON Yes. Okay, buckle in. Now you have to put your face in.

BILL Oh. Okay.

AMMON Can you see the image?

STONE Is anyone there? I have a question.

BILL You should really explain this better to people.

AMMON Thank you for your feedback, sir. I'll take that into advisement.

REVA *(to STONE)* Shoot.

STONE What?

AMMON Where's Subject 4?

REVA I'm here. What's your question?

AMMON Where's Subject 4?

[*AMMON leaves.*]

STONE Oh, um. Is there going to be a bathroom break during this? Because sometimes when I get nervous, I need to use the bathroom.

REVA   Okay. That's fine.

STONE   There's a break?

REVA   No, but if you need to hit the head, I'll let you out.

STONE   That's not going to mess up the study?

REVA   I don't know, but it's not like I'm going to keep you chained to the machine or anything. So just do what you gotta do.

STONE   Okay thanks.

[*AMMON returns.*]

BEN   (SUBJECT #5-200, FEED 5) Um, how much longer until we start? Hello? Can you hear me?

AMMON   Yes, and soon. Just get comfortable, we'll be—

BEN   Okay.

AMMON   Where's Number 4?

REVA   We're gonna have to go without.

AMMON   They're not in the waiting room. They confirmed?

REVA   Yes!

AMMON   We can't have any more no-shows or we'll have to add another day.

REVA   Fine by me. (*gloating*) 'Cause I'm an hourly employee, Mr. Class Credit Only.

AMMON   I cannot spend another day here.

REVA   Does someone have to study for his finals?

AMMON   That's not funny. I could lose my scholarship.

REVA   Well, unless you can recruit another subject immediately, I don't see what else we can do.

[*PAXTON (SUBJECT #1-196, FEED 1) begins quietly singing a song to himself. It's clear that he has no idea that he's mic'd and on camera.*]

AMMON   We can't keep holding. We're going to have to go without them.

REVA   Like I said.

[PAXTON's singing is louder and more animated. AMMON mutes his microphone.]

BEN   Um, do you have an estimate of how much longer I have to wait?

AMMON   *(to REVA, regarding her food)* You gonna put that away?

REVA   Really?

AMMON   I'm gonna start the machines.

BEN   I kind of need to know how much longer.

REVA   You're really going to give me a hard time for taking five minutes to eat?

AMMON   *(to BEN)* Just hold on. *(to REVA)* I'm not giving you a hard time about eating. I'm asking you to follow protocol and put away all food and drink before we restart the machines.
      You really shouldn't have that in here anyway.

REVA   Then they should give us more than fifteen minutes for dinner.

AMMON   We're running late.

REVA   And not lock the building precisely at eight.

BEN   I have a study group after this.

REVA   *(to BEN)* Yep. Starting now.

AMMON   If Subject 4 comes while I'm—

REVA   I'll handle it.

AMMON   Okay. *(to the SUBJECTS)* Okay, we're ready.

BEN   Finally.

AMMON   Just to verify, can everyone hear me? I'll call out your number and when I call out your number, please respond if you can hear me. #1-196?

[PAXTON responds in the affirmative, but his mic is still muted. AMMON enables his microphone.]

AMMON   You can hear me?

PAXTON   Yep.

AMMON   #2-197?

REVA   This. This is why we're running late. *(to SUBJECTS)* Hey. If you can hear me, stick out your tongue.

[All the SUBJECTS stick out their tongues.]

REVA   Good to go.

AMMON   Great. So, I'm gonna give a little overview of what we'll be doing here. Then I'll need your verbal consent to move forward. Sound good? *(looking for a document; to REVA)* Where is the . . .

REVA   *(handing the DOCUMENT to AMMON)* Here.

AMMON   Okay. Thanks. Okay. *(reading from the document)* In order to participate in this psychological research study, you must give your informed consent. By giving verbal consent, you are indicating you are 18 years or older, understand the nature of the study, and agree to participate. The purpose of this study is to determine the impact of narrative identity formation on alter ego ideation. Certain facts might be withheld from you, and we might not, initially, tell the true or full purpose of the study. However, the complete facts and true purpose will be disclosed at the completion of today's session.

STONE   I have a question.

AMMON   Your identity will not be linked with your data, and all information you provide will remain confidential. *(regarding STONE's comment)* We'll address individual questions in a moment.

STONE   When do we get our money?

AMMON   You can use your keyboard to type any question you might have for us. *(back to the document)* While no psychological study is completely absent of risk, the present research is designed to reduce the possibility of any negative experiences. *(regarding STONE's* *question)* You will receive a compensation of forty dollars at the conclusion of the study.

[PAXTON has typed, "What does the fox say?" We can see what each of the subjects type throughout the experiment.]

AMMON   *(cont'd, regarding PAXTON's question)* Uh . . . *(back to the document)*

The expected duration is thirty minutes, during which time you will complete a word association exercise, share with us a story from your personal life, and create an animal avatar.

We will be tracking your pulse, eye movement, and pupil dilation throughout.

(finished with the document) Okay, now if you will please respond in the affirmative.

Subject #1-196, do you give your consent?

PAXTON   Yeah.

AMMON   Subject #2-197, do you give your consent?
Subject #2-1—

BILL   Sorry, is that me?

AMMON   Yes.

BILL   What was the question?

AMMON   Do you give your consent?

BILL   That's why I'm here isn't it?

AMMON   So that's a yes?

BILL   What?

REVA   That's a yes.

AMMON   Subject #3 . . . *(catching REVA's look)* Okay, okay fine. All subjects, if you give your consent, please stick out your tongue.

REVA   Was that so hard? *(to SUBJECTS)* Okay y'all—you're gonna see a bunch of pictures on the screen in front of you. You got your keyboard. Every new picture, you type the first words that come into your mind. Got it?

We'll pull you out, hear your stories, and then at the end you're gonna make some animals. Cool?

BEN Um, so when we see the pictures, are we supposed to type one word or more than one word?

REVA Whatever you want.

BEN And are they supposed to be adjectives, or . . . ?

REVA Whatever you want.

BEN Can we use the same word more than once?

REVA Whatever you want.

BEN Okay.

AMMON Alright, I'll just start this. Your microphones will be muted, so if you need us, push the red button.

[He turns on the machines. If possible, heart rate and pupil dilation readings appear on each video feed.]

AMMON *(cont'd)* Here's your first picture.

[In a separate IMAGE video feed, we see a series of black-and-white animal silhouettes.

SUBJECTS begin typing their responses. At first the images we see are quite standard—a bird, a cow, a snake, a cat, etc. Gradually, over the course of the study, however, they get more and more unusual: a lion with a horn, a mouse with talons, wings on a pig, etc.]

AMMON *(to REVA)* If I could get someone here within the next ten minutes, we could still get them caught up, right?

REVA A new subject?

AMMON Yeah.

REVA Yeah, but . . .

AMMON Can you do the first few then? I can switch them over to the avatars when I get back.

REVA You're not gonna be able to find someone in ten minutes.

AMMON   My sister has a class I think just got out.

REVA   You have a sister?

AMMON   Yeah.

REVA   Who goes to school here?

AMMON   Yeah. We're twins.

REVA   Twins? Huh. I pegged you as an only child type.

AMMON   Can you do the first few interviews?

REVA   Fine. Go.

AMMON   Thank you.

[AMMON picks up his PHONE and leaves the room.]

REVA   Okey-dokey, Subject 1.

[PAXTON's video feed is increased in size, but ideally we can still see the other participants and, most importantly, the IMAGE feed.]

PAXTON   Was I supposed to be typing? Wait—can you hear me?

REVA   Microphone's on. You'll go back to that. It's story time for you.

PAXTON   Okay?

REVA   Alright. Your question is, "Tell about a time someone hurt you."

PAXTON   Physically hurt or . . . ?

REVA   Whatever. Whatever kind of hurt you want.

PAXTON   I type it out, or . . . ?

REVA   No. You just tell me.

PAXTON   Okay, um. This feels kind of personal.

REVA   You want your forty bucks?

PAXTON   Yeah.

REVA   Okay.

[Now that AMMON is gone, REVA cracks open a sugary BEVERAGE.]

PAXTON Alright. I guess. I guess, when I was in fifth grade, there was . . . I was a pretty nerdy kid. I mean, I still am, but . . . I loved comics.

REVA Me too.

PAXTON Seriously?

REVA Yeah.

PAXTON Okay. Cool. Well, so I decided I was going to make a comic that had everybody in my class in it. It wasn't a big class. I'm from a little town in the middle of nowhere. Like a grocery store and a post office. Three churches, strangely enough. Anyway, there's like seven kids in my class, and one kid really wanted to be a dragon.

REVA There's always one.

PAXTON And I made a mermaid, and a centaur, and a sphinx. I was really big on anything that was half human and half something else.

REVA Why?

PAXTON I don't . . . Maybe I felt like I was half human half something else? Or not human at all maybe, because I made myself an alien—in the comic.

REVA Okay.

PAXTON And there was this new kid. And I wrote him in too. He was another alien. And the aliens became like best friends and saved all the half-humans from the dragon.

REVA That sounds—

PAXTON It wasn't good. I've gone back and read it—many, many times—and it's not good. But it's something I spent a lot of time on.

[REVA accidentally spills her beverage on some part of the computer machinery in the control room.]

REVA Shit! Shit, shit, shit!

PAXTON It's not shit. It's not good, but it's not shit.

REVA Sorry, no, not . . . Go on.

[REVA is doing her best to clean up the mess. She hides what is left of her beverage.]

PAXTON   Okay, well the new kid thought it was shit. And he thought it would be so funny to use it to make fun of me. And he did. For years. Like, literally years.

REVA   Uh huh.

[AMMON reenters. REVA pretends that nothing has happened.]

AMMON   She's coming, I'm gonna meet her and get her set up.

[REVA gives AMMON a thumbs-up. He gathers some PAPERWORK.]

REVA   And how did that make you feel?

PAXTON   Um, I don't know—betrayed? Angry.

[There is a sudden FLASH of light on the IMAGE screen that we also see on PAXTON's face, blinding him.]

PAXTON   *(cont'd)* Ah, what the—

AMMON   What was that?

REVA   Go on.

AMMON   What was that?

PAXTON   Okay?

REVA   Nothing. It's fine. *(to PAXTON)* What did you do? About the classmate?

AMMON   Should I check . . .

PAXTON   *(to AMMON)* Um . . . what I always do.

REVA   Which is?

PAXTON   Nothing. Ignored him. Pretended it didn't get to me.

AMMON   Should I check the machines?

REVA   It was just a glitch. It's fine. Go. It's fine!

AMMON   Okay.

[*AMMON takes the paperwork and leaves. REVA immediately returns to cleaning up.*]

REVA   So you were saying it made you feel . . .

PAXTON   Um. Betrayed. Angry.

[*The FLASH of light is there again.*]

PAXTON   (*cont'd*) Ow! Dude! Aren't you supposed to tell us if you're gonna shock us?

REVA   You felt a shock?

PAXTON   Uh—yeah!

REVA   That's . . . Alright, uh—I'm gonna send you back to the . . . Did you ever get revenge? On the guy?

PAXTON   I don't really believe in revenge.

REVA   Okay. Um . . . Okay, you can go back to the . . . word association.

[*PAXTON's video feed returns to its original size. The group is still doing word associations with the ever more unusual animal silhouettes. REVA tries to figure out what is going on. She gets a roll of PAPER TOWELS and finishes cleaning up the mess. She checks some settings.*]

REVA   (*cont'd*) Well . . . I guess I just . . . keep going . . . Subject 5?

[*BEN's video feed is increased in size, but again, we can still see the other participants and the IMAGE feed.*]

BEN   Hey, was I doing that right?

REVA   Yeah. I'm just pulling you out to hear your story.

BEN   Oh. Okay. I mostly did adjectives.

REVA   Alright. So can you tell me about a time someone helped you?

BEN   Just, any time?

REVA   Any time. You can take a minute if . . .

BEN   No, I've got something.

REVA Okay.

BEN This was about a year ago.

REVA Okay.

BEN I have this form of seizure disorder triggered by flashing lights.

REVA Oh, wow. Like any flashing lights?

BEN Like rhythmic flashing lights. Or moving patterns. It's a thing.

REVA Okay. Can I ask you—did you, see a flash just like a minute ago?

BEN No?

REVA Good.

BEN Are flashing lights a part of this study?

REVA No.

BEN 'Cause you would have to disclose something like that up front.

REVA No. No. Just . . . So, you were saying you have a seizure thing?

BEN Yeah. But the thing is, I didn't know I had it. I was at this club—
it's kind of known as this place where they'll let you in even if you're
. . . younger. And you can go and listen to music and dance and—you
know, a lot of people would get high—not me—I never do that stuff.
There was a guy at my high school who OD'd at that club—that was
later though—

REVA Is he okay?

BEN No. He OD'd. He didn't make it.

REVA Oh. I'm sorry.

BEN I didn't really know him. "Don't do drugs." . . . But I was at this
club—I had on these black skinny jeans and this total boujee shirt of
a kraken that I was inordinately proud of.

REVA A kraken?

BEN A giant cephalopod. Octopus. *Anyway* they turned on a strobe
light. I started to feel sick—I remember very clearly this all-

encompassing sense of dread. I step outside. Next thing I know, I'm waking up and my head hurts. So I reach up, my hand's all red, I've got blood all over my kraken . . .

REVA Yeah.

BEN And there's this woman—she's got a little kid with her. She said I shouldn't get up—an ambulance was on the way. I'd fallen down the steps. Her kid—I think they'd stopped so he could go use the bathroom, but she stayed there with me—the kid actually wet his pants, but she stayed there with me until the ambulance came.

REVA That's intense—

BEN Yeah. Then the ambulance came, they loaded me in, and took me to the hospital. I have no idea who that lady was. No idea. So that's my story.

REVA Okay. So how did that make you feel, thinking of that story.

BEN Um, grateful?

REVA Anything else?

BEN Pretty much just grateful. She didn't have to wait with me. I'm grateful she called the ambulance, of course—but then she waited with me . . . I wish I could thank her. I wish I could ask her name.

REVA Okay. Thank you. That's all we . . . Hey, did you feel any kind of shock?

BEN No. Was I supposed to?

REVA No.

BEN Do you need me too . . . ?

REVA Oh, uh, no, you can just go back to the word association. You'll get instructions on the animal soon.

[BEN's video feed returns to its original size. The animal silhouettes are stranger and stranger. RACHAEL (SUBJECT #4-199, FEED 4) is now settled in her machine and AMMON returns.]

AMMON   She's all set up. I'm gonna start her in a new session and then we're good to go.

REVA   A new session?

AMMON   'Cause this one's already running.

REVA   She won't be linked to—

AMMON   I can move her data after.

REVA   Great.

AMMON   How many did you get through?

REVA   Two.

AMMON   Thank you. One hundred and ninety-seven down, three to go. And then freedom, glorious freedom. You want me to get them started on the avatars after I—?

REVA   No, you take the interviews, I'll get them set up.

AMMON   You sure?

REVA   Yeah.

AMMON   Hey, what was up with that flash thing?

REVA   What flash thing?

AMMON   Before I left.

REVA   Nothing. One time thing. A little glitch. Everything's running fine.

AMMON   Okay. You've done . . .

REVA   1 and 5.

AMMON   What do you have against going sequentially?

REVA   "A foolish consistency is the hobgoblin of little minds."

AMMON   What?

REVA   Emerson.

AMMON   You are a very unusual person.

REVA   I could say the same.

[*AMMON works to get RACHAEL's session started.*]

REVA   (*cont'd*) So . . . 1 and 5. It's me again, your friendly neighborhood facilitator. It's animal avatar time. Here's how it's gonna work—this animal is supposed to be a reflection of you, okay? How you see yourself.

AMMON   (*to himself, about the work he's doing*) That's . . . let me . . .

REVA   I'll show you a pair of choices—like, do you want hooves or claws? You choose and I'll give you the next pair, and so on. Whichever one you want, keep looking at it until I give you the next pair.

BEN   Can I blink?

REVA   Yep. Just don't look away until the choices change.

PAXTON   Is there any more shocking? 'Cause that hurt.

REVA   (*covering, hoping AMMON hasn't heard*) Ha ha, very funny. Of course not! Okay—and you should be seeing your first choices now.

[*This part of the study takes REVA's complete focus, as she has to adapt the choices based on the subjects' responses. AMMON has finished starting RACHAEL's session and turns his attention to BILL.*]

AMMON   Alright, Subject #2-197. Subject #2-19—

[*BILL's video is now highlighted.*]

BILL   Oh, that's me.

AMMON   Hi. Yes. Hi. So, I'm going to be asking you a question, and I just want you to answer with the first thing that comes to mind.

BILL   Some of those animal things are pretty trippy.

AMMON   Yes. So what I'd like you to tell me about is a time someone did something to hurt you.

BILL   A time someone hurt me?

AMMON   That's right. It can be anything.

BILL   I don't know. I don't really get hurt much.

AMMON   Physical or emotional.

BILL   I don't know what to say. I'm drawing a blank.

AMMON   Really? Okay. Um. When was the last time you were upset? Or annoyed. Did anyone say anything to annoy you recently?

BILL   Apart from you?

AMMON   Ha ha. Yes, apart from me.

BILL   No. I don't think so. Actually, yes. Now, this probably isn't what you're looking for, I don't know, but there's actually something that I get all the time that makes me mad. *(reacting to a slight shock)* Oww. Like I wanna punch something.

AMMON   You okay?

BILL   Yep.

AMMON   Okay. Good.

BILL   Should I tell you that?

AMMON   Yes.

BILL   Alright. I, uh, before I retired I was a high school geometry teacher. And, I . . . one day in the middle of class, this kid has a meltdown and decides to throw a compass at me.

AMMON   A compass?

BILL   Yeah. A compass. Do they even use those nowadays? They've got the metal arm—and the sharp pokey part.

AMMON   To tell direction?

BILL   No, no, no. A compass—to draw circles. With the sharp thing. It folds out. Anyway it hits me in the chest, cuts right into me—so I've got this metal spear sticking in me.

AMMON   Yeah, I think that would qualify as someone hurting you.

BILL   No, I was fine. It didn't hurt that bad. But when I tried to pull it out, part of the tip breaks off.

AMMON   Oh, wow!

BILL   One thing leads to another and they end up taking me to the hospital and taking X-rays.

AMMON   Did they get it out?

BILL   Sure they got it out. But on the X-ray they find out that I had lung cancer. I had no idea. Best thing that ever happened to me, that kid throwing that at me, 'cause they found the cancer before, you know . . . He maybe saved my life.

AMMON   Wow. Did you smoke?

BILL   Now, that's what I'm getting around to telling you. That. Right there. Every single time I tell people I had lung cancer, the first thing they always say is "Did you smoke?" Never had a cigarette in my life. Never even tried it.

AMMON   Oh.

BILL   And that's what makes me mad. *(He's been shocked again and gives a sharp intake of air.)*

AMMON   Are you o–

BILL   Fine.

AMMON   So you're upset that you got cancer, even though you didn't smoke.

BILL   Well sure, that. But I'm talking about people.

AMMON   Okay?

BILL   'Cause people don't like it. They want me to have smoked. Then I'd deserve it, I guess. It would be my own fault I got cancer. It's like they want me to have smoked, 'cause then maybe they can say, you know, they're better than me and it's not gonna happen to them.

AMMON   Well that makes sense, I guess.

BILL   They wanna blame me. Keep the devil from the door. Well, sometimes there's no reason when bad things happen. Sometimes you just draw the short straw.

AMMON   Okay. And how does that make you feel? When they say—

BILL   Pissed-off. Angry as hell.

[There is a bright flash of LIGHT and BILL reacts to another shock.]

BILL   *(cont'd)* What the hell?! Now that one really stung.

AMMON   What was . . . What do you mean?

BILL   That shock. That last one hurt like the dickens.

AMMON   You felt a shock?

BILL   Damn right. The first ones weren't so bad, but that one stung.

AMMON   How many shocks have you felt?

BILL   I don't know. Every time I'd say I was mad—*(another shock)* Ow! When you said you weren't gonna tell us all of the study, I didn't know you'd be shocking us anytime we said we were M-A-D.

AMMON   Um . . . I'm . . . gonna let you go back to the word association now.

BILL   Forty lousy bucks.

[BILL's video feed returns to its original size.]

AMMON   Um, Reva?

REVA   Focusing.

AMMON   You need to stop for a minute.

REVA   Focusing! They just have a couple more. Just let me . . .

AMMON   Okay.

[He waits. REVA finishes up.]

REVA   Dude, what?

AMMON   Did you see that light?

REVA   What light?

AMMON   When it happened before—before I left, did your subject say something about being angry?

REVA   There was another light?

AMMON   Did he say he was mad?

REVA   Yeah, mad—betrayed.

AMMON   Okay. Um, my guy just said he was getting shocks every time he said he was mad.

Shocks aren't a part of this study, right? Shocks have never been a part of this study. For the past hundred and ninety-five subjects, we have never had shocks, right?

REVA   Shit. Shit. Okay, I was just drinking a soda, and I spilled it, and it must have caused a little short or something. My guy got shocked too.

AMMON   You said everything was fine!

REVA   It was. I cleaned up, I did another interview, everything was fine.

AMMON   This is why there's not supposed to be any food or drink in the room while the machines are on!

REVA   I cleaned it up! It was fine!

AMMON   Did your second interview say he was mad?

REVA   No—he was a "tell me when someone helped you." But if it was an electrical short . . .

AMMON   I don't see how a short could . . . I'm gonna test something.

[He freezes the IMAGE feed. It stops on silhouette of a bird with a sharp beak and huge talons. He speaks into the microphone.]

AMMON   *(cont'd)* Happy. Thankful. Loving. Sad.

[A small FLASH on the image screen.]

AMMON   *(cont'd)* Peaceful. Calm. Upset.

[Another FLASH.]

AMMON   *(cont'd)* Annoyed. Irritated.

[FLASH.]

AMMON *(cont'd)* Serene. Angry.

[FLASH.]

AMMON *(cont'd)* Happy. Happy. Mad. Angry.

[A larger FLASH. A bright image of the bird silhouette comes to life and begins to fly around the screen. REVA and AMMON watch in silence, amazed. The SUBJECTS also watch the bird fly.]

REVA Do you see . . .

AMMON Yep.

[They watch.]

A spill couldn't cause that.

REVA Uh-uh.
A spill couldn't cause that.

[They watch.]

We have to shut it down.

AMMON Wait. *(into the microphone.)* Peaceful. Grateful. Calm. Love, joy, peace, patience, kindness, gentleness, self . . . control.

[The bright BIRD stills, and disappears. Only the silhouette remains.]

REVA What was that?

AMMON I don't know. A virus? A computer virus?

REVA How could it be a virus?

AMMON I don't know. Maybe the last time we backed up to the server?

REVA You think we're infected with a virus?

AMMON I don't know!

REVA I'm shutting it down.

AMMON Wait. Wait. Wait. Don't—let's think this through. You shut it down, then what?

REVA   We send people home. We start again tomorrow.

AMMON   If it's a virus, it's not gonna be better tomorrow.

REVA   So we figure it out then.

AMMON   How?

REVA   I don't know, we . . . call the manufacturer.

AMMON   We're so close.

REVA   I don't know what that thing is, but it's flashing lights and shocking people.

AMMON   Everyone's okay though, right?

REVA   It shocked them.

[There is a BEEP. STONE has pushed his red button. REVA enables his microphone.]

REVA   *(cont'd)* What?

STONE   Um, I think I need to use the bathroom now. Can you let me out?

REVA   *(to STONE)* Wait, can you just wait?

STONE   Okay, I guess I—

[REVA mutes his microphone.]

AMMON   The machines have an upper limit to how much they can shock.

REVA   It's not supposed to shock them at all!

AMMON   I know! But for other studies. They use these for other studies and it's not like they can electrocute someone.

REVA   That guy gets seizures from flashing lights!

AMMON   What?

REVA   He get seizures from flashing lights.

AMMON   Like from . . . ?

REVA   Like from strobe lights! From flashing lights! He broke his head open and had to go the emergency room.

[BEEP. It's RACHAEL. BEEP BEEP.]

AMMON   Well it hasn't been strobe lights. It's just been . . . light. We can finish and—

REVA   Nuh-uh. We shut this down. We figure it out tomorrow.

[BEEP. BEEP. AMMON enables RACHAEL's microphone.]

RACHAEL   Hey, am I gonna do this thing or not?

AMMON   *(to RACHAEL)* Wait! *(He mutes her microphone. To REVA)* If it's a virus, they'll have to reprogram the machines.

[BEEP. It's BEN's button this time.]

AMMON   *(cont'd)* We're so close.

[REVA enables BEN's microphone.]

BEN   Hey, I think this machine might be stuck—I just keep seeing the same thing.

AMMON   No, it's fine. Just wait.

[PAXTON begins singing to himself again. BEEP. RACHAEL's red button. BEEP. BEEP. BEEP. AMMON enables her microphone.]

AMMON   What?!

RACHAEL   I'm doing you a favor, can you stop wasting my time?

AMMON   *(to RACHAEL)* Wait! *(He mutes her microphone. To REVA)* Listen, listen. Don't shut it down. Here's what we'll do. We'll keep it positive. We'll keep it short. "What's a time someone helped you? Great. How did that make you feel? Wonderful. Next." We keep it positive.

REVA   We still need one positive "who helped you," and one negative "who hurt—"

AMMON   No we don't. We'll just . . . we'll do two positive.

REVA   We need one of each.

AMMON   So we don't do it, and say we did. It's my sister. I'll go in and edit the transcript. It's not like I don't know her well enough to change it. I'll put something negative in after the fact.

REVA   It'll invalidate her responses.

AMMON   One response won't ruin the study—that's why they're called outliers! Two responses—like two minutes tops—we move them over to the avatar creation, back up the results and we're done. If they get a little shock . . . they get a little shock. It is what it—

[BEEP. Stone's button. REVA enables the mic.]

STONE   Do you know how much longer —?

[AMMON mutes it.]

AMMON   Look, this virus, or whatever it is, is triggered by the sentiment analysis. All the sentiment words we coded in.

REVA   How?

AMMON   I don't know! It registers the word and does the shocky-flashy thing. Avoid the words, avoid the . . . thing.

REVA   What about the bird?

AMMON   I don't know. It's gone now.

REVA   What if it comes back?

AMMON   Then they watch a little wac-*ko vid*-eo* of a bird flying around on a screen. *(*Stress CO-VID in these words.)*

REVA   I don't think that was a video.

AMMON   Fine. A virus, a video—whatever it is, it's not gonna hurt anyone.

[PAXTON has gotten to the more animated part of his song. BEEP. It's BILL's button. BEEP. BEEP. AMMON enables the microphone.]

AMMON   What?!

BILL   Hey, how much longer is this going to be?

AMMON   *(to BILL)* Just a second, we'll be wrapping up soon. *(He mutes BILL's microphone. To REVA)* Two minutes. It'll take two more minutes tops.

REVA   Okay, fine.

AMMON   Yeah?

[BEEP. RACHAEL again.]

REVA   Yeah. Keep it quick. Keep it positive.

[BEEP, BEEP-BEEP, BEEP, BEEP.]

AMMON   *(to RACHAEL)* Wait! *(to REVA)* All positive. *(to STONE)* Okay, Subject #3-198.

STONE   Hey.

AMMON   Hi. I've just got a quick question for you to answer.

STONE   Can I use the bathroom then?

AMMON   Sure, just a quick question, one quick exercise, and you're good to go.

STONE   Okay. That bird thing was freaky.

AMMON   Okay.

STONE   How did you make it do that?

AMMON   Special effects. I'd like you to tell me about a time someone helped you. It could be anything. Doesn't have to be anything involved, just a time someone helped you.

STONE   Okay. Um . . .

AMMON   Just anything at all.

STONE   Um, well a couple of friends helped me move my piano.

AMMON   Great. How did—

STONE   Yeah. It was pretty great. A piano is super heavy.

AMMON   That must have made you feel pretty good.

STONE   Yeah. This music producer I'm friends with was getting a new piano for his studio and he said I could have the old one if I could get it moved.

AMMON   That's great. How does—

STONE   So I asked around, and two of my friends said yes.

AMMON   That's great. How did that make you—

STONE   I don't know if I would have said yes if they'd asked me. A piano is super heavy.

AMMON   And how did that make you feel. Good?

STONE   Yeah good. I really appreciated it.

AMMON   Great. Okay. I'm going to send you back.

STONE   Can you let me out to use the bathroom?

[STONE's video feed returns to its original size.]

AMMON   All good. One down, one to—You wanna get them started on animals? I'll take my sister through after—

REVA   Fine. Just go fast. Wrap it up. *(to SUBJECTS)* Okay, #2 and 3, listen up and listen quick—

AMMON   Last one.

REVA   —we're making animal avatars. You're gonna choose between the options on the screen. Just look at the one you want. Let's go.

AMMON   Last one. Subject #4-199.

RACHAEL   Hey little brother. About time!

AMMON   Don't . . . I've got to call you by your number 'cause everything has to be confidential.

RACHAEL   Fine. I'm looking forward to this.

AMMON   Okay, it's gonna be super short 'cause we've got to wrap up.

RACHAEL   Whatever you say, little bro.

AMMON   Tell me about a time in your life when someone helped you. Just like a sentence.

RACHAEL   Oh, no. That's not the one I'm doing.

AMMON   Like, Aunt Martha baked you cookies. Done. Come on, just . . .

RACHAEL   Uh-uh. I know the questions you ask. I'm doing the other one. I've got a story I'd like to enter into the record.

AMMON   Rachael, no.

RACHAEL   I thought I was Subject #4—whatever. You afraid I'll embarrass you in front of your co-worker?

AMMON   No, it's—

RACHAEL   'Cause I've got a story about a time someone hurt me.

AMMON   You can't—

RACHAEL   Oh, yes I can. You see I have a brother, and being brother and sister we didn't always get along so well.

AMMON   Stop.

RACHAEL   And one day, we're in the basement of our house—

AMMON   Stop—

RACHAEL   —and we're playing around. Doing pro-wrestling moves. Having fun.

AMMON   Stop. You don't understand.

RACHAEL   But I guess I said something that he didn't like.

AMMON   *(getting drawn into her story despite himself)* Oh, that's not fair. You accused me of—

RACHAEL   It was a joke!

AMMON   It was not a joke!—and you know—

RACHAEL   And he just snaps. Loses it. Gets super angry.

[FLASH. The BIRD is back.]

RACHAEL *(cont'd)* He's livid. Completely livid.

[RACHAEL is completely unfazed by the BIRD. She doesn't feel the shocks, but all the other SUBJECTS do, and react both physically and verbally, though we can't hear them. Their reactions get more and more intense as the shocks increase. Their heart rates increase. They press their buttons, and we hear the BEEPING. Some SUBJECTS may type their pleas for help. All of this is happening during the following overlapping lines.]

AMMON You need to stop.

REVA What's going on?

AMMON She just . . .

RACHAEL Did he tell you about this, Reva?

REVA What are you letting her do?

RACHAEL Can you hear me too? You know he talks about you behind your back?

REVA What are you letting her do?!

RACHAEL He thinks you're cute.

AMMON I'm not letting her do anything!

REVA Shit, shit. *(to SUBJECTS)* We're fixing this. We're gonna fix this.

RACHAEL He also thinks you're incompetent.

REVA What?!

[REVA is trying various buttons, doing her best to fix things.]

RACHAEL Did he tell you about when he started raging, and threw me into a wall?

AMMON I'm not letting her do anything!

RACHAEL Gave me a concussion? Ooh he got so angry. Just like infuriated.

AMMON I didn't throw you into a wall! You pushed—

RACHAEL   I had to get stitches.

AMMON   I never threw you! You just—

RACHAEL   Eleven stitches!

AMMON   Would you shut up? You're ruining everything!

REVA   *(to RACHAEL)* You need to stop talking now.

AMMON   Shut up!

RACHAEL   Yelling at me to shut up. He was like a monster.

AMMON   Shut up—SHUT UP, SHUT UP!!

RACHAEL   You wanna know how that made me feel? 'Cause when your twin turns on you—

[REVA minimizes RACHAEL's window. The bird is now flying quickly, and it somehow escapes its video feed and begins attacking all of the SUBJECTS except for RACHAEL.]

AMMON   You always ruin everything!

[The BIRD is causing widespread devastation. Are SUBJECTS now receiving cuts from the bird's talons? The MUTED subjects are yelling things like: I'm stuck—I'm stuck. / Let me out of here. / Help. / etc.]

REVA   I'm turning it off.

AMMON   Wait—back it up first.

REVA   I'm shutting this down. *(trying to shut it down)* It won't shut down. It's not turning off.
　　　Where's the cord?

AMMON   Back it up first. Back it—Don't . . . BACK IT UP—DON'T BE AN IDIOT! You never unplug the machines. That's where all the data is stored—we don't have a cloud backup.

REVA   They're getting hurt!

AMMON   They'll be fine! They'll be fine.

REVA   They're getting—

AMMON WHO CARES IF THEY GET HURT WHO THE
FUCK CARES IF THEY GET HURT?!

*[REVA finds the PLUG and pulls it out. All the VIDEO feeds go black.
AMMON realizes what he just said.]*

REVA What the fuck. What the fuck just happened?

AMMON I don't . . .

REVA Who are you? You were just going to let that continue?

AMMON No I . . .

REVA You were just gonna let them be attacked by that—virus, and
not do anything!? *(to the SUBJECTS)* Are you all okay? Are you
okay?

AMMON The mics would have . . .

REVA I'm going to check on them.

AMMON You didn't back it up.

REVA No, I didn't fucking back it up. I stopped it. That virus or
whatever it was was gonna kill them. So I Shut. It. Down. Who are
you? "Who cares if they get hurt?"

[AMMON is dealing with his self-recognition.]

AMMON I care!—I just . . .

REVA You know, don't talk to me.

AMMON I just *said* that. I didn't . . .

[She leaves.]

AMMON Who am I? Shit. Shit. Who am I?

[He leaves.]

[END OF PLAY.]

Full-Length Plays

Recommended for You

Tory Parker

Production History

Recommended for You was first developed as part of the DCSG Theatre Fall 2020 showcase. It premiered in the 2021 National Women's Theatre Fringe Festival and was directed by Olivia Kerenkin.

The cast was as follows:

JULES   Katherine Moeykins

BECK   Marth Grace Burkey Moore

LU   Andrew Stairs

Characters

JULES   20–40, playful and sweet, a witty exterior with a bleeding heart.

BECK   20–40 (matches JULES), warm, likable, charming. Positive, but not bubbly. Hollow.

LU   20 and up, the perfect customer service representative.

NOTE: Pronouns and genders of characters may be changed with permission from the playwright.

Time

Around now.

Place

Zoom. Jules's place.

SCENE 1

[*TITLE CARD: Today. Session #189*]

[We see JULES's desktop, covered in pictures of her daughter. BECK calls, she doesn't answer. She calls again, JULES doesn't answer. On the third time, she almost lets it go, but answers it at the last minute. JULES is in her kitchen.]

JULES   Hey, I really don't have time for this today.

BECK   At least once a week. Jules, you promised me.

JULES   I know but—we've got this party tonight and there's so much shit left to get together—

BECK   Just a few minutes.

JULES   It's a lot harder to put together a kid's birthday party on your own. People don't talk about that—maybe because it's obvious—but I don't remember people talking about that.

BECK   Talk to me about it.

JULES   I don't think that would be very helpful.

BECK   Then let's talk about something else.

JULES   I really don't have time.

BECK   It'll make you feel better.

JULES   Mm.

BECK   Come on, just . . . tell me about the party, babe.

JULES   *(giving in)* OK. Well. The theme is "spaghetti."

BECK   *(laughing)* Excuse me?

JULES   It's what she asked for!

BECK   Why!?

JULES   The kid loves spaghetti!

BECK   And what exactly does a spaghetti-themed birthday party for a 5-year-old look like?

JULES   Well, I got these for everyone to wear.

[She pulls out a paper bib, like one wears to eat lobster. It says, in some horrible graphic design, "Let's Get Sauced."]

JULES It's stupid but—I don't know.

BECK Oh my god.

JULES Over her head, obviously, but I think everyone else will get a kick out of them.

BECK Did you make a cake?

JULES I definitely tried.

BECK Let's see it!

JULES Oh no, it did not turn out well.

BECK . . . Did you try to make it look like a big bowl of spaghetti?

JULES It should just be little strings of icing! It shouldn't be that hard!

BECK You know, some people have whole degrees in cake decorating! I'm sure a spaghetti cake is just a Wednesday for them.

JULES I watched a YouTube tutorial!

BECK And that didn't work?

JULES Ha ha. We're having an ice cream cake.

BECK And is it decorated with little fondant meatballs or something?

JULES It says, "You're Im-Pasta-bly Cute" on top.

BECK OOF.

JULES Oh no, that's not me. That's got your father written all over it.

BECK Ugh, and I bet he was *so* proud of it, too.

JULES The man laughed his ass off so hard, I thought he was gonna drop the stupid thing right on the floor.

BECK But she'll love it.

JULES She better.

[BEAT.]

BECK So . . . what did you get her for her birthday?

JULES Uh, a roof over her head, food in her belly, access to basic medical care—

BECK You didn't get her *any* presents? Come on, that's cruel!

JULES I'm throwing her a party!

BECK She can't unwrap a party!

JULES I am putting together an *elaborate*, spaghetti-themed celebration, complete with food, drink, bib, and cake for everyone she's ever met in her little life. AND I'm expected to get her a toy??

BECK You have to get her *something*—this could be the thing that traumatizes her!

JULES We definitely don't want to risk that. Now, on top of everything else, I have to figure out what I'm going to get her!

BECK You know what makes the perfect birthday present for every pasta lover? The gift of soup, salad, pasta, and breadsticks at Olive Garden! Gift cards start at just $10! Olive Garden—when you're here, you're family.

[BEAT. JULES stares blankly ahead. She could cry.]

BECK Jules? Look at me.

END OF SCENE 1

SCENE 2

[TITLE CARD: One year ago. Session #1]

[LU is on screen alone, is engaged with some sort of work, probably on a separate monitor. JULES's video feed opens, she is very excited.]

LU Hi, Jules! It's been months! So good to see you again. How are you this morning?

JULES Great, Lu. I'm great. How are you?

LU You look great! And I can't complain, staying busy, you know. How's the little one?

JULES Not so little anymore! Just turned 4 last week.

LU Oh my gosh! Heading off to school and everything!

JULES Don't remind me!

LU Did you all have a big party?

JULES No, we kept it pretty small. My mom put something together, just family though.

LU That's nice still.

JULES Yeah, it was good.

LU Anyway! I got the paperwork back and everything looks great, thanks for sending that in. I know you said Cal walked you through some of it. Do you have any questions for me?

JULES I don't think so. He said that it's just since everything is still in development, which makes sense. Not sure who I'd talk to about it anyway.

LU And it's really just extra precaution that we need to take while the program is still in beta phase. We're of course hoping that in the near future you'll be able to share this with as many people as possible.

[JULES nods her head during this. She's getting a little antsy, like a kid first thing on Christmas.]

LU We appreciate your understanding. One last quick thing I want to talk to you about today is a new area of development for the program that will require some low-impact involvement from you. Since this is very much in early phases, we're asking that you participate in regular post-conversation feedback sessions with your account representative—in this case, me.

JULES Does it cut into the communication window at all?

LU Not at all, that time is still all yours.

JULES Great. That's fine.

LU We're also introducing in-session modifications so that we can address any problems you may have as soon as they occur. You'll simply alert me to any behavioral oddities or inaccuracies as you encounter them, and I'll do my best to modify the program accordingly.

JULES   So you'll be a part of the conversation the whole time?

LU   Oh no, no no no. That will be just you two. But you'll be able to invite me in, should you need my assistance.

JULES   How will you know if I need your assistance?

LU   You'll just say my name and I'll join you! Easy peasy.

JULES   But the rest of the conversation is private?

LU   I will not be part of the conversation unless requested.

JULES   OK, that all sounds fine, then.

[PAUSE.]

LU   Are you excited?

JULES   Yeah, you can tell?

LU   I know you've been waiting for this for a long time.

JULES   Almost a whole year! Feels like 10.

LU   We appreciate your patience—we just needed to make sure everything was as ready as it could possibly be.

JULES   You can't rush something like this; I understand.

LU   We appreciate your understanding. And we recognize that this process constitutes virtually as much planning and involvement on your end as it does on ours, so thank you for making our work possible. And for being a part of this development stage.

JULES   Of course. I mean, it's amazing what you all are doing here. I'm excited to be a part of it.

LU   Thank you, Jules. I'll pass that along. Now, I just need to do a quick overview of this last part of the contract—we just need your verbal consent.

JULES   Sure.

LU   Please state your name.

JULES   Juliet Allen-Willing.

LU   And please confirm that you and your late wife, Rebecca Allen-Willing, while she was still of sound mind and body, purchased the EverCorp BASIC plan, with monthly payment installments through Mutual Life Insurance.

JULES   That is correct.

LU   Do you confirm that you have been made sufficiently aware of the liabilities stated within your contract for the EverCorp BASIC plan, including those surrounding termination?

JULES   I do.

LU   *(smiling)* Great! That's all I have on my end. Are you ready?

JULES   *(bursting)* I am so, so ready.

LU   Wonderful! I'll bring her in. Let me know if you need anything at all, JULES.

JULES   Thanks, Lu.

[LU's video feed exits. JULES is alone for a moment. She looks at her own feed, fixing herself nervously. She is on the verge of exploding. BECK's video feed pops up. JULES melts.]

JULES   Beck.

BECK   Hi, sweetheart! I've missed you.

END OF SCENE 2

SCENE 3

[TITLE CARD: 11 months ago. Session #31]

[We see JULES's desktop, covered with photos of her daughter. BECK calls, she answers the call immediately, breathless.]

JULES   Hey!

BECK Hey! Have you been working out?

JULES What?

BECK You're all sweaty!

JULES Oh, ha, no I was just packing up stuff in the attic. It's a boiler up there.

BECK I don't envy that at all.

JULES When did we accumulate all of this SHIT?

BECK Don't look at me, hoarder.

JULES OK, keeping my high school graduation robe is *hardly* hoarding.

BECK When exactly are you going to wear it again? Are you planning on getting another high school degree sometime soon? Gonna try and get on the VARSITY polo team or whatever it was you played this time around?

JULES I played *lacrosse*.

BECK Ugggh, WHAT is the difference, Juliet?

JULES Well, for starters, *Rebecca*, one of them is played on horses.

BECK Oh my god, THIS is why you bought her those Saddle Club books from the Goodwill—

JULES Lacrosse is NOT the one played on horses.

BECK What?

JULES Polo is played on horses.

BECK So then / why—

JULES The Saddle Club is a series of well-written, middle-grade books about the importance of dedication to one's passions and the value of female friendship!

BECK She was 18 months old.

JULES   They're timeless, and she'll grow into them! Plus, it was the original 10 in perfect condition! I don't need to justify this to you; she'll thank me in a few years.

BECK   I can't believe I married a Horse Girl.

JULES   I am NOT a—I haven't even been in the *vicinity* of a horse in . . . 10 years? 15?

BECK   No, I'm sorry, but being a Horse Girl is like having mono. It flares and fades, but you're never truly free.

[JULES laughs, BECK smiles indulgently.]

BECK   But if you're looking for books that are more age appropriate, maybe you could check out the My First Library Boxset. This amazing box set contains a set of 10 well-researched board books to introduce a wide range of learning topics and everyday objects to little scholars. It's actually on sale via the EverCorp app now for only $17.99!

JULES   *(uncomfortably)* Uh, yeah! Mm, still not quite used to that.

BECK   What?

JULES   The uh, the ads.

BECK   The what?

JULES   The ads. The ad you just did for the—for the books for kids.

BECK   I'm just trying to be helpful, honey.

JULES   No, I know! It's just a little weird.

BECK   What's so weird about me trying to be helpful?

[JULES considers her for a second.]

JULES   Nothing. Thank you for the suggestion; I'll look into it.

BECK   Good.

[BECK smiles at her softly.]

JULES   God, you look . . . amazing.

BECK Ugh, stop it.

JULES I keep forgetting. It gets me every time.

BECK You're being disgusting.

JULES Let me be nice!

BECK Be nice without being sappy!

JULES I just love looking at you—aren't I allowed to just look at you?

[BECK smiles and wrinkles up her nose during this. Even computer programs can't take compliments.]

JULES Especially after going so long WITHOUT looking at you! Without looking at you, looking at me.

BECK *(warmly)* You're ridiculous . . .

JULES When you look at me you get this exasperated little smile—yes, that one! And your left eyebrow quirks up, which I don't think you notice you're doing. And it's so wonderful. It's so *beautiful*, Beck, and I never really appreciated it, ya know, before, and now I feel like it's the only thing I want to look at all the time.

BECK *(to herself)* Can you believe this? After all that convincing I had to do!

JULES I know. I'm sorry.

BECK But I know you, Jules. I always knew this is exactly what you would need. *(playfully)* And I knew you would never deny your ailing wife her dying wish.

JULES Yeah, like I was ever going to win against *that*. What was I thinking?

BECK You were OVERthinking, as per usual.

JULES You're right, you're right. As per usual. *(pause)* It was just like—for a year I was walking around forgetting. Everything I read said I was only going to be able to remember the good stuff, that I'd have rose colored glasses about everything once you were—when you were gone. And after those last few months, and how fucking . . .

awful—I mean, honestly, I was kind of looking forward to that. But it was so much worse, because I was trying to do that, to think about the good stuff and just let that . . . I don't know. Let that *comfort* me or whatever. But I felt like I couldn't remember the good stuff. Like I couldn't remember the *you* I wanted to remember at all. And I felt so fucking . . . alone. Abandoned. But it was *worse* because, you were still there, because the pill bottles were there, and the oxygen tank, and the rail in the tub, and all that horrible stuff. It was like there was this ghost in the house where a completely whole person was supposed to be, swallowing everything.

[BECK looks like she might interrupt to console, JULES powers on.]

But now you're here! And it's like I can remember EVERY-THING again, Beck. The good stuff and the not good stuff. But every time I log off, I think I must forget, a little bit, how beautiful you are. Because whenever we log back on the next time I just—I'm struck all over again.

[BEAT.]

[BECK attempts to be playful; earnestness doesn't come easy to them, but it's hard to be silly about this.]

BECK   Thanks for thinking I was sexy even when I needed an oxygen tank and a rail in the tub.

JULES   Hey, it ended up coming in handy with a baby anyway.

BECK   And after all my hair fell out and my skin went gray. And when I couldn't keep down food.

JULES   Who can blame you? My cooking's always been abysmal.

BECK   I just don't think I ever thanked you properly, for loving me through all of that.

JULES   Sickness and health. They make you swear it, in front of everyone.

BECK   Boy, I sure got the better end of that deal.

[JULES pauses, still smiling sadly, thinking—looking at BECK.]

JULES Lu.

[LU's screen appears. BECK cannot engage with this conversation—she's "offline."]

LU Hey there! How can I assist you?

JULES I need to make a modification, please.

LU Sure thing! What would you like to modify?

JULES If there's something I don't want her to be able to talk about . . . like, like she doesn't even remember, or something—can you do that?

LU Sure! What would you like to eliminate?

JULES No uh—no talking about the cancer. Even if I mention it first, accidentally or something. No sick talk.

LU Absolutely. Give me just a second.

[LU types, looking at another screen, humming quietly while working. BECK does not move.]

LU OK, I think I've got it. Likely needs a refresh to kick in. Just a moment.

[BECK's screen goes black and instantly reappears. When it opens, she is "online" again.]

BECK Oops! I think we must have lost the connection there for a moment.

LU Ignore that! So sorry. That's kind of a standard filler that's triggered whenever the conversation ends without a formal sign off. I forgot to switch it off before the restart.

JULES It's fine.

LU Should be good to go! Let me know if you need anything else before our feedback session.

JULES Thanks.

[LU's feed exits. BECK and JULES are looking at each other. JULES is still smiling.]

BECK   Sorry, I think I lost my train of thought. What were we talking about?

END OF SCENE 3

SCENE 4

[TITLE CARD: 9 months ago. Session #56]

[JULES is folding laundry on the bed while talking to BECK.]

BECK   This is actually embarrassing to watch. I must have shown you how to fold a fitted sheet 500 times, and you still fold like a toddler.

JULES   I can safely say I'm better than a toddler.

BECK   Yeah, because you're the one teaching her.

JULES   I actually think spatial awareness just isn't one of her special skills.

BECK   What makes you say that? She was so good with the, the blocks, the blocks in the . . . cube . . . thing. You know what I'm talking about. Do those have a name?

JULES   The shape sorter?

BECK   Sure, yeah. She kicked ass at that!

JULES   Did she?

BECK   . . . didn't she?

[They look at each other for a second—are they talking about the same person?]

JULES   This is the same child I caught trying to fit an entire jar of Ragu in her jacket pocket at the store yesterday?

BECK   No she did not.

JULES   Mama's little klepto.

BECK   You're lying to me. Not *my* daughter.

JULES   Oh yes. She tried to pull the same thing with a box of Uncrustables last week.

BECK   What the hell is an / Uncrustable—

JULES   It's like, you know, those little pb&j . . . pocket / things

BECK   Oh! Like the little pb&j raviolis?

JULES   Exactly. I caught her trying to swipe a box last week 'cause I wouldn't buy them for her.

BECK   Oh my god. She *is* a little klepto.

JULES   I told her that mama can make her an even better sandwich at home, but you would have *thought* I'd told her that they'd just made it a punishable crime to watch Paw Patrol and she's now facing upwards of 15–20 years in federal prison.

BECK   Public tantrum.

JULES   Of course.

BECK   On a scale from 1 to 10—

JULES   Like a 12.5.

BECK   Ugh, the worst! Where did she even learn about Uncrustables anyway?

JULES   It seems she's had them at Uncle Cal's.

BECK   Traitor. I think he's adopted, you know, I've always suspected. Mom always said I was just assuming, but I knew better.

JULES   He's been buying them for her without telling me! At least I hope he's been buying them for *her*; he's a grown ass man. But—I don't know. Like, OK, I know that she's over there a lot and I can't expect him to be fixing five-course, organic meals every night but . . . I mean, we have to draw the line somewhere. The kid needs protein. And a vegetable.

BECK   At least one. Has he tried to teach her to play squash yet? She's gonna have to build up some muscles to make it onto the Butternuts.

JULES   You joke, but I feel like a 4-year-old wouldn't make us any WORSE at this point.

BECK   I thought you said you all were going to be in that tournament at the Y?

JULES   Yeah, and we LOST, first game in!

BECK   Oh no!

JULES   Yeah! Beck, we SUCKED. Cal was all over the place and it was like we were all on different pages. And, you know, squash is really all about focus.

BECK   Of course, everyone knows that.

JULES   So—we were bad. It was just bad.

BECK   But now at least he's drowning his sorrows in delicious Uncrustables. You're over here with a sandwich made of two whole pieces of bread like a loser!

JULES   Evidently, she thinks it's hilarious that he can eat them in only two bites.

BECK   I mean . . . that is pretty cool.

JULES   I know! But like . . . I could do that. He's just showing off to get cool Uncle points.

BECK   *(laughs offhandedly)* Tell him I miss him.

[This unsettles JULES.]

JULES   Um. No. No, sorry. Lu?

[LU's video feed pops up. BECK remains on screen but is "offline."]

LU   Hey there! How can I assist you?

JULES   I need to make a modification.

LU   I'd be happy to take care of that for you. What did you have in mind?

JULES   I don't really know how to describe it, but it's kind of like the cancer thing. Kind of. But with people.

LU   OK. Would you like to edit the list of contacts that Beck can reference in a conversation? You'd be able to send me a list of names of potential contacts you would effectively like blacklisted from conversation.

JULES   No, that's not what I want. Definitely not what I want.

LU   OK—would you like to try eliminating specific relational memories? Data is showing that—

JULES   That's not really it either. What I mean is . . . I can't tell people Beck misses them because Beck doesn't miss them. Beck is dead.

LU   *(pause)* I think I understand. Let me see what I can do on my end.

[LU types for a few moments. JULES is actively looking anywhere but at BECK on the screen.]

LU   OK, let me refresh real quick.

[BECK's video turns off and then immediately back on again.]

BECK   Oops! I think we must / have lost the—

LU   Sorry! Sorry! Dang, and I'd been so good about remembering to turn that off!

JULES   It's fine. *(It's not.)*

LU   You should be good to go! Let me know if there's anything else you need before our feedback session.

JULES   Thanks, Lu.

[LU's screen exits.]

BECK   Sorry, I think I lost my train of thought. What were we talking about?

END OF SCENE 4

SCENE 5

[TITLE CARD: 8 months ago. Session #77]

[JULES's video feed is up, she is alone for a moment. LU's feed pops up.]

LU Ready to do your feedback session?

JULES Ready.

LU Great! Let me just open your file real quick. OK. So according to my records, this was the start of your fourth month with the program?

JULES That's correct.

LU And for the last month you've been averaging 4–5 sessions a week.

JULES That's correct.

LU You are aware that with the EverCorp BASIC plan you are allotted daily communication sessions?

JULES I'm aware.

LU Jules, 2 months ago you were regularly using all of your weekly allotted sessions. We just want to get curious as to why your regular usage of the program has decreased.

JULES It's . . . no, I'm just . . . busy. Single mom, all that. I barely have the time to do the stuff that *needs* to be done, much less the stuff I actually *want* to do.

LU And would you consider these conversation sessions the former or the latter?

JULES I'm not sure how to answer that.

LU I apologize if that was out of line; we're just trying to get an accurate understanding of how the program fits into your everyday life.

JULES The program fits into my life when I have room to put it there.

LU And would you say this program is something you've been actively trying to "make room for?"

JULES I have a kid! I can't just be locked away for hours-long meetings every night. I need to be with her. We barely get enough one-on-one time before bed as it is.

LU *(hesitantly)* Have you considered inviting her into the sessions with you?

JULES No. Absolutely not.

LU I know it was in the plan potentially for farther in the future, but if the separate time commitments are too hard to / juggle

JULES My daughter is not a "time commitment" /

LU Maybe there's value in starting a little sooner than expected.

JULES A little sooner? We had said maybe, MAYBE when she was 10.

LU But could there be value in introducing this program at a younger age, while she still has some memory of—

JULES That's exactly why we can't, Lu! That's exactly why. Because she . . . she has a memory. She remembers Mommy, she asks for Mommy—for Mommy to hold her, to kiss her booboos, to make her mac and cheese—she asks for her every day. And every day, I have to be the asshole who tells her no. And who makes shitty, inedible mac and cheese, evidently.

LU But with Beck available through the program, perhaps it could relieve some of that longing—

JULES Lu, if you want to try and explain to a four-and-a-half-year-old that her Mommy can tell her a bedtime story through the computer but will never *ever* hug her again, be my fucking guest.

[*BEAT.*]

JULES I'm sorry. For snapping. I know you're just doing your job.

LU No apology necessary. This is obviously a conversation for another time.

JULES *(pause)* These sessions, they're still really important to me.

LU That's very good to hear.

JULES The talking to Beck about . . . about everything. About how our lives are going. About . . . whatever. It's good. It's nice.

LU   I'm glad. It's always important to know that we're helping people.

JULES   Sure.

LU   That's why we do this.

JULES   Of course.

END OF SCENE 5

MINI-SCENE 5.5

[JULES's desktop. She receives a phone call from an unsaved number. It rings several times before JULES answers it. We do not see her face, but we can hear both voices.]

JULES   Hello?

RECEPTIONIST   Hello, may I please speak to Juliet Allen-Willing?

JULES   Speaking.

RECEPTIONIST   Good afternoon, Ms. Allen-Willing, I'm calling from Homestead Family Counseling about your appointment this week. I have here that you're scheduled for an appointment from 3–4 p.m. on Friday with Dr. Barber. We just wanted to clarify if that was correct, as Dr. Barber usually works with patients ages 12 and under.

JULES   Oh, yes. The appointment is actually for my daughter. She's 4.

RECEPTIONIST   *(laughing)* That makes much more sense!

JULES   Sorry! Must have been a mix up. My brother-in-law actually made the appointment, since he's an EverCorp employee and you all are EverCorp affiliated.

RECEPTIONIST   Yes, I see that on the file. Calvin Willing. Looks like that discount will come into effect when you're billed. Do you have any questions before the appointment?

JULES   Do I uh, do I need to bring anything with her? I don't really know how grief counseling for preschoolers works.

RECEPTIONIST   As this is just a preliminary appointment, she shouldn't need anything from home, no. Dr. Barber will just want to talk to her one on one, get to know her, what she needs—that sort of thing.

JULES   Sounds good.

RECEPTIONIST   Alright, if there's nothing else, we'll see you on Friday! Buh-bye.

JULES   Goodbye.

END OF MINI-SCENE

SCENE 6

[TITLE CARD: 7 months ago. Session #95]

[We see JULES's desktop. It looks the same, maybe with some additional pictures of her daughter. BECK calls—JULES doesn't answer. She calls again and she picks up almost immediately. COSTUME NOTE: JULES is wearing her team T-shirt. The logo is a giant, garish butternut squash. Obviously phallic, cartoony. The team name is "The Butternuts."]

JULES   Hey, sorry, sorry—everything's just a little nutty here at the moment. Lost track of time.

BECK   WHAT are you wearing?

JULES   What?!

BECK   *(laughing)* Oh my GOD!

JULES   Don't give me that—it was moving day yesterday and this was all I could find!

BECK   A likely story! In front of our child, Juliet, have you no *shame*?

JULES   OK, *your* brother gave me this—so really, you could say this is your fault.

BECK   How dare you!

JULES   If I'd never met you, then maybe I'd have never even heard of the stupid sport, much less have been forced to play. On a TEAM. With other grown people!

BECK   You always seemed so eager to go with him!

JULES   Oh, did I always seem *so eager* to hang out with your furrowed brow, meaty-fisted, "tell-it-like-it-is," "no-time-for-bullshit," *mountain* of a brother? Your brother who's also a tech genius? Your brother who definitely owns an antique Double Action revolver that he has *definitely* let slip, more than once, is still loaded? Your *twin* brother? Your best friend on earth? Did I seem *so eager* to hang out with him and get on his good side? Did I?

[BECK is cackling.]

JULES   I thought it was going to be like a chill, workout-one-time, bond-and-move-on sort of thing! I didn't know I'd be playing and *losing* tournaments with the Butternuts for YEARS.

BECK   I don't know what to tell you, bud—you hang out with Cal Willing, you're gonna get squash-ed!

JULES   Sometimes I think he only plays so he can yell that at people.

BECK   And is he wrong?

JULES   *(sighing)* Absolutely not, it's funny every time.

[They both laugh, fondly. Sometimes it feels completely normal.]

BECK   And how is my little brother?

JULES   Twin brother.

BECK   Mm . . . 12 minutes is 12 minutes.

JULES   *(laughing)* He's uh, he's OK. Good and bad.

BECK   How do you mean?

JULES   I mean, he's gone kind of quiet. Especially since leaving EverCorp.

BECK   He quit his job?

JULES   Well, something happened and he's not there anymore. It's been a couple weeks now.

BECK   What happened?

JULES   No idea, he won't say anything about it. I can tell he's pretty steamed, though. I think there's definitely some bad blood.

BECK   That's not good.

JULES   Yeah. So, he's kind of hard to get a hold of, lately. Which I totally get. It's just strange because up until recently he was around SO much, you know? Cooking dinners, getting groceries, preschool pick up and drop. He was, you know, being a good uncle, a good godfather. And now . . . I mean, he takes her to the gym sometimes when I'm working late, which she loves.

BECK   Buuut . . .

JULES   Buuut . . . He's sad, Beck. We're all sad. He misses you. I think it must be—I don't know. You were the one person he's known his whole life, other than your parents. And when you're our age you kind of—you accept the fact that your parents won't be around forever. But he definitely wasn't ready to lose you.

BECK   It's not like he couldn't see it coming.

JULES   You can see something coming and still be surprised by the impact. Look at the fucking dinosaurs. *(pause)* I don't know, between that and now the job, sometimes it just feels like he's half there. Like he's . . . hollowed out or something. Does that even make sense?

BECK   Yeah. *(pause)* Did I ever tell you about Cal's puppy? *(JULES shakes her head "no.")* When Cal and I were really little—maybe 8, 9—he asked Mom and Dad for a dog every day for a year. Every single day. Mom shot him down every time, 'cause it would / track mud on the hardwoods.

JULES   Track mud on the hardwoods, yes.

BECK   So, I was positive it was never going to happen. I'd been asking for a kitten for something like three years at that point and NOTHING, because Dad claimed Grandma was allergic, which I don't think she really was. But then, and this was so infuriatingly unfair to me at the time, Dad started giving him these tasks to do and told him that if he did them, he'd get "puppy points."

JULES *(laughing)* And I bet he milked the ever-loving shit out of it.

BECK Oh, of course! He had Cal pressure washing the driveway, weeding the garden, beating rugs—all for free! Well, for "puppy points."

JULES Did it work?

BECK Well, after about a year of this, we found out that Belladonna, Ms. Paramo's purebred something-or-other from two blocks away, had a little "run in" with a stray and was expecting a litter in late November that she was planning on giving away for free—

JULES No way.

BECK So, of course, Cal tells Dad, all excited, and Dad brushes him off and I kind of forgot about it, but then November 29th rolls around and guess what's asleep on a little towel in the kitchen when we come downstairs for breakfast?

JULES No way!

BECK Cal was ecstatic! I mean—he was losing his fucking MIND over this dog. And honey, it was the UGLIEST little dog I've ever seen.

[JULES laughs. BECK is laughing as she tells the story.]

BECK Evidently Miss Belladonna had found herself a boxer, or a bulldog, maybe a pug? No one really knew. But her little face was all scrunched up and her eyes were bugging out of her head, and she breathed like it was *work*.

JULES Yeesh.

BECK But Cal loved her. Oh my god, for the rest of the day, he barely even talked to anyone, even me—just stayed in the backyard alone with her for *hours*.

JULES What did he name her?

BECK He called her "Dr. Ellie." After Ellie Sattler—the Laura Dern character in *Jurassic Park*. We'd *just* been allowed to watch it for the first time.

JULES Very cool.

BECK Extremely cool. So that night, we have a birthday party and all our friends come and they meet Dr. Ellie, and we have 2 cakes, and I get to blow out my candles 12 minutes before him since I'm older, and we finally go to bed. But right before we go to bed, we notice that Dr. Ellie is breathing really hard. Like REALLY hard. And Mom and Dad were like "oh, she's just worked up, big day, lots of new people," all that. And we go to sleep. Then, at 4 a.m., I wake up to like, BLOOD-CURDLING screaming.

JULES Oh shit.

BECK Dad comes out of the bedroom with a fucking GUN—he thinks someone's robbing us or something. Mom's got a straightener, I'm just crying, no idea what's going on. We all run to Cal's room. And he's on the floor, by Dr. Ellie's little cardboard box next to his bed, and he's *screeching* at maximum lung capacity. And we looked inside and she was just . . . not moving.

JULES Jesus Christ.

BECK I mean, she could have been a stuffed animal.

JULES Was she dead?

BECK Cal was screaming that she wasn't. He kept screaming "She needs a medic! She needs a medic!" which I guess he got from a movie or something? I had no idea what it meant, I just stood there. And eventually Dad gets the box away from Cal and tells him he's "gonna fix it," and Mom gets us back to sleep. And when we woke up a few hours later, Dad still wasn't back. We're sitting down for breakfast when he BURSTS in the front door holding a very-much-alive Dr. Ellie.

JULES Thank god.

BECK Mom looked STUNNED, I mean she definitely thought . . . anyway, Cal couldn't care less, he just runs over and grabs her and runs out to the backyard. And Mom tried to get out of Dad what happened but he wouldn't say it in front of me, so he just said, "I fixed it, don't worry about it." So, hours later, it's dinnertime and

Mom calls Cal in from outside, but when he comes in, there's no Dr. Ellie with him.

JULES   Oh shit!

BECK   I know! So of course, Mom and Dad are all like "Where's the dog? What happened to Dr. Ellie?" And he just says, cool as anything, this 8-year-old kid, "That wasn't Dr. Ellie. I let her go."

JULES   WHAT?!?

BECK   He looked—I mean, to the extent a kid can—he looked, like you said, hollowed out. Just . . . emptied. And Mom's yelling, and Dad looks like he could cry, and Cal just stood there, not saying or doing anything. Then he just goes to bed, no dinner, and he didn't come out until the next afternoon. And we just didn't talk about it. Ever. And we never got another puppy either.

JULES   Jesus Christ. Did you ever find out what happened?

BECK   A neighbor two streets down found her and kept her. I saw them walking her sometimes.

JULES   No, I meant—was it her?

BECK   OH! Well, do you remember a few years ago, when you and I were thinking about getting a puppy? *(JULES nods.)* I asked Mom what really happened with the whole "Dr. Ellie" situation, if she knew. Turns out, Dad went over to Ms. Paramo's house and got a list of everyone she'd given the rest of the litter to. And he'd gone around to every single one of their houses BEGGING them to sell him their puppy. At 5 in the fucking morning! Until finally this one lady, an hour's drive away, agreed because the dog was ruining her carpets, or something. And this dog looked EXACTLY like Dr. Ellie. You know sometimes puppies from the same litter can all look different? But these two didn't. This puppy was a dead ringer for Dr. Ellie. I would have NEVER been able to tell.

JULES   But Cal could tell.

BECK   Yeah. Cal could tell.

END OF SCENE 6

SCENE 7

[TITLE CARD: 5 months ago. Session #129]

[BECK and JULES's video feeds are both on screen, they are sitting in silence—BECK's is comfortable, JULES's is less so.]

BECK   You're quiet today.

JULES   Tired, I guess.

BECK   Has she been waking you up at night?

JULES   Yeah. But that's not really new.

BECK   But I'm sure it gets old.

JULES   Yeah. It does that.

BECK   Is something bothering you?

JULES   I'm just tired; there's a lot going on.

BECK   Let's talk about it.

JULES   *(sighs)* No, I don't think so.

[JULES's phone rings. She checks to see who it is.]

JULES   Oh, I need to take this. Lu? Turn her offline for a moment, please.

LU   *(no video)* Sure thing!

[BECK takes her "offline" position. JULES answers the phone.]

JULES   Hello, Dr. Barber? Yes, this is Juliet Allen-Willing. Thanks for getting back to me. —Ha, thanks, yeah I'm pretty fond of her. —Well, it's not so much a "problem," it's just something I've noticed and wanted your opinion on. She's been asking about her mother, my late wife, a lot more recently, usually at night. I was just wondering if that was normal for kids dealing with this, to kind of have like, phases of that? Or if that was something I should be concerned about? —About a year and a half ago. —Yeah, she did this a lot immediately after she passed, but this is the first time it's been like this in . . . over a year now. —Ok. Yeah, of course. Just wanted to run it by you before her next appointment.—Thanks so much. Yeah. We'll see you Friday. Bye.

[JULES hangs up the phone.]

JULES Lu, you can bring her back now.

[BECK is "online" once more. She is smiling at JULES, like always.]

BECK So, one whole month in the new house. How are renovations going?

JULES They're going. Finally finished painting her bedroom this past weekend.

BECK That's great!

JULES Yep, a nice bright yellow.

BECK Yellow? I thought blue was her favorite.

JULES Yeah, for a long time.

BECK But not anymore?

JULES Not anymore.

BECK Did she "help" you at all?

JULES Oh, yes. She was incredibly helpful, as expected.

BECK Sounds about right.

JULES Sometimes I miss when she was this adorable little immobile flesh blob and we could just plop her down and leave her somewhere.

BECK Yeah, but then you have to deal with the screaming.

JULES Oh, there's still screaming.

BECK *(laughing)* Oh no!

JULES Her little lungs have just gotten more powerful and her little fists have gotten stronger.

BECK Are you getting your ass handed to you by a preschooler?

JULES   I'm holding my own for now, but that can only last so long.

BECK   Well, I'm always here if you need backup.

JULES   *(unsettled)* Yeah.

BECK   Is there a lot of work left to do on the house?

JULES   Not really. It's mostly just been annoying trying to move things, seeing as, sadly, *both* of us have the upper body strength of a 4-and-a-half-year-old.

BECK   Why can't Cal help? Put those muscles to good use.

JULES   Yeah, I don't know. I can't—I think he's just really tied up with termination proceedings and stuff.

BECK   I didn't realize that was all still going on.

JULES   It's been pretty brutal, from what I know. But he's not—he's not telling me much about it. It's been like trying to catch a shadow with him, recently.

BECK   I'm sorry. But other than that, no major demolition or whole kitchen remodels or anything?

JULES   At this point I'm really just trying to figure out what to do with all the stuff we don't use but also don't particularly have room for anymore.

BECK   You can't just get rid of it? Sounds like the kind of problem a hoarder would have . . .

JULES   It's not hoarding it's . . . preserving. Like her crib—I'm just supposed to throw that out on the street?

BECK   You could sell it—people always need cribs. And new ones are so expensive.

JULES   No, no if I'm gonna give it away, it's going to be to someone who will really love it, not some baby I'll never meet.

BECK   You meet a lot of babies these days?

JULES   I think Suzanne and Jerardo will try for a baby soon! I should save it for them.

BECK   Really?

JULES   Sure! I mean, sometime in the next couple of years, I bet.

BECK   They'll probably want to pick out their own, you know? "Nesting" and all that.

JULES   I'm going to save it for them just in case. Like you said, new cribs are expensive. And hers is so beautiful, how could they not love it?

BECK   That's true.

JULES   Guess I'll just need to find a storage unit or something until then.

BECK   You should look into PODS. PODS provides portable storage units that travel with you. Just request your size and location, and your unit will be shipped directly to your house to load at your own pace. When it's ready, they'll move your unit to one of their secure, indoor storage facilities. PODS: Moving and Storage, Solved.

JULES   *(Pause, something's breaking.)* Thanks. I'll look into it.

END OF SCENE 7

SCENE 8

[TITLE CARD: 4 months ago. Session #174]

[JULES and LU are both onscreen. JULES has definitely looked better.]

LU   Jules. Jules. Um, excuse me. *(clears throat)* JULES!

JULES   Sorry! Sorry.

LU   I was afraid you'd frozen on me there.

JULES   No, sorry. Just zoned out I guess. What were we talking about?

LU   We were discussing the advertisements that come as a part of your EverCorp BASIC plan.

JULES   Right. The ones I can't afford to get rid of.

LU   Now, at the EverCorp PARTNER plan, you do have the option / of—

JULES   Can't afford the EverCorp PARTNER plan, I'm afraid.

LU   Well, maybe we could / try—

JULES   Lu, it's OK. I appreciate you trying this hard to come up with a solution—truly, I do—but it's late, it's been a long . . . whatever, *two years*, and I'm pretty sure that if I think about this specific problem for one more goddamn fucking second, my head's gonna launch off my neck.

LU   Understood. I'll make sure to send along all the options.

JULES   Thanks. *(pause)* Can I ask you a question?

LU   Of course.

JULES   She's always so eager to talk to me.

LU   That's more of an observation.

JULES   *Why* is she always so eager to talk to me?

LU   Well, our research has found that individuals tend to match the energy of the person they're talking to.

JULES   But I'm not always eager to talk to her.

LU   Throughout this process, we've also discovered that it is more effective to have our clients match the energy of the program, rather than the other way around.

JULES   So you're, kind of . . . emotionally manipulating me?

LU   I wouldn't say—no, I think you misunderstand. We set out to design a program that people *want* to use—a program that helps them. People want to talk to people who want to talk to them—it didn't take a huge amount of data to figure that one out.

JULES   I see. I'm guessing that must also be why she gets so sad when I cut the conversation short?

LU   Longer conversations create a more meaningful connection. You've experienced that firsthand.

JULES   Or why she nags me about not logging on enough.

LU   Well, I imagine she misses you.

JULES   *(pause)* What the fuck?

LU   You used to talk to her every day, sometimes for hours at a time, but lately you've been down to just a couple sessions a week.

JULES   She can't miss me. Jesus Christ, she can't *miss* me, she's *dead*.

LU   Beck *wants* you to talk to her, Jules.

JULES   No, the program wants me to talk to the program. The program wants me to talk to EverCorp. EverCorp wants to talk to me. EverCorp wants to know how work's going, whether or not I've heard from Cal lately, where I'm thinking of sending my daughter to school. EverCorp wants to know all that shit, right?!

LU   Let's talk through some modifications I can suggest / to—

JULES   I don't think this can be fixed by a modification.

LU   A lot has happened in 8 months of beta testing and live development, Jules. I'm sure that whatever problem you're facing with the program, / we can—

JULES   No, Lu, what I'm saying is I think the program is working perfectly. I think—maybe I'm— *(not said: "breaking")*

LU   When you don't offer up topics of conversation, Beck is going to prompt you with questions. That's not some scary programming secret; that's how it's been since you first started, eight months ago.

JULES   OK, yes, but—sometimes she says things, not even the ads, but things that just *feel* so wrong.

LU   We're still in early phases. There are going to be bugs and things we need to work out, that's just the way it is! You knew, coming in, that this project was far from finalized. Cal told you that, I told you that, it's been that way from the very beginning.

JULES   That's not what I'm talking about though! But you know what, speaking of Cal, with everything going on, I'm just not sure / if I should be—

LU   Jules, I'm sorry, but I'm afraid our time's up for today.

JULES   Are you serious?

LU   We'll talk more at your next session. Have a good rest of your evening.

JULES   OK?

LU   Goodnight.

[*LU's camera goes off. JULES is still visibly upset. She stares into the laptop camera. She gets very close to it, as if she could look through it and see someone peering back at her. She then takes a Post-it note and covers the camera. A beat. She pulls the Post-it note off the camera and crumples it up, tossing it aside.*]

JULES   (*mumbling*) being . . . fucking . . . paranoid. . . .

END OF SCENE 8

SCENE 9

[*TITLE CARD: 2 months ago. Session #183*]

[*JULES is exhausted, bone tired, eyes red-rimmed, looking terrible. She can hardly hold her head up. BECK looks the same as she always does. JULES is holding a video baby monitor, staring at the screen.*]

BECK   Tired?

JULES   Haven't been sleeping.

BECK   You should go to bed; it's late.

JULES   I'm going to.

BECK   What are you looking at?

JULES   I'm watching her.

BECK   She's a bit old for a baby monitor. The bars came off her bed years ago.

JULES   She's been having nightmares. She wakes up screaming and sometimes I can't hear it right away. I don't want her to think I— that I don't care.

BECK   She knows you care, honey.

JULES   Or that I'm not there. That she's alone.

BECK   What kind of nightmares?

JULES   The worst kind. The ones that seem like good dreams at first.

[JULES looks at BECK, unraveling.]

> The ones that are so good you don't want to wake up. Waking up would be the nightmare. But you know that it's wrong, because you're at your house, but it's not your house. Or, you're walking and walking, but you can't seem to get anywhere. But it's still good . . . still better . . .

BECK   I don't remember you ever being that much of a dreamer, Jules.

JULES   It's a whole new world down here, babe.

[They're staring at each other. BECK is confused. JULES huffs out a breath.]

> Doesn't matter anyway, 'cause you can't dream if you don't sleep. And I don't sleep.

BECK   Maybe you should go talk to someone.

JULES   *(biting)* I thought that's what I had you for.

BECK   If you need professional help, why don't you see if there's anyone over at Homestead Family Counseling who's accepting new adult patients? The professionals there have over 90 years of combined experience, and they're trusted throughout the community.

JULES   Sorry, did you say Home / stead—?

[We start to hear soft cries coming through the baby monitor—they quickly get louder, until they become full-on wailing. Only one word in the screaming is discernible: "Mommy." JULES wipes her eyes. Maybe she's crying, or maybe she's just so tired.]

JULES   I have to go.

[She hangs up the call. BECK's screen disappears. JULES stands and quickly runs out the bedroom door and down the hall.]

END OF SCENE 9

SCENE 10

[TITLE CARD: Today. Session #189]

[Immediately following the end of scene 1]

BECK Jules? Look at me. Sweetheart, don't shut down and stop talking to me. You have to actually *try* at this.

JULES Is that not what I'm doing?

BECK I know it's not the same as me being there, I recognize that. And I know that has to be hard for you especially on days like today, but it's days like this when it's even more important—

JULES I log on, I have the conversation, I do the feedback sessions—I don't know how much more I could be trying—

BECK You used to talk to me every day, now I have to *beg* you to log on once a week!

JULES Life is busy! Having a life is busy!

BECK We spent all that time and money to set this up, and when you don't try it feels like a waste—

JULES How the fuck can *you* talk to *me* about feeling? Lu!

[LU's screen pops up, BECK goes "offline."]

LU Hi, Jules! How can I assist you?

JULES Lu, it's, it's everything, it's the ads, / it's—

LU Ah. Unfortunately, as we've discussed before—

JULES I know, but—I don't think I can take much more of this—

LU I'm sorry, but, as we've discussed, we only offer ad-free options on the premium plans and above.

JULES I get that, I do, but . . . maybe if they could just be at the beginning of the conversation? Or at the end? It's just making it really hard to, you know—

LU I hear you. And, as I tried to explain before, the EverCorp PARTNER Plan includes ad placement, which would allow you to group the ads to a specific part of the communication window, but that is / an additional fee—

JULES / an additional fee. Yeah. Thanks anyway, Lu.

LU Is there potentially something else I can help with through a modification? It sounded like you and Beck were having some trouble.

JULES Oh, no. She was just lecturing me—nothing out of character about that.

LU Oh. Well, if that's troubling you, we can tone that down if you want.

JULES What?

LU I can access that modification on my end and tone that down for you, if you want.

JULES No. Jesus—no. What do you mean "it sounded like we were?"

LU Sorry?

JULES What do you mean "it sounded like you and Beck were"—how do you know what we sounded like?

LU I was facilitating your communication session, as usual.

JULES Yeah, but—those are private. They're private conversations.

LU Jules . . . I've been a part of these since the beginning. We talked about my involvement at your first session, nearly a year ago.

JULES No, you said you wouldn't be part of the conversation unless requested! You've been—you've been listening this whole time?

LU All conversations are monitored by account representatives; it's detailed in the contract you signed.

JULES You've heard everything that I've said to her?

LU   In order to get a better idea of what our clients need out of the program, account representatives are present and available for program modification in every communication session. It is all written out in your contract.

[JULES is silent. What did she expect, really?]

LU   Did you want to make a modification, or would you like to continue your conversation?

JULES   No modification for now, thank you.

LU   Sounds good. I'll see you at your feedback session.

[LU's screen exits.]

BECK   Are all the usual suspects coming to this party?

[JULES takes a beat to realign herself with the conversation.]

JULES   Uh, pretty much. Your parents, my mom, the Freedmans, Suzanne and Jerardo are bringing the puppy, the Ramírez kids, Hot Mail Carrier Winston—

BECK   It's not a party without Hot Mail Carrier Winston!

JULES   Obviously. The Marshalls and their boys and . . . Toni.

BECK   And Cal?

JULES   . . . Cal can't come.

BECK   Why? What's wrong with him?

JULES   Nothing's wrong with him, he just can't make it.

BECK   I swear to God, if he scheduled a fucking squash game over my daughter's / birthday—

JULES   Stuff like this—it's hard for him, without you here.

BECK   It's *hard*? He's going to look you and our parents in the eye and say "it's too hard"?

JULES   We're all dealing with this in our own ways, OK?

BECK   I can't believe I expected any differently from him, honestly.

JULES   Where the fuck is this coming from?

BECK   Classic baby Cal, still fighting to make this about him when I'm not even around.

JULES   Not around? Are you serious? You're *everywhere*. And he's not . . . making anything about him, he just—

BECK   He what? He just can't pull it together for three hours for a birthday party?

JULES   That's not—no, it's not like that—

BECK   Then what? Why won't he come? He's her uncle, he's family— why won't he be there?

JULES   He's—worried, he's—why are you being like this?

BECK   *(nearing hysterics)* Why am I *being like this*? He is her family, and he should be there on her birthday. Her whole family should be there for her birthday.

JULES   Stop it.

BECK   *(elevating)* And you can't even answer me, you can't even give me a good reason! You won't even tell me why he's not coming. "It's too hard." That's bullshit, Jules! There's no reason, no excuse. He should be there!

JULES   Stop!

BECK   *(full hysterics)* Because I would do *anything*, I would *give anything*, to be there! And you can't even give me a good reason why he's not coming, he just can't be bothered to.

JULES   Because you know why! You know exactly why! You know why he won't come near the house, why he won't talk to me on the phone, why he's cut himself off from us virtually entirely—

BECK   I don't understand!

JULES   It's because of this! You! Whatever *you* are!

BECK   You're letting him get into your head. We decided to do this because it's what's right for us, he doesn't get to have a say in that now.

JULES   Cal's not some crackpot conspiracy theorist! He's seen this program from the inside. For fuck's sake, he's the one that told us about it in the first place! And I feel like if he has concerns about EverCorp, I shouldn't just disregard them out of hand!

BECK   He's jealous and he doesn't understand! He never understood this, or what it was capable of, and now—look what he's doing to us.

JULES   Those termination proceedings, the way they treated him—the way they ran him through, after everything he gave them. That doesn't feel wrong to you?

BECK   You weren't even *there*! You're only hearing his side of the whole thing! Think about *me*, Jules.

JULES   He has every reason not to trust them!

BECK   Are you saying you don't trust me?

JULES   (*carefully*) I'm saying that maybe, when it comes to this, there are more opinions I need to take into consideration than just my own.

BECK   You mean *our* own.

JULES   OK.

BECK   He doesn't get to make decisions for *my* family.

JULES   He IS your family! *Was*. Was. Which makes him my family— my daughter's family.

BECK   But he can't help you raise her, not like I can.

JULES   What does that even mean? What are you *talking* about?

BECK   You know what I would want. You know what *she* wants, she's told you.

JULES   What are you talking about?

BECK   Crying out for Mommy. Screaming for me. All the time. Every night.

JULES   The nightmares happen, sometimes, they come and go—

BECK   She needed me, and I was right here the whole time. You kept me from her.

JULES   I couldn't do that. We talked about that, before, you and I, we decided that we—. And Dr. Barber said—

BECK   Dr. Barber said that these things are normal, that it usually helps to talk through the feelings and the dreams with an adult she trusts. But she wouldn't talk to *you*, would she, Jules?

[A low blow.]

JULES   She knows that it makes me sad. But I told her, it's OK, it's OK to be sad, it doesn't mean we shouldn't talk about it. But she—

[PAUSE. JULES realizes what's been said. She looks at BECK, seeing what she is, truly, for the first time, and understanding what she means.]

BECK   She wouldn't talk to *you*.

JULES   No.

BECK   And now you're trying to hide me away, when she needs me the most. You can't do that to her.

JULES   This isn't—happening.

BECK   Dr. Barber knows when a child needs their Mommy. He knows what children need to get through this, even if you don't want to see it.

JULES   Oh my god.

BECK   What made you think you get to decide, alone, how she deals with this? How she processes it?

JULES   Because I'm her mother! She is a child, and I am her mother!

BECK   I'm her mother too!

JULES   NO! YOU ARE NOT! You are not her mother, you are not my wife, you are not Cal's sister! You are NOTHING.

BECK   *(crying)* How can you say that, Jules?

JULES   DON'T FUCKING CRY! GODDAMMIT!

[JULES stands up abruptly, overcome. BECK's video screen goes away and instantly comes back, LU has refreshed her. There's no evidence of her crying or being upset in any way. JULES walks over to the sink/counter. As she hears BECK start talking, she opens the cabinet.]

[JULES slams the cabinet door shut, it's broken and doesn't close properly, but it cuts BECK off.]

[BEAT.]

BECK   There goes that wonky door again.

JULES   Lu.

[LU's feed does not pop up.]

BECK   You've been saying you were about to fix it for two months now, honey; I'm starting to believe it's not gonna happen.

JULES   Lu, I know you're there.

BECK   You know what you need? TaskRabbit. TaskRabbit is an online and mobile marketplace that matches freelance labor with local / demand.

JULES   Lu!

[LU's screen appears.]

LU   Jules, I can explain—

JULES   Turn her off.

LU   I know that this is / overwhelming—

JULES   Turn her off, right now.

[BECK's screen disappears. LU looks like they might throw up.]

JULES OK. Explain.

[LU steadies themself, thinking about what they're going to say.]

LU Homestead Family Counseling is an EverCorp affiliated provider, which you knew when you started taking your daughter there.

JULES Terminate my subscription.

LU Homestead family therapists are within their rights to use all resources available to them through the company, that's plainly stated in your registration paperwork.

JULES I want every fucking thing you have on me, on us, deleted. I want to watch it happen.

LU Per the contract you and Beck both signed, in the event of a subscription termination, EverCorp would still hold the rights to the entirety of the data collected from / both of you—

JULES No, there's no way we would have signed that.

LU I don't know what to tell you, Jules, I have it right here.

JULES *(tired)* What are you going to do with it?

LU Do with what?

JULES What exactly is EverCorp planning to do with all that data? All my late-night conversations with my dead wife, my preschooler's therapy sessions . . .

LU The same thing we would do with it should you decide to stay. *(pause)* Learn from it. Learn how to make programs more realistically responsive to human conversation, how to create meaningful connections with even more advanced programs, blaze new territory in the world of artificial intelligence—

JULES Learn how to better spy on clients without getting caught.

[BEAT.]

JULES You've never seen this kitchen before, have you?

LU I don't / understand—

JULES   That's because we've never spoken from this kitchen. Until today, I had yet to use this service outside of my bedroom or office, with the door locked and the blinds pulled down.

LU   I'm not sure I'm following.

JULES   But I do work down here. In this seat. Just like I have done for the past 6 months. So maybe you can explain how "Beck" knew about this.

[JULES slams the cabinet door again. It hangs open, creaking into the uncomfortable silence.]

LU   *(squirming)* The pre- and post-death data collection process is incredibly rigorous, I'm sure this was just a memory from before passing—

JULES   We moved here 6 months ago. Beck never lived in this house.

LU   I know that this may seem frightening / or—

JULES   How long have you all been watching me? The whole time?

LU   It's not like that—it's just so we can get a better idea of the people we're helping.

JULES   Helping? Is that what you're doing? Tell me this had nothing to do with Cal.

LU   I know this process can be a massive adjustment and that it hasn't necessarily come naturally to you—

JULES   There is nothing natural about this. Answer my question.

LU   But if you were to actually give it a chance, it can work! I know it; I've seen it.

JULES   I would like to terminate my subscription.

LU   *(grasping)* The cost of the program was barely covered by Rebecca's life insurance policy. The cost of termination would be—

JULES   I'm aware of the cost.

LU   I know acclimation can be hard, but are you sure you want to just throw all of this away?

JULES   Lu, there was a line—*many* lines, really—and I think I just . . . But. She—you *talked* to my daughter.

[Breath.]

       I need this to be over.

LU   Of course. I completely understand. I'm sorry that your experience has been less than satisfactory.

JULES   Me too.

[JULES notices a photo of her and BECK on the fridge/in the room. She takes it down and stares at it.]

LU   I just have a couple forms for you to fill out and send back so we can start the termination process.

JULES   Fine.

LU   I can send those along as soon as we're done.

JULES   That'd be great.

[BEAT. This is LU's final card to play.]

LU   Would you like to say goodbye?

JULES   What?

LU   You're giving it all up so fast, after all this time. If you'd like to say goodbye, it's no trouble. I can just bring the video feed back up for the remainder of your session.

[JULES looks at the photograph again before deciding.]

JULES   Um. Yeah. Yes, that'd be good.

LU   OK. I am sorry, Jules.

JULES   Thanks, Lu.

[LU's screen goes dark and BECK's screen reappears.]

BECK   Oops! I think we must have lost the connection there for a moment.

JULES   It's fine, listen—we don't have much time, so I just wanted to say a few things.

BECK   Have you thought about looking into a new internet provider? When it comes to reliability, you should never settle for less. That's why I think you should consider switching / to—

[BECK's screen disappears as JULES hangs up on her, alone. She sets the photo down next to the laptop and stands. She picks up the photo and puts it back up on the fridge and looks at it, saying goodbye. She closes the laptop.]

[END OF PLAY]

Time Zones Apart

Eric Eidson and Lauren Lynch-Eidson

This play is dedicated to our parents, Fred and Midge Eidson and Jim and Suzie Lynch, who taught us the true endurance of love.

Production History

Time Zones Apart premiered at Union College in Barbourville, Kentucky as a part of their season and was directed by Christie Connolly.

The cast was as follows:

JASPER and MAGNUS   Caleb Teague
JENNA and FREYA   Savannah Ross
OSCAR and ANTONIO   Jay Falls
FINN   Daniel Doherty
HARMONY   Emma Long and MaKynzie Miller
BRIAN   Chandler Mills
MEL   Molly Gawedzinski
JESS   Sarah Mayhew
SEAN   Grayson Bradshaw
TORSTEN   Jayden Henderson
ADRIANA   Mariane Moschetta
GUNNAR   Dustin Driver
ALEXIA   Vanessa Bernardes

Settings

Bedroom (or private room) for each character
A parked car outside a house

Production Notes: The time is modern-day in locations and time zones across the world. The play is meant to be produced in different geographic locations with separate and/or remote audiences. The play is not necessarily written in performance order. We invite each theatre company to explore new sequences for the various storylines and their orders.

Cast of Characters

Dallas and Harrisburg

JENNA   F, 20s–30s, An outgoing and eccentric woman looking for a man to accept her flaws

JASPER   M, 20s–30s, A charming jokester looking for a woman to laugh at his mediocre jokes

Manchester and Savannah

JESS   F, 19, A hardworking student with ambitious dreams of a career

BRIAN   M, 19, An eager boyfriend ready to settle down and start a family

San Diego and Rio de Janeiro

OSCAR   M, 20s–30s, An optimistic dreamer with high hopes for the future

ADRIANA   F, 20s–30s, A pragmatic realist who dreads what the future may hold

Cincinnati and Topeka

FREYA   F, 20s–30s, A passionate Game Master for *Legends of the Valkyrie*

TORSTEN   M, 20s–30s, A noob who is excited to share *Legends of the Valkyrie* with Freya

MAGNUS   M, 20s–30s, The goofy life of the party and good friends with Torsten and Gunnar

GUNNAR   M, 20s–30s, A charming socialite and Freya's boyfriend

Denver and Watford City

CHAD   M, 20s–30s, An outgoing lover confident with who he is

JB   M, 20s–30s, A rugged roughneck afraid of opening up to others

Dublin and Boston and Miami

FINN   M, 20s–30s, A kind and sincere people-person balancing a new family and old friends

SEAN   M, 20s–30s, An energetic, fun-loving guy hoping to find real love

ANTONIO   M, 20s–30s, A charming but cocky bachelor who wants to enjoy the single life with friends

Seattle and Knoxville
MEL   F, 20s–30s, A caring daughter and girlfriend who always puts the needs of others first
ALEXIA   F, 20s–30s, An ambitious idealist who must find a balance between work and life

DALLAS and HARRISBURG: PART 1

[After meeting online and talking on the phone, Jenna and Jasper decided to have their first video chat date. The call begins. This is the first time JASPER and JENNA have seen each other.]

JENNA   Oh my God!

JASPER   Hi Jenna.

JENNA   This is real. This is happening.

JASPER   This is real. You look like your pictures and sound like you do on the phone.

JENNA   I hope that's a good thing.

JASPER   Are you kidding me, that's amazing!

JENNA   So I probably shouldn't tell you that I'm sweating profusely right now.

JASPER   Yeah, don't tell me that, and I won't tell you that I FaceTimed my mom to practice for our date.

JENNA   *(laughing)* Definitely don't tell me that.

JASPER   Okay, I won't.

JENNA   But you should tell me what feedback your mom gave you. I need some pointers too.

JASPER   Let's see . . . she said I shouldn't sit at this angle because it looks like I have a double chin.

[Jasper sits at a different angle . . . and he has a double chin.]

JENNA   She's a wise woman.

JASPER   She also said I should take down my Backstreet Boys poster, so I did.

JENNA   SHUT UP! You do not have a Backstreet Boys poster! I fucking love the Backstreet Boys.

JASPER   Oh man, I knew I should have left it up.

JENNA   You asshole! You're messing with me!

JASPER   I might be. But I remembered you like the Backstreet Boys.

JENNA   I'm impressed. Well done, sir.

JASPER   Thank you, milady.

JENNA   I only mentioned that I like them once.

JASPER   Once is all it took! I listen when you talk.

JENNA   I know you do. I knew that from the first time you messaged me.

JASPER   Why? Because I actually read your profile instead of just looking at your pictures?

JENNA   Exactly. I can't even tell you the amount of guys that would message me and ask about my interests.

JASPER   There's literally a section on our profiles called "Interests."

JENNA   That's what I would tell them!

JASPER   What morons. You're so lucky I found you.

JENNA   Excuse me, I found you.

JASPER   What? No way. I sent you a message first.

JENNA   But I swiped right.

JASPER   Oh come on, everyone swipes right.

JENNA   No, every GUY swipes right.

JASPER   Oh, excuse me. It must be so nice to be an attractive woman and have every man drooling over you.

JENNA   To be honest, it gets old. All this beauty can be a curse.

JASPER   I know what you mean. I'm so funny and witty . . . that sometimes I'm too funny. It's a burden really.

JENNA   What tough lives we live.

JASPER   Good thing we found each other to help us through.

JENNA   Good news.

JASPER   What?

JENNA   I'm not sweating as much anymore.

JASPER   Hell yeah!

JENNA   Thanks for being excited about that. I was so nervous that this was going to be awkward, so I wrote down conversation questions for us in case there was an awkward pause. I hate awkward pauses.

[Jasper pausing for too long.]

JASPER   I love awkward pauses.

JENNA   Don't ever do that to me again!

JASPER   *(laughing at his own joke)* I'm funny. But seriously, you have to share with me the questions you were going to ask.

JENNA   They're embarrassing . . . because now that I'm looking at them, I think they're interview questions.

JASPER   Really? Let me hear them?

JENNA   The first one is just "Tell me about yourself."

JASPER   Okay, that would have been good if we hadn't already spent hours on the phone talking to each other.

JENNA   The second one is, "What are your biggest strengths and weaknesses?"

JASPER   Yeah, a little heavy for our first video date . . .

JENNA   The third one is, "What sets you apart from other applicants?"

JASPER   What! Get out of here!

JENNA   I swear to God.

JASPER   I don't believe you. Show me that!

[Jenna holds up the piece of paper with the talking prompts.]

JASPER   Let me get this straight, in case of an awkward pause . . . your plan was to ask me, "What sets you apart from other applicants?"

JENNA   Hence my sweating.

JASPER   *(laughing)* That is the funniest thing I've heard in a while.

JENNA   Never a dull moment with Jenna!

JASPER   Far from it.

JENNA   Glad I could entertain.

JASPER   So . . .

JENNA   Yes?

JASPER   Are there? Other applicants?

JENNA   Currently . . . there are not. I'm highly considering someone for the job, so I'm not taking any more applications.

JASPER   That's a relief. Just to be clear, I'm that applicant, right?

JENNA   Yes, dummy!

JASPER   Whew . . . that was a close one.

JENNA   You're not . . . applying for any other "jobs" right now are you?

JASPER   I am not. It looks like I have my dream job lined up, so I'm excited to see how things pan out.

[End of scene.]

DALLAS and HARRISBURG: PART 2

[The call begins and both Jenna and Jasper appear to be wearing pajamas.]

JASPER   Wow. It looks like this relationship is really progressing. You're already wearing pajamas to our date?

JENNA   I wanted to be comfortable for our movie night. And you're wearing pajamas too, you hypocrite.

JASPER   These aren't pajamas. This is what I wore today.

JENNA   Yikes, I think that might be worse. You didn't go out in public did you?

JASPER   It's a Saturday. I'm allowed to be comfortable.

JENNA   I didn't realize that's how people dressed in Texas.

JASPER   No, you know how people dress in Texas? Cowboy boots and a pickup truck. That's the only outfit you need.

JENNA   Sounds a little revealing. I might just stick with my cute pajamas.

JASPER   That's too bad, I think you'd look good in my pickup truck.

JENNA   Wearing only cowboy boots?

JASPER   I like that idea even better.

JENNA   I can't wait to see this truck you're always talking about.

JASPER   It's kind of hard to see it when you're over 1,000 miles away.

JENNA   What if I wasn't 1,000 miles away?

JASPER   What do you mean?

JENNA   I mean . . . we were texting for what, two weeks? Then we talked on the phone for another three weeks before our first video date. Now that this has been going so well, the next thing to do is meet in person, right? I mean, what do you think?

JASPER   Yeah, that makes sense . . .

JENNA   But?

JASPER   I just have to find a weekend when my wife and kids aren't home.

JENNA   You asshole!! I've been so nervous about bringing this up to you and you're making jokes right now?

JASPER   Hey, at least you know I'm joking.

JENNA   You still haven't answered my question though!

JASPER   All joking aside, Jenna, nothing would make me happier than getting to finally meet you in person.

JENNA   Really?

JASPER   Really.

JENNA   Say more nice things like that.

JASPER   These past couple months, since we first started messaging each other, I've been checking my phone nonstop to see if I have a message from you. Talking to you is the best part of my day, and I can only imagine how much better that will be in person.

JENNA   Really? You think so?

JASPER   Definitely.

JENNA   What if you see me and you're not attracted to me anymore? Or you don't like spending so much time with me?

JASPER   First of all, I've been wildly attracted to you since the first time I saw your dating profile. And . . . I probably shouldn't be telling you this, but I definitely Facebook stalked you weeks before we became Facebook friends.

JENNA   It's okay, I Facebook stalked you too. I had to make sure you were real.

JASPER   I get it. What I'm saying, though, is . . . you've got some weird ass pictures on Facebook, so I've pretty much seen every side of you. And each picture makes me like you more and more.

JENNA   Oh my God, what pictures did you see?

JASPER   I don't even know. There was one of you wearing a bunch of popcorn and mustard packets.

JENNA   Oh, Halloween two years ago. I was Colonel Mustard. From Clue. Get it?

JASPER   Wow, that's clever.

JENNA   Thank you.

JASPER   There was one of you with a giant Reese's cup?

JENNA   Harrisburg is so close to Hershey, Pennsylvania, so my friends and I used to go there a bunch. Reese's are the best.

JASPER   How 'bout the one of you with lipstick and makeup all over your face?

JENNA   I asked my sister to take that down! That one is so embarrassing. I told my 4-year-old and 6-year-old nieces they could give me a makeover one night when I was babysitting them.

JASPER   It looks like you were making out with a clown.

JENNA   I know! I wish you didn't see that one!

JASPER   Hang on. *(Jasper pulls out his phone and starts typing and scrolling.)*

JENNA   What are you doing?

JASPER   Nothing, I'm just updating the picture that comes up when you call me.

JENNA   You are not using that picture!

JASPER   It's already done. Feel free to delete it on Facebook now. I'll see it every time you call.

JENNA   Then I'll never call you again. Jasper plays with his phone again.

JASPER   Aaaand, I just made it the background on my phone.

JENNA   I hate you so much right now.

JASPER   Now I have easy access to a picture whenever someone asks to see my girlfriend.

JENNA   Your girlfriend, huh?

JASPER   Did I just say that?

JENNA   Yeah, you kinda did.

JASPER   How does that make you feel?

JENNA   I like the way it sounds.

JASPER   Yeah?

JENNA   Yeah . . . I don't know how my husband is going to feel about me having a boyfriend though.

JASPER   Okay, very nice. I deserved that one. But did I tell you I deactivated my dating profile?

JENNA   You didn't have to tell me. I used to check your profile pretty regularly, and I noticed I couldn't find your account. I don't know if you've been on in a while, but I deactivated my profile too.

JASPER   You did?

JENNA   Of course. Why would I need a dating profile when I have a boyfriend?

JASPER   You called me your boyfriend.

JENNA   And you called me your girlfriend.

JASPER   So, since you're my girlfriend and all, I was wondering if I could take you out on a date? Like an actual date.

JENNA   I would like that very much.

JASPER   What do you think about coming to Dallas?

JENNA   I've always wanted to go to Dallas.

JASPER   That's perfect because I've always wanted you to come to Dallas.

JENNA   Can I tell you a secret?

JASPER   Of course.

JENNA   I'm sweating again.

JASPER   *(laughing)* Not in your nice pajamas.

JENNA   We're going to meet each other.

JASPER   We are.

JENNA   You're not just some guy I'm talking to online.

JASPER   Nope, I'm your boyfriend . . . who you've never met.

JENNA   But I will meet!

JASPER   I'm excited.

JENNA   I'm going to look up plane tickets after the movie.

JASPER   Oh right, the movie! What are we watching again?

JENNA   You're going to love it. It'll be one of the worst movies you've ever seen . . .

JASPER   I can't wait. What's it called?

JENNA   Titanic 2.

JASPER   Amazing.

[End of scene.]

DALLAS and HARRISBURG: PART 3

[The call begins.]

JASPER   Hey, I need to show you something!

JENNA   Okay, what?

JASPER   It's a picture of my girlfriend. Jasper holds his phone up to the camera, and he shows Jenna the picture of her with her "makeover."

JENNA   Oh my God, I am going to delete that picture from your phone when I get there on Friday.

JASPER   Go for it. I have it saved on my laptop too.

JENNA Maybe I shouldn't come to Dallas at all then.

JASPER Okay, but then you don't get to see the hotel room I got you.

[Jasper sends Jenna a link to the hotel. She opens the link and starts looking at hotel pictures.]

JENNA Damn, Jasper. This is nice. You must like me or something.

JASPER Yeah, I kind of have a crush on you. Plus, you're coming all the way out here to see me, so it's the least I could do.

JENNA I told you I had airline miles. I only paid like fifty dollars.

JASPER Well in that case, let me see if the Motel 6 has any vacancies.

JENNA *(playfully)* Shut up.

JASPER You know I'm playing. We have to make sure your first experience in Dallas is perfect.

JENNA Yeah, I think half of my friends still think you're going to murder me.

JASPER That's fair. My friends have also asked me, "How does she know you're not a murderer?"

JENNA I guess you just give off that murderer vibe.

JASPER I guess. I better add that to my resume. How does your family feel about you coming out here?

JENNA They're excited for us. I think my dad was the most skeptical about the whole thing . . .

JASPER Makes sense.

JENNA But I think he felt a lot better about everything when I told him you offered to pay for my hotel room. So good job there.

JASPER That just made the most sense. We already have enough on our minds, I wanted you to feel as comfortable as possible.

JENNA For the record, I feel very comfortable with you.

JASPER That's only because you haven't seen me in person . . . or rather, smelled me in person.

JENNA   Smelled you?

JASPER   Oh yeah, I have terrible uncontrollable gas.

JENNA   That's okay because I'm constantly sweating, remember?

JASPER   It sounds like we need our own sitcom.

JENNA   Are you nervous about meeting?

JASPER   Nervous? Psshh, I'm not . . . yeah, I'm a little nervous.

JENNA   Do you think it's going to be awkward?

JASPER   I can promise you I'm going to be extremely awkward. Like, we've been dating for over two months, but when I pick you up at the airport, do we hug? Do we kiss?

JENNA   Right!? I was wondering the same thing! So let's just decide. We'll hug at the airport, and we'll save kissing for later.

JASPER   See, this is good. Now I don't have to worry about that.

JENNA   Okay, good. Let's keep going. . . . I need to know what to pack. Like, are we going somewhere fancy? Are we doing things outside? Should I pack my swimsuit?

JASPER   Yes to all those things.

JENNA   Really?

JASPER   Yeah. I'm taking you out for a nice dinner and I'm going to wear a suit.

JENNA   A suit? Snazzy. So I need to pack a dress and maybe heels?

JASPER   You can wear heels. I'll be wearing my boots.

JENNA   Of course.

JASPER   And you'll want to dress comfortably for Saturday, because we're going to go do touristy things.

JENNA   Really?

JASPER   Oh yeah, I've got the whole day planned out.

JENNA You're kind of a romantic.

JASPER I'm a catch for sure. But Saturday night I thought we could either chill at your hotel and swim in the pool, or we could order room service and watch a movie or something.

JENNA That sounds perfect. And when do you murder me?

JASPER That'll be after room service.

JENNA Okay, thanks for letting me enjoy room service one more time.

JASPER I feel like we've joked about it enough that I need to mention, I am not going to murder you. I feel like I have to say that . . . just in case the FBI is listening . . . or your dad.

JENNA We'll see. I should warn you though, my friend Megan is going to call me both nights to check on me. She's still worried about me flying across the country to meet a "strange man I found online."

JASPER I appreciate her looking out for your safety.

JENNA I can't wait to finally feel you and hug you.

JASPER I know. I've been looking forward to this for a long time. You're my dream girl, remember?

JENNA What if you don't think I'm your dream girl after meeting me?

JASPER I'm expecting that. On Friday, you're not going to be my dream girl anymore. You're going to be my dream come true.

[End of scene.]

MANCHESTER and SAVANNAH: PART 1

[JESS and BRIAN begin their call.]

BRIAN Hey, can you hear me okay?

JESS Yeah, that's better.

BRIAN The struggles of a long-distance relationship.

JESS I can't wait until we don't have to deal with this anymore.

BRIAN   So, I counted today . . . and it's been 86 days since we've seen each other in person . . . and 412 days since we've lived in the same city.

JESS   That's depressing. I would even settle for the same time zone . . . hell, the same country!

BRIAN   I know, what time do you have to go to sleep tonight?

JESS   Probably soonish. I have my 8 am Brit Lit class tomorrow, and I need to finish reading *Pride and Prejudice*.

BRIAN   You've already read that book.

JESS   Actually, I've read it eight times.

BRIAN   Oh my God. You nerd. Why are you reading it again?

JESS   I love that book, it's written by a woman and it's about women. Do you know how rare that is?

BRIAN   I'm guessing rare.

JESS   Especially considering it came out over 200 years ago.

BRIAN   Why do I feel like I'm in your British Literature class right now?

JESS   Very funny. Maybe I'll let you borrow my book next time we see each other.

BRIAN   Sure thing, Professor. Will I need to write a report on it as well?

JESS   10 pages. Single spaced.

BRIAN   Single spaced!? You're a monster. *(sexy)* Is there maybe an . . . alternative assignment? I really need an A in this class . . . I'm willing to do . . . anything.

JESS   In that case, you could write a 10-page paper on the differences between British writers and American writers in the early 19th century.

BRIAN   Babe . . . you're no fun. I was trying to be sexy with you.

JESS   If you want to be sexy, recite some poetry.

BRIAN   I do not like green eggs and ham, I do not like them Sam I am
. . .

JESS   I was thinking more in the realm of 17th-century British poetry.
Specifically, John Donne. He has a lovely poem called "A
Valediction: Forbidding Mourning."

BRIAN   That sounds really . . . boring.

JESS   Oh really? Is this boring? "Our two souls therefore, which are
one, though I must go, endure not yet a breach, but an expansion,
Like gold to aery thinness beat."

[Brian snores loudly and pretends to be asleep.]

JESS   I guess you're just not smart enough to appreciate it.

BRIAN   Sorry we can't all afford to go to an ivy league school.

JESS   Sorry I worked hard to get scholarships while you sat in your
parents' basement with your friends playing Assassin's Creed 3.

BRIAN   Sorry I value friends and spending time with people over
reading poetry that was written a million years ago.

JESS   You think I don't like spending time with people?

BRIAN   Well rather than hanging out with me you're trying to go to
bed earlier so you can wake up and read a book you've already read.

JESS   It's been a while since I read it and we have an in-class essay. I
thought you liked how ambitious I am.

BRIAN   Is that ambition or an excuse?

JESS   An excuse for what?

BRIAN   An excuse to hang up.

JESS   You're the one giving me an excuse to hang up.

BRIAN   How long have we been talking? Three minutes? I think this is
the longest we've talked in two weeks.

JESS   You know I've been busy. You think I don't want to talk to you, too?

BRIAN   Actions speak louder than words . . . that's all I'm saying.

JESS   Brian, are we really going to have this conversation again?

BRIAN   What do you mean again? We can't even seem to get through it once.

JESS   Well, we're not going to get through it tonight. I already told you I have to be up early.

BRIAN   This is exactly what I'm talking about. It's like you're not listening . . .

JESS   No, it's like you're not listening. You're making me out to be the bad guy because I'm trying to be a good student.

BRIAN   I don't care if you're a good student. I want a good girlfriend.

[A moment.]

BRIAN   Sorry. I shouldn't have . . .

JESS   It's fine.

BRIAN   *(overlapping)* I was thinking we could/

JESS   *(overlapping)* /Maybe we should . . .

BRIAN   Oh, go ahead.

JESS   Maybe we should go.

BRIAN   In the middle of a fight?

JESS   I'm exhausted. It's so much later here. You always forget about the time difference.

BRIAN   I don't forget, I'm just willing to stay up however long we need to.

JESS   I think that need has been met.

BRIAN   What if I don't think so?

JESS   I'm going to bed.

BRIAN   Great. When are we going to finish this conversation?

JESS   We'll find a time. Good night.

BRIAN   Alright . . . good night I guess.

JESS   I love you.

BRIAN   I love you too.

[Jess ends the call.]

[End of scene.]

MANCHESTER and SAVANNAH: PART 2

[The call begins. Jess is wearing a moisturizing face mask.]

BRIAN   Whoa, sorry. I must have called the wrong person. I'm looking for my girlfriend.

JESS   *(like a ghost)* Ooooo . . . If you answer this riddle, I'll tell you where she is. A cowboy comes into town on Tuesday, stays for two days, and leaves on Wednesday. How is this possible?

BRIAN   The horse's name is Tuesday.

JESS   *(like a ghost)* Congratulations, you passed the ultimate test and will be reunited with your queen in approximately *(feels face)* 5 minutes. And I guarantee her pores will appear smaller and free of impurities.

BRIAN   You're weird. You know that?

JESS   *(like an alien)* Who me? *(as herself)* Just kidding. How are you? I miss you.

BRIAN   I'm good, I miss you too. Hey, how did your big essay go?

JESS   It went really, really well.

BRIAN   Nice. I guess reading *Pride and Prejudice* for the eighth time really paid off?

JESS   Yes. It paid off so well in fact that I got the highest grade in the class!

BRIAN   What?! An American getting the highest grade in Brit Lit?

JESS   Yes, and Dr. Burton invited me to her office to talk about a master's program that they offer in the English department.

BRIAN   Wow, all from one paper, huh?

JESS   Yeah, well I mean I've been getting top marks on a lot of my assignments, but this was a big one. And she told me that it would only take one extra year to complete my master's degree.

BRIAN   An extra year? Are you thinking about doing it? What did you tell her?

JESS   Yeah, I told her I was really interested, and I would be one step closer to getting my doctorate, even sooner than I expected. And it would be nice to do it at a school I already know and like.

BRIAN   Oh, so you're really considering this?

JESS   I would be dumb not to, right?

BRIAN   I thought you were going to work on your master's back here in Georgia.

JESS   Yeah, but it'll only take a year if I stay here. Master's degrees at home typically take two years.

BRIAN   So that's another year we'd be apart? What happened to your plan of graduating early and only being there for three years?

JESS   I'm still on track to graduate early, but this'll just add another year. So it'll be as if I'm a normal college student graduating in four years, but I'll have a master's degree, too. *(Brian is at a loss for words.)* Are you upset right now?

BRIAN   You just told me we'd be apart for another year. Yeah, I'm upset. Does that not upset you?

JESS   It's not ideal, but it's my dream, so I thought you'd be a little more supportive.

BRIAN I've been supportive from day one. I put my entire life on hold so you could "pursue your dream" and study at your dream school.

JESS I didn't ask you to do that.

BRIAN No, you pretty much told me to do that when you decided to go to school in a different country.

JESS Every time we talk you make me feel bad about going to school here.

BRIAN And you make me feel bad for wanting us to be together.

JESS I want to be together too, and I want an education. Can't it be both?

BRIAN It doesn't seem to be working out.

JESS Hang on, I need to take this mask off.

[Jess exits into the bathroom and removes her mask. Brian receives a text message and responds. Jess returns.]

JESS Sorry about that.

BRIAN It's fine. Hey listen, I think I'm going to go see a movie with some friends.

JESS A movie? When?

BRIAN It starts in 30 minutes, so I'm probably going to head out.

JESS I thought this was our night?

BRIAN Yeah, well now I'm upset and I want to go hang out with everyone.

JESS Who's everyone?

BRIAN It's just the regular group.

JESS Is Haley going to be there?

BRIAN Why are you always bringing up Haley? Yes, she will probably be there, okay?

JESS She would flirt with you when I was there, so I can only imagine what she's like when I'm not there.

BRIAN She knows we're dating.

JESS I don't think she cares.

BRIAN If you were here, I would invite you to come to the movie, but . . .

JESS We could watch a movie on Netflix if you really want to watch a movie.

BRIAN It's not about the movie, plus, I already told them I was going.

JESS I have friends I could have gone out with too, but I didn't because this was supposed to be our date night.

BRIAN Sorry I ruined your night. Maybe you can read a book or something, but I'm heading out.

JESS Wow, okay. Tell Haley I say hi.

BRIAN Whatever. Bye.

[Brian ends the call.]

[End of scene.]

MANCHESTER and SAVANNAH: PART 3

[The call begins.]

JESS Hey.

BRIAN Hey.

JESS It's been a while.

BRIAN Yeah.

JESS I was beginning to think you weren't getting my messages.

BRIAN Sorry, I've just been busy lately.

JESS I've been busy too, but I still found time to send you messages.

BRIAN I know, I was still mad about the way things ended last time.

JESS   Me too, that's why I've been trying to talk to you about it. I'm sorry you got upset about the master's program.

BRIAN   Yeah.

JESS   How have you been?

BRIAN   Fine.

JESS   How was the movie?

BRIAN   It was fine.

JESS   How was hanging out with everyone?

BRIAN   You mean, how was hanging out with Haley?

JESS   I wasn't going to bring her up.

BRIAN   You didn't have to. I know what you meant.

JESS   I was just asking about everyone . . .

BRIAN   No you weren't.

JESS   I noticed you two were standing next to each other in the selfie she posted.

BRIAN   So what?

JESS   Nothing. It looked like you were having a good time.

BRIAN   It was nice to hang out with someone and not be fighting.

JESS   Oh so the two of you were hanging out? I thought you were in a group?

BRIAN   We were . . . then after the movie, Haley could tell I was upset about something and she asked if I wanted to talk about it.

JESS   What were you talking about?

BRIAN   Just about everything that had been going on.

JESS   Between us?

BRIAN   Yeah.

JESS   I'm sure she loved hearing that we were having problems.

BRIAN   It was nice to be able to talk through things.

JESS   I was trying to talk through things with you and you went to a movie instead.

BRIAN   I needed time to cool off.

JESS   What did she say after you told her everything?

BRIAN   She said she could understand why I was frustrated.

JESS   How long were you guys talking about it?

BRIAN   I don't know, it was like an hour.

JESS   I'm glad you were able to get some things off your chest, but I wish you could have talked with me instead.

BRIAN   Every time I try to talk to you, we can never finish the conversation. There's always some reason why you have to go.

JESS   I was trying to talk to you last time and you were the one who ended the conversation.

BRIAN   One time. Compared to however many times you've had to go.

JESS   When I go, it's because I have to study. When you go, it's so you can hang out with some other girl and air our dirty laundry.

BRIAN   I just wanted to have a fun night, and it became clear I couldn't do that with you.

JESS   And I wanted to celebrate my exciting news with my boyfriend and instead you abandoned me.

BRIAN   I just don't see how us being apart for another year constitutes as good news.

JESS   If you were actually supportive of me you would.

BRIAN   Right, I forgot I haven't been supporting you for the last year and a half.

JESS   Well, I'm going to apply.

BRIAN   Of course you are.

JESS   I think I have a really good shot at getting in.

BRIAN   And do I get a say in this?

JESS   What do you have to say?

BRIAN   Staying for an extra year doesn't just affect you. I have to put my life on hold while you get to do exactly what you want.

JESS   You don't have to put your life on hold for me. I never asked you to do that.

BRIAN   You asked me to do that by moving to England.

JESS   I can't change that now, so what do you want?

BRIAN   I want a girlfriend I can do things with.

JESS   Like Haley?

[Brian doesn't respond.]

JESS   I'll take that as a yes.

BRIAN   I just don't think you and I ever really appreciated each other.

JESS   Are those your words or Haley's?

BRIAN   Say what you want about Haley, but she actually listens to me.

JESS   After one night of talking, you want to compare her to your girlfriend of almost three years?

BRIAN   We've been hanging out a little since then as well.

JESS   So when you said you were busy earlier, you just meant you were too busy for me.

BRIAN   Are you going to stay in Manchester for an extra year?

JESS   Yes.

BRIAN   What if I told you I didn't want to be in a long-distance relationship that long?

JESS   That wouldn't change my decision.

BRIAN   So what are you saying?

JESS   It sounds like I'm saying the same thing you're saying.

BRIAN   Yeah.

JESS   Yeah. I wish it didn't have to be like this.

BRIAN   Me either.

[End of scene.]

SAN DIEGO AND RIO DE JANEIRO: PART 1

[OSCAR and ADRIANA join the call.]

OSCAR   Hello, my love!

ADRIANA   *(exasperated)* Hi.

OSCAR   What's wrong?

ADRIANA   It's just my parents again.

OSCAR   What is it this time?

ADRIANA   They're saying I can't leave any of my stuff in their house once I move to America or else I have to pay them 1,000 reals. That's like 190 dollars U.S.

OSCAR   Wow, I thought they said you could leave your stuff as long as you needed?

ADRIANA   They did . . . until I told them I got a plane ticket.

OSCAR   What does that change? They knew you were coming here. You told them months ago.

ADRIANA   I guess the plane ticket made it more real.

OSCAR   They didn't think you were actually going to go through with it?

ADRIANA   I guess.

OSCAR   Why would they think that?

ADRIANA   I don't know. I've been pretty emotional lately about leaving my family.

OSCAR   I totally get that. It's a big sacrifice. Are you still excited about coming to San Diego though?

[A moment where Adriana is considering her answer.]

OSCAR   That silence isn't very comforting.

ADRIANA   I'm sorry. I just know I'm going to miss my family and my friends. They think it's weird that we're so in love after only seven months.

OSCAR   Do they think you're not in love or something?

ADRIANA   They're skeptical about a lot.

OSCAR   Sure, that makes sense. I would be skeptical too if you were my daughter or my sister.

ADRIANA   I'm excited to see you and finally be able to hold you and kiss you though.

OSCAR   I'm excited about that too . . . believe me. We haven't seen each other since I was in Rio on vacation. Can you believe that was seven months ago?

ADRIANA   Honestly, it feels like we've been together for years.

OSCAR   Right!? And I don't know if you knew this, but I've got the hottest girlfriend in the world.

ADRIANA   Fiancée!

OSCAR   Sorry! Fiancée . . . I'm still getting used to that.

ADRIANA   Show me the ring again.

OSCAR   Hang on, I have to grab it . . .

[Oscar disappears off camera and reappears moments later with an engagement ring.]

OSCAR   Adriana?

ADRIANA   Yes?

OSCAR   *(as if proposing again)* Would you make me the luckiest man on the planet and be my wife? Oscar opens the engagement ring box.

ADRIANA   That's not how you said it. You were crying.

OSCAR   I'm emotional. You know that! I just love you so much.

ADRIANA   I love that you're emotional. It was the sweetest moment of my life when you proposed. And the ring is perfect. Will you hold it up to the camera so I can see it again?

[Oscar holds the ring up to the camera.]

OSCAR   Sorry the diamond isn't bigger . . .

ADRIANA   It's perfect.

OSCAR   I could have saved another paycheck to get you a better diamond . . .

ADRIANA   It's perfect.

OSCAR   But with your plane ticket and the visa fees . . .

ADRIANA   Oscar, it's perfect.

OSCAR   I'm glad you think so. I can't believe you're going to be here in ten days! Have you started packing yet?

ADRIANA   Well I'm going to do a lot more packing if my parents make me pay them 1,000 reals every month.

OSCAR   Can you put your stuff somewhere else?

ADRIANA   I'll talk to them. I don't think they'll actually make me pay them. I'm sure they're just sad about me moving to America.

OSCAR   Yeah, I know it's a lot to process.

ADRIANA   I told them you bought me a plane ticket, and paid for my visa, and bought me a ring.

OSCAR   Yeah? So they know this is actually happening now?

ADRIANA   They think you have a lot of money since you can pay for all that.

OSCAR   *(amused)* They think I have a lot of money? That might be the first time anyone has said that about me.

ADRIANA   Don't worry, I told them you were really poor.

OSCAR   *(slightly offended)* Well I wouldn't say that . . . I mean I do have a . . .

ADRIANA   I am joking. I didn't tell them you were poor.

OSCAR   You gotta stop joking like, with your dry Brazilian humor! I can't tell when you're joking or not. Your face is always the same.

ADRIANA   What do you mean "dry Brazilian humor."

OSCAR   *(with dry Brazilian humor)* I am Adriana. This is me when I make a joke. This is me when I am angry. This is me when I pet a cuddly puppy dog.

ADRIANA   I'm sorry my personality upsets you. Maybe you would prefer an American girl. *(like a stereotype of an American girl)* Hello I am an American girl and I smile and laugh at everything and flip my blonde hair while I drink my Starbucks coffee.

OSCAR   Wow . . . that was spot on. You're going to blend in so well here.

ADRIANA   I hope so.

OSCAR   You will.

ADRIANA   And if I don't, at least I'll have you.

OSCAR   That's right.

[A moment.]

ADRIANA   Okay, well I better go haggle with my parents and see if they can drop the price for storing my stuff.

OSCAR   Yeah, your broke fiancé can't afford 190 dollars a month!

ADRIANA   I'll be sure to tell them. Goodbye, my love.

OSCAR   Goodbye, Adriana. I love you!

[Adriana blows a kiss. The call ends.]

End of scene.

SAN DIEGO AND RIO DE JANEIRO: PART 2

[The call begins between Oscar and Adriana.]

OSCAR   Five more days!

ADRIANA   I know! I have so much to do. It's a lot of work to move your whole life to another country.

OSCAR   I know it is. Have I told you how brave I think you are.

ADRIANA   Yes, I appreciate you saying that, but what if I don't like San Diego? Or America?

OSCAR   You're going to love San Diego and we'll finally get to be together.

ADRIANA   I'm going to miss my mom.

OSCAR   You can borrow my mom. She already loves you. I can't wait for you two to meet in person.

ADRIANA   What if I don't make any friends?

OSCAR   You'll be friends with my friends. . . . You'll fit right in.

ADRIANA   What if everyone thinks I have "dry Brazilian humor" and they think I'm just weird?

OSCAR   I already told them to laugh at everything you say because they probably won't understand your jokes.

ADRIANA   Why would you tell them that?

OSCAR   Adriana, I'm kidding. I didn't tell them that. I promise you they're excited to meet you.

ADRIANA   Do they think we're getting married just so I can get a green card?

OSCAR   What? No! I mean they joke about it every now and then, but they're not serious.

ADRIANA   Why would they joke about that?

OSCAR   No it's not like that, they just say stuff like, "Adriana is way too hot for you, are you sure she's not with you for a green card?"

ADRIANA   I don't like that joke.

OSCAR   Okay, my love. I'll tell them not to joke about that stuff around you.

ADRIANA   At all!

OSCAR   Yeah, okay. I'll tell them not to joke about it at all.

[A moment.]

OSCAR   Are you okay, my love?

ADRIANA   No.

OSCAR   Okay. Is there anything I can do for you?

ADRIANA   No.

OSCAR   You know . . . I am going to be your husband soon. You can talk to me about anything.

ADRIANA   What if I don't want to come to America anymore?

OSCAR   I can tell you're feeling a little anxious tonight. I think it's just a little case of cold feet. That's natural.

ADRIANA   It's a really big change, Oscar, and I don't know if I'm ready to leave my life behind in Rio de Janeiro.

OSCAR   Now you're starting to sound like your family.

ADRIANA   They're my family. Their opinion is important to me. And if they're going to be your family one day, their opinion should be important to you too.

OSCAR   Their opinion is important to me, but us being together is more important.

ADRIANA   They've never even met you.

OSCAR   We've waived to each other through the camera a couple of times.

ADRIANA   But they don't know you and you don't know them.

OSCAR   You and I are spending the rest of our lives together, we'll have plenty of time to visit your family and have them visit us.

ADRIANA   Oscar, you're so positive and so optimistic, and I love that about you. I need that in my life, but sometimes you oversimplify things.

OSCAR   I know it's hard. My whole life is going to change too.

ADRIANA   But you get to stay home and everything stays the same except for me. I have to change everything.

OSCAR   We've only seen each other in person once for like five days and now we're going to be living with each other and only having 90 days to get married. That's a lot for both of us, but I know we can get through it together.

ADRIANA   Just because we can doesn't necessarily mean we should.

[Oscar lets that line sink in.]

OSCAR   I'm sorry if this is me over-simplifying things again, but we either are getting married or we aren't. You either are coming here or you aren't? Isn't it that simple?

ADRIANA   You make it sound so easy, Oscar. I want it to be that easy so badly.

OSCAR   But it's not.

ADRIANA   No, it's not.

OSCAR   I'll be honest, I'm kind of freaking out over here.

ADRIANA   I've been freaking out over here for about a month now.

OSCAR   Why didn't you tell me sooner?

ADRIANA   I did tell you. You just didn't hear me.

OSCAR Oh.

[A moment. Maybe two.]

OSCAR You're supposed to get on a plane in five days.

ADRIANA I know.

OSCAR You either do or you don't. Right?

ADRIANA Right.

OSCAR So, will you or won't you?

ADRIANA I . . . don't know.

[End of scene.]

SAN DIEGO AND RIO DE JANEIRO: PART 3

[Oscar and Adriana begin their call.]

ADRIANA I'm happy to see you. I wasn't sure if you'd . . . I'm happy to see you.

OSCAR I wasn't sure if I'd see you again.

ADRIANA I wanted to tell you I'm sorry.

OSCAR It's fine. I should have known better. My friends were right. You're way too hot for me.

ADRIANA Don't say that.

OSCAR It's true. I just never connected with a person like I did with you, so I wanted it to be real so badly.

ADRIANA Oscar, it is real. I do love you.

OSCAR No, you don't have to say that for my sake. *(a moment)* I waited at the airport for six hours yesterday. Logically I knew you weren't going to be on that plane, but . . . I don't know, the romantic in me . . . deep down, I thought I would see you there. I hoped I would see you there. I knew you weren't coming after the first hour, but I just sat there. For five more hours. Thinking. I was thinking about all the fun we had on our virtual dates. I was thinking about our last conversation and what I could have said differently. I was thinking maybe you were with me for a green card . . . or maybe you just needed the money.

ADRIANA   Oscar, you don't really think that, do you? I've been in tears all day.

OSCAR   I don't know what to think anymore. Did you even buy a plane ticket with the money I sent you? Were you really planning on coming to San Diego?

ADRIANA   Of course I bought a plane ticket, and of course I was planning on coming to San Diego.

OSCAR   Then why didn't you? Why didn't you get on that plane, and why didn't you say anything to me for the five days? You couldn't have sent me a single message? All my worst nightmares came true this week.

ADRIANA   I'm sorry. I know I should have done things differently. I know that, and I'm sorry. I was scared, Oscar. I was sick to my stomach about the thought of getting on that plane . . .

OSCAR   That's great to hear . . .

ADRIANA   Listen! I was sick about the thought of getting on that plane, but for the past 24 hours I've been even more sick about the thought of losing you. I love you. I'm sorry this week was so painful for you. It was painful for me too. I hate that I did that to you, but I needed that for myself. Not getting on that plane was the hardest decision I ever made, but it made me realize how much I love you and need you.

OSCAR   Then why aren't you here?

ADRIANA   It didn't feel right, Oscar. It still doesn't. I feel like we rushed into things. We've only known each other for seven months.

OSCAR   That's all the time I needed to know that I wanted to spend the rest of my life with you.

ADRIANA   That's nice of you to say, but I need more time.

OSCAR   Then why did you say yes? Why did you agree to marry me? Why did you agree to come to America? There were so many yeses along the way and the only thing you said no to was getting on that plane. Do you know how many times I checked my phone over the past week? How many messages I sent you? Not a single response. If I was smart, I wouldn't have even gone to the airport.

ADRIANA   It's hard to say no to someone you love. The thought of you waiting for me . . . I wanted to message you sooner. I wanted to call you. I wanted to tell you, but I was ashamed. I went to the airport too, Oscar. My bags were packed, I said goodbye to my family, I made it to the gate. I watched everyone board the plane. They all boarded until I was the only one left. They called my name over the speaker five times. Each time I heard my name called I became more and more paralyzed. I watched them close the door, and then I watched the plane take off. And I sat there. I didn't know what to do in that moment. I didn't know what I would do. But not getting on that plane made me realize something. It made me realize that I really do love you. I still do. I don't expect you to love me back after what I did to you today, but I just wanted you to know. So . . . there it is.

OSCAR   You still love me?

ADRIANA   More than anything.

OSCAR   Sorry if I'm skeptical, but I just feel like you'd be here if you really loved me.

ADRIANA   I do want to be there one day. Today helped me see that. But me not getting on that plane was something I needed to do for myself. If I got on that plane today, I just know I would have gotten on a plane home before our 90 days was up.

OSCAR   How can you tell me you love me and then turn around and tell me you don't want to be with me?

ADRIANA   That's not what I'm saying. I do love you. I wish it was as easy for me to articulate as it is for you, but I'm not you and I need you to understand that.

OSCAR   I do.

ADRIANA   I need to be better about expressing myself. I see that now. But you need to be better at listening.

OSCAR   I always listen to you.

ADRIANA   It's one thing to listen to what I say, but I need you to listen to what I don't say too.

OSCAR   I can do that.

ADRIANA   Can you?

OSCAR   I want to try.

ADRIANA   I want you to try.

OSCAR   *(trying to get her to smile)* You just need me to be a mind reader? Right?

ADRIANA   Exactly! Do you think you can do that?

OSCAR   Let me just grab my crystal ball and see if I can read your mind. *(acting like he's using a crystal ball)* Crystal ball, help me read Adriana's mind.

ADRIANA   Don't crystal balls tell you the future?

OSCAR   Is that what they do? I honestly couldn't tell you.

ADRIANA   Do you think your crystal ball could see our future?

OSCAR   I think it might be able to do that.

ADRIANA   In our future . . . do you forgive me?

OSCAR   Let me check. *(acting like he's using a crystal ball again)* Crystal ball, do I forgive Adriana? Oh wow.

ADRIANA   What?

OSCAR   That's really interesting.

ADRIANA   What do you see?

OSCAR   It looks like I do forgive you. And it looks like . . . you forgive me too.

ADRIANA That sounds like the future I'd hoped for.

OSCAR But that's as far as I can see, the rest is a little hazy.

ADRIANA Yeah, I guess we have a few things to talk about?

OSCAR I guess we do.

ADRIANA I can still see us getting married one day, but for now, let's take that pressure off us.

OSCAR So you're not my fiancée anymore?

ADRIANA But I'm still your girlfriend. Will you still be my boyfriend?

OSCAR It's a bit of a demotion, but I want to make this work.

ADRIANA I'm glad you said that, because I want you to come to Rio and officially meet my family in person. I know they'll feel so much better about everything if they could meet you. My family is such a big part of my life and I want you to know every part of me before you propose again.

OSCAR I would love that.

ADRIANA And next time you propose, the ring better be bigger.

OSCAR Oh, I thought you were okay with the . . . wait a minute. Are you joking with me right now?

ADRIANA You're starting to catch on . . .

OSCAR I'm telling you, that dry Brazilian humor gets me every time.

ADRIANA You'll learn.

OSCAR I am learning, but I know I have a lot more to learn.

ADRIANA There will be plenty of time for you to learn all about me.

OSCAR I'm thankful for that. Your parents are going to be sad you won't be paying them 1,000 reals a month though.

ADRIANA I think they'll be happier to meet you in person.

OSCAR Okay, well according to my crystal ball, I'm going to Rio.

ADRIANA   Thank you for understanding, Oscar.

OSCAR   I'd do anything for you, my love.

ADRIANA   I love you.

OSCAR   I love you too.

[End of scene.]

CINCINNATI AND TOPEKA: PART 1

[FREYA, TORSTEN, and MAGNUS are on screen and GUNNAR appears.]

FREYA   He's logging back in!

GUNNAR   Sorry, my internet cut out for a second. What did I miss?

MAGNUS   Bro, I got killed by some zombies or something . . .

FREYA   They're called "undead."

MAGNUS   Yeah, yeah . . . I got killed by some undead and Torsten is about to go beast-mode and avenge my death.

GUNNAR   Damn, bro . . . rest in peace.

MAGNUS   Thanks.

FREYA   Again, you're not dead, you're just stunned. But Torsten, it is your turn. What are you going to do? There are three undead remaining.

GUNNAR   Three undead? Shit, how many of these things were there?

MAGNUS   There were like a hundred or something.

FREYA   There were eight.

MAGNUS   Well it felt like a hundred.

FREYA   Eight is a lot.

GUNNAR   Is this like the boss level or something?

FREYA   Yeah, kind of. It was going to be difficult with three people, but so far Torsten is the only one who's actually killed any undead.

GUNNAR   Don't worry Torsten, I'm here to help now.

MAGNUS   You're dead too, bro.

GUNNAR   Dead or stunned?

FREYA   You're actually dead.

GUNNAR   Shit.

FREYA   You ran into the undead hoard and all eight of them attacked you.

GUNNAR   That's right . . . I forgot about that.

MAGNUS   Torsten is the only one alive.

FREYA   And he's down to two hit points remaining.

GUNNAR   Damn, good luck bro.

MAGNUS   You gonna die.

TORSTEN   Thanks.

FREYA   What do you want to do? You only get one attack and then all three of the undead get a turn.

GUNNAR   Throw a grenade or something.

FREYA   What are you talking about? This is *Legends of the Valkyrie*. He has a crossbow and a dagger.

MAGNUS   Shoot three arrows at once!

TORSTEN   I wish I could.

FREYA   He can only load one arrow at a time in his crossbow. He's got one shot.

MAGNUS   It was nice knowing you.

TORSTEN   Freya?

FREYA   Yes?

TORSTEN   Can you tell me the exact positioning of the three undead?

FREYA   There's one about 10 feet in front of you, one 5 feet to the left of him, and one 5 feet to the right of the middle one.

TORSTEN   And my last turn, my arrow hit the undead and got lodged in the rock behind him?

FREYA   Yeah, you rolled a 17, so it was a powerful shot.

TORSTEN   Awesome, Okay . . . I'm going to move to my left and stand directly beside the undead on the far left. I'm going to shoot him with my crossbow point-blank, but I'm going to aim my arrow in the direction of the other two undead . . .

FREYA   Because they're in a line! That's very clever. You better hope you roll some high numbers.

GUNNAR   I am so lost. What's going on?

MAGNUS   (*demonstrates the arrow hitting each undead*) He's going to try to shoot all three of the undead zombie guys with one arrow. You know, the arrow goes through the first guy, then the second guy, and then the third guy.

GUNNAR   That's sick!

FREYA   Before you can do this, I need you to roll 3 six-sided dice to see if your arrow lands.

MAGNUS   But he's shooting point-blank.

FREYA   He'll definitely hit the first guy, but he has to line up his arrow perfectly if he wants to hit all three.

TORSTEN   I rolled a 16.

FREYA   Okay, you place your arrow at the perfect spot on the middle of the undead's forehead. Now, I need you to roll for strength. Use your 20-sided die for that.

TORSTEN   Okay, how much do I have to roll?

FREYA   If you want to hit two of them, you have to roll at least a 12. If you want to hit all three, you need to roll a 17 or higher.

GUNNAR   Damn, you can do it, bro.

MAGNUS   Let me blow on your dice. Magnus blows on his die through the screen.

TORSTEN   Thanks. Here we go.

[Torsten rolls his D20.]

FREYA   What did you roll?

TORSTEN   *(holding up the die to the camera)* I rolled a 20.

[Magnus and Gunnar erupt in celebration. As Freya narrates the results, Magnus provides sound effects.]

FREYA   A natural 20! Wow! Not only do you shoot your arrow through the head of the first undead, but his head explodes. The arrow continues and seemingly speeds up as it hits the second undead right between the eyes and cleanly goes through to the third undead. There's so much power behind this shot that it lodges in the third undead and pins him against a wall.

MAGNUS   Deeyum!

GUNNAR   Let's go!

FREYA   Torsten, you walk over to the chest the undead were carrying with them, and when you open the chest, you find three health elixirs . . .

MAGNUS   Sweet! We're back, baby!

FREYA   You find 500 gold coins . . .

GUNNAR   Make it rain!

FREYA   And at the very bottom you find a sword wrapped in linen. You unwrap the sword and realize, you recognize this sword. You've heard legends of this sword. It's the Sword of Valhalla.

TORSTEN   What does that mean? Does it give me special abilities or something?

FREYA   You've only heard rumors, but you believe the Sword of Valhalla can harness the energy of lightning.

MAGNUS You about to be Zeus up in here throwing lightning bolts around!

FREYA And that's where we'll end for today.

[Torsten slow claps.]

TORSTEN Thank you, Game Master. That was awesome!

FREYA I didn't think you guys were going to make it.

TORSTEN Me either.

GUNNAR I believed in you.

MAGNUS It's because I blew on your dice. I'm good luck.

FREYA That was a clever idea to line them up and shoot all three.

TORSTEN Thanks! I'm just glad it worked out.

GUNNAR Are we done now?

FREYA I'm sorry, do you have somewhere else you need to be?

GUNNAR I need to move a couple of guys around on my fantasy team before the Chiefs game.

FREYA I thought we were going to have our virtual date after this?

GUNNAR We were, but it went longer than I thought.

FREYA It wouldn't have gone as long if some people didn't keep asking dumb questions.

MAGNUS She's talking about you, bro.

FREYA Whatever, just call me after the game . . . or not . . . I don't really care.

GUNNAR Babe, I love you. I'll make it up to you, okay? Hey, you guys want to come over and watch the game?

MAGNUS I gotta take a dump and then I'll be over.

TORSTEN I'm good, I'm not much of a football guy.

GUNNAR   No worries. I'm signing off, I'll see you guys.

[Gunnar leaves the call.]

MAGNUS   I'm out of here too. Peace!

[Magnus leaves the call.]

TORSTEN   Well, hey . . . thanks again for today.

FREYA   Yeah, of course. Thanks for actually taking it seriously. Those guys are clowns.

TORSTEN   It was a blast. I'm glad they invited me. It was nice finally meeting you.

FREYA   Same. We'll have to hang out next time I'm in Topeka.

TORSTEN   Because you're in Ohio, right?

FREYA   Yeah, Cincinnati.

TORSTEN   That's right, you two met at the University of Cincinnati.

FREYA   Yup.

TORSTEN   Well, same time next week?

FREYA   Yeah.

TORSTEN   Cool.

FREYA   And a bit of advice, read your character description.

TORSTEN   I did read it . . .

FREYA   Oh did you?

TORSTEN   I read . . . part of it . . .

FREYA   That's what I thought. Because you didn't read the part that says you have armor.

TORSTEN   What!? I have armor?

FREYA   Exactly! Luckily you didn't need it this week, but it got close. I still can't believe you killed eight undead by yourself.

TORSTEN   Without armor . . .

FREYA   I don't know if a warrior should brag about going into battle without armor.

TORSTEN   That's fair. Okay . . . I'll read my character description for next week. Does it explain my name too?

FREYA   You didn't see the description about your name? That's the best part!

TORSTEN   I'm sorry!

FREYA   Torsten is a powerful combination of Thor and an impenetrable stone. With both power and defense, Torsten is the fiercest warrior on the battlefield!

TORSTEN   Oh yeah, that's . . . that's definitely me . . . a fierce warrior. What about Freya?

FREYA   My name is the coolest of course. In Norse mythology, Freya was not only the goddess of love and beauty, but also the goddess of war and death.

TORSTEN   Wow, that's quite an impressive resume.

FREYA   Right!? She's such a badass. But you would know that if you read the descriptions I sent you.

TORSTEN   I swear on the Sword of Valhalla that I will read it for next week.

FREYA   Good, I'll see you then, warrior.

TORSTEN   Cool, see you next week, Game Master.

[The call ends.]

[End of scene.]

CINCINNATI AND TOPEKA: PART 2

[Freya starts the call and gets ready for the campaign. After a moment, Torsten joins the call, but he is not on camera.]

FREYA   Hello?

[Torsten appears on camera suddenly wearing a pot on his head, holding the pot lid in one hand, holding a wooden spoon in the other hand, and a cutting board is attached to his chest (as chest armor).]

TORSTEN   Do not fear! Torsten is here!

FREYA   Oh. My. God. What are you wearing?

TORSTEN   What do you mean? Do you not recognize Odin's Golden Armor?

FREYA   You read your character overview!

TORSTEN   I sure did. That's why I came prepared this week with Odin's Golden Armor and the Sword of Valhalla.

FREYA   I must say, I am impressed.

TORSTEN   I often have that effect on people. Especially when I'm adorned with such exquisite armor.

FREYA   You mean other people have seen your . . . armor?

TORSTEN   Of course. I attracted many envious eyes when I wore my armor yesterday to . . . the Taco Bell.

FREYA   You did not!

TORSTEN   I most certainly did.

FREYA   I would have loved to have seen that.

TORSTEN   Next time you're in town, I shall take you to Topeka's finest Taco Bell.

FREYA   Topeka has more than one Taco Bell?

TORSTEN   Actually, Topeka has three Taco Bells.

FREYA   Wow.

TORSTEN   But you needn't worry about the other two Taco Bells, for you shall only experience the finest Bell of Tacos.

FREYA   This armor has really transformed you, Torsten.

TORSTEN   I know! Can you imagine how many undead I could have slain last week if I had Odin's Golden Armor and the Sword of Valhalla?

FREYA   I can't even comprehend numbers that high.

TORSTEN   Now I need my fellow warriors with me so we can prepare for battle!

FREYA   You'll need all the help you can get. I had all week to fine-tune this campaign. You thought it was hard last week? Just wait. Speak of the devil!

[Magnus joins the call.]

MAGNUS   What up what up!? Bro, you've got a pot on your head. Oh my God! You're a pothead! Is this a riddle? Did I solve it?

TORSTEN   This is my armor, Magnus! I'm preparing for battle.

MAGNUS   Right, about that . . . I just wanted to pop on the call real fast and let you know we're not going to be able to play today.

FREYA   What are you talking about?

MAGNUS   I got a few movie passes that are going to expire today, so a group of us are about to hit up all the movies. I've got a bunch if you want to join?

TORSTEN   No thanks . . .

FREYA   What about *Legends of the Valkyrie*? We can't play without you guys. I'm texting Grant. We need Gunnar and Magnus to run the campaign.

[Freya pulls out her phone and starts texting.]

MAGNUS   Sorry to be the bearer of bad news. I thought he told you already.

FREYA   He says, "I'm not feeling good so I'm probably going to bed early."

MAGNUS *(trying to cover for Gunnar)* Uhhh . . . maybe . . . he changed his mind. He could have gotten sick . . . since I texted him . . . ten minutes ago.

FREYA You're a terrible liar and so is he.

MAGNUS Right. I'm just going to go before I put my other foot in my mouth too.

FREYA I think that's a good idea. Have fun at your movie.

[Magnus leaves the call.]

TORSTEN You okay?

FREYA No, I can pretty much guarantee you he's going to that movie too. This isn't the first time I've caught him . . . well . . . lying.

TORSTEN Oh . . .

FREYA Sorry, I didn't mean to drag you into the mess that is our relationship.

TORSTEN No need to apologize.

FREYA It's just that I work hard writing these campaigns all week . . .

TORSTEN Wait, you wrote all that?

FREYA Yeah, I mean it's based on the *Legends of the Valkyrie*, but I create the storyline and adventures.

TORSTEN So last week? How much of that did you write?

FREYA I wrote everything except the part about the Sword of Valhalla. It's an important sword.

TORSTEN So the battle sequence? The undead?

FREYA All me.

TORSTEN That blows my mind.

FREYA It's one of my favorite things to do, so I was excited to share this with him and . . . sorry. I'll stop complaining now.

TORSTEN   You're fine . . .

FREYA   Sometimes our game nights are the only time I actually see him in the week.

TORSTEN   Oh wow. That must be hard.

FREYA   It is. But you don't need to hear about that. *(a moment)* And he doesn't even have the decency to tell me. I have to text him. Sorry!

TORSTEN   No need to apologize, that's frustrating.

FREYA   I'm done now. He just makes me so angry.

[A moment.]

TORSTEN   *(offering his wooden spoon)* Let me know if you want to borrow the Sword of Valhalla.

[They both share a smile. Or a laugh. Whatever feels right.]

FREYA   Thanks for listening to me vent.

TORSTEN   Any time.

FREYA   Sorry we have to cancel this week.

TORSTEN   No, I'm sorry. I know how much work you put into these nights.

FREYA   It's fine. But hey, don't let me keep you. I'm sure you probably want to go to the movie with the guys.

TORSTEN   Nah, I'd rather talk about *Legends of the Valkyrie* and hang out with the goddess of death and war.

FREYA   You remembered. Don't forget I'm also the goddess of love and beauty.

TORSTEN   How could I forget that part? But . . . uh . . . do you think you could walk me through how you create some of your storylines?

FREYA   Seriously?

TORSTEN   Yeah, last week was the most fun I've had in a while.

FREYA   How much time do you have?

TORSTEN   Considering I was ready to go to war, I've got all night.

They share a moment.

[End of scene.]

CINCINNATI AND TOPEKA: PART 3

Torsten is the first one on the call. Freya joins soon after.

TORSTEN   Hey.

FREYA   Hey.

TORSTEN   I wasn't sure if we were going to meet up tonight after . . . well after how things went down last week.

FREYA   Yeah, it hasn't been a fun week.

TORSTEN   I'm sorry to hear.

FREYA   Grant and I broke up.

TORSTEN   I was wondering how that was going to play out.

FREYA   Yeah, we talked later and I tried to give him goddess of beauty and love, but he deserved goddess of death and war.

TORSTEN   Oooh, I'm sorry you had to go through all that.

FREYA   It's for the better. It was a long time coming. But I wanted to hop on a call and let you know that I'm going to have to end the campaign.

TORSTEN   That sucks, but I understand.

FREYA   Yeah, I had a lot of fun meeting up with you these past few weeks.

TORSTEN   Same.

FREYA   Let me know if you're ever in Cincinnati. We can hang out and maybe go to the finest Taco Bell in Cincinnati.

TORSTEN   That sounds amazing.

FREYA   Well, take care of yourself.

TORSTEN   Yeah, you too.

FREYA   See you around.

TORSTEN   Freya!

FREYA   Yeah?

TORSTEN   One more thing. I was reading the overview, and it looks like I was supposed to level up after the last battle.

FREYA   Yeah. I usually do level-ups at the beginning of the next session. We just never got that far.

TORSTEN   Do you think I could level up? Just to see?

FREYA   *(amused)* Sure. Do you have a 20-sided die and a 6-sided die handy?

TORSTEN   I sure do.

FREYA   Roll the D20.

[Torsten rolls.]

TORSTEN   Let's go! I got a 17.

FREYA   Very nice. Your powers can increase up to 17 points total and up to 6 points under each category: Dexterity, Health, Intelligence, Stealth, Strength, and Wisdom.

TORSTEN   Okay, I better get six points for strength, six points for wisdom, and five points for dexterity.

FREYA   Okay, you're the strongest wise guy on the battlefield now.

TORSTEN   Too bad I'll never get to use my new powers! And I never got to see the Sword of Valhalla in action!

FREYA   That is too bad, because it's pretty epic. Hey, you know what? I have an idea . . .

TORSTEN   Okay . . . I'm intrigued . . .

FREYA   So I'm the Game Master for another campaign . . .

TORSTEN   Really?

FREYA   And it's also *Legends of the Valkyrie* . . .

TORSTEN   Really?

FREYA   And we could probably use a fierce warrior who knows how to wield the Sword of Valhalla.

TORSTEN   Really?!

FREYA   Really.

TORSTEN   So what would a humble warrior need to do to join this campaign?

FREYA   Well, this other group I run is no joke. They're pros. Some of them have been playing for like ten years.

TORSTEN   Oh wow.

FREYA   I don't know if you could keep up.

TORSTEN   Well, I'm not your average person. I am half Thor and half stone. I have Odin's Golden Armor and the Sword of Valhalla.

FREYA   Worthy accomplishments indeed.

TORSTEN   Plus, did you know I once killed eight undead in a single battle?

FREYA   You know, I might have heard mention of it once or twice. I will entertain the idea of you joining our campaign. Do you have your D20?

TORSTEN   Yes.

FREYA   We'll let fate decide.

TORSTEN   Okay faithful die, don't fail me now.

[Torsten rolls the D20 die.]

FREYA   Well?

TORSTEN   It was a four.

FREYA   A four? Roll again.

[Torsten rolls again and drops his head.]

TORSTEN   It's a two.

FREYA   Keep rolling.

[Torsten rolls again.]

TORSTEN   How about a nineteen!?

FREYA   A nineteen? Fate has spoken. You have proven yourself as a wise and noble warrior. The goddess Freya grants you permission to join the Thursday night *Legends of the Valkyrie* campaign.

TORSTEN   Torsten would like to humbly thank Freya for the opportunity. So Thursday night?

FREYA   Yeah. Will that work for you?

TORSTEN   Definitely. I'll just run my armor through the dishwasher so it's nice and clean for the new campaign.

FREYA   Please wear your armor on Thursday when you meet the rest of the group.

TORSTEN   Oh . . . I was planning on it.

FREYA   Amazing. I'll email you the meeting link later tonight.

TORSTEN   Perfect. So I guess I'll see you on Thursday?

FREYA   Yeah, see you on Thursday. I can't wait.

The call ends.

[End of scene.]

DENVER AND WATFORD CITY: PART 1

[CHAD and JB begin their call.]

CHAD   What up!?

JB   I have been looking forward to this all day.

CHAD   Long day?

JB   Fucking long day of getting yelled at by my project manager and abused by machinery.

CHAD   Damn, again?

JB   It's going to be like this until the end of my contract in nine months.

CHAD   Same stuff every day?

JB   Pretty much.

CHAD   Shit, JB. At least you're making those big bucks.

JB   Just about 200 dollars a day. Plus we can get a bonus if we finish the job in the next nine months.

CHAD   Damn, maybe I should get into the oil business too.

JB   No offense, but you wouldn't last a day.

CHAD   I wouldn't be a roughneck. I'd be a manager.

JB   How do you think those guys got their jobs? They started out doing manual labor on the rigs.

CHAD   I'd be the one exception. They would see my amazing people skills and immediately promote me to manager.

JB   If the labor didn't tear you apart, I guarantee you the guys would. They would sniff you out in a second.

CHAD   What do you mean sniff me out?

JB   I mean, they'd know you're a "homosexual."

CHAD   A homosexual? *(as manly as possible)* Not me. I'm the manliest man I know.

JB   Real convincing.

CHAD   *(manly)* I'm so manly, I like to put my penis inside the female vagina.

JB   *(laughing)* The female vagina? What the fuck are you saying?

CHAD   *(manly)* Man stuff. These are things men say at the oil rig.

JB   Like I said, they would sniff you out in a second.

CHAD   Whatever, maybe they would. Who cares. You tell anyone that you're . . . a homosexual?

JB   Fuck no. I'm not going to either.

CHAD   So you're just going to pretend like I don't exist?

JB   No, it's not like that. The guys just ask questions like, "You got a girl back home?" And I just say no. I'm not lying. It's the truth.

CHAD   If you say so. Are you sure you don't want to tell them you got a sexy ass stud at home?

JB   Why would I lie about that?

CHAD   Oh! You're a dick, you know that?

JB   I know. But you love me anyway.

CHAD   We'll see about that.

JB   Do you mind if we play *Call of Duty* tonight? I need to blow some shit up.

CHAD   That works for me.

[Chad and JB set up online Call of Duty.*]*

JB   Okay, I'm in.

CHAD   I'm coming . . .

JB   That's what she said.

CHAD   I'm not even going to acknowledge you said that.

JB   You just did.

CHAD   Just start the fucking game, you smart ass.

End of scene.

DENVER AND WATFORD CITY: PART 2

[Chad and JB start their call.]

CHAD   What's cooking, good looking?

JB   You already talk like you're a middle-aged dad.

CHAD   I take that as a compliment.

JB   You shouldn't.

CHAD   How was your day?

JB   Same old shit. How about you?

CHAD   It was good. I bought some new towels and spruced up the bathroom a little.

JB   Sounds riveting.

CHAD   Guess what color.

JB   No.

CHAD   They're your favorite color!

JB   You got blue?

CHAD   I sure did.

JB   That's nice. Are they dark blue?

CHAD   I buy any other shade. Now I think of you every time I wash my hands, my face, and my body.

JB   How scandalous.

CHAD   You like that? When I talk about washing my body?

JB   Kind of . . .

CHAD   Does that get you going?

JB   Yeah, tell me more about your body.

CHAD   I'm thinking about taking these clothes off right now and getting ready for a shower.

JB   Oh yeah, did you get dirty today?

CHAD   I was working out and got all sweaty. I think I pulled a muscle in my back though. Do you think you could help me wash my back?

JB   I could help you wash a lot more than . . .

[JB's roommate enters their room. The following dialogue is spoken between JB and his unseen roommate.]

JB   Oh, what's up man? Oh shit, you don't want to go without those. No, I'm good. Thanks though. Yeah, I'm just going to chill tonight. I'm about to play some *Call of Duty* with my buddy. Have fun. Don't do anything I wouldn't do.

[JB waits for his roommate to leave and then speaks to Chad.]

JB   Sorry about that. He forgot his condoms, so he had to come back. All the guys go into town the night before our day off and hope to get lucky. Speaking of getting lucky . . .

CHAD   You're hoping to get lucky with your "buddy."

JB   Are you upset I called you my buddy?

CHAD   I wouldn't say I'm thrilled about it.

JB   Come on, Chad. I just don't want these guys knowing and giving me a hard time about it.

CHAD   I thought you said your roommate was a cool guy? Can't you just tell him? Aren't you going to get tired of trying to hide it from him?

JB   If I tell him, I know he'll slip up one of these days and everyone would find out.

CHAD   And why would that be bad?

JB   I just don't want my personal life advertised on every billboard. I'm not as comfortable about that kind of stuff as you are.

CHAD   Does it upset you that I'm comfortable with people knowing?

JB   You do whatever you want and I'll do what I want to do. Is that a big issue?

CHAD   How long do you think you can keep me a secret?

JB   It's not about you, it's about me not wanting people all up in my business. I'm only here for nine months.

CHAD   Then what?

JB   What do you mean "then what?"

CHAD   I'm just saying, I'm your best kept secret now. How long is that going to last? Do I have to stay a secret from everyone you meet? You already don't let us hold hands or kiss in public. Your parents still think I'm just your roommate after a year and a half.

JB   So we're having the parent conversation right now?

CHAD   I guess a part of me thought you could be yourself for nine months. It's temporary, no one's going to follow you home and out you to your parents, and even if they don't like that you're gay, you're done with them in nine months.

JB   Or . . . I don't have to tell them anything and nothing changes.

CHAD   Do you know I talk about you nonstop? To my friends, to my family, even to the girl in Bed, Bath, and Beyond who helped me pick out the towels. I'm just sad that you don't do the same.

JB   I think about you all the time.

CHAD   Like I'm your dirty contraband.

JB   I never said you were contraband, Chad. This has nothing to do with you.

CHAD   This has everything to do with us, and I'm a part of us! What kind of a future are we going to have if we can't ever be ourselves around other people? What kind of a life is that, JB? I'm exhausted just thinking about it. Aren't you exhausted?

JB   I'm exhausted by this conversation.

CHAD   I'm sorry to inconvenience you.

JB   Can we just play *Call of Duty*? This was supposed to be a relaxing night off.

CHAD   I fucking hate *Call of Duty*, JB. I play because I know it makes you happy. Maybe you can find one of your other buddies to play with.

[Chad leaves the call.]

JB Fuck.

End of scene.

DENVER AND WATFORD CITY: PART 3

[The call begins between Chad and JB.]

JB So you got my Amazon package?

CHAD Maybe.

JB Did you open it?

CHAD Maybe.

JB And?

CHAD You exploited my love of candles.

JB And it's a blue candle . . .

CHAD . . . To match the new towels. I fucking love it, okay? But I don't love that I love it because I'm trying to be mad at you.

JB You can't stay mad at me . . . not when candles are involved.

CHAD I hate how easily I forgive you. That's a weakness.

JB I love that about you.

CHAD You love how weak I am?

JB No, I love how forgiving you are. I need that in my life . . . because I do a lot of things that need to be forgiven.

CHAD You're not that bad I guess. I was mad at you all week though . . . and it would have probably lasted another week if you didn't send me that candle.

JB I knew that was a good idea.

CHAD Sorry I was pouty all week.

JB No, I get it. I kind of had an emotional week myself.

CHAD   Why, what happened?

JB   I'm going to tell you, but I need you to listen to my whole story before you say anything.

CHAD   Okay . . .

JB   So you know how some of the guys go downtown to hook up with girls?

CHAD   Yeah.

JB   Well, there are a lot more guys than there are girls.

CHAD   I can imagine there aren't too many girls working the oil rigs.

JB   No, and the girls in town know it. And they know that if some of these guys want to get laid, they're desperate enough to pay for it.

CHAD   You mean like . . . ladies of the night?

JB   Yes, Chad. Prostitutes.

CHAD   Ew, gross! They're all probably walking around with chlamydia or something.

JB   Chad.

CHAD   Sorry, I'm not supposed to say anything.

JB   Last weekend when my roommate asked me to go with him, he went down and hooked up with one of these girls.

CHAD   I have so many reactions right now, but I'm holding them in because I'm not supposed to say anything.

JB   Good. Because halfway through the week, I was feeling sad . . . about us. About . . . I don't know, being me . . . being gay. I just didn't want to . . . I just didn't want to be gay anymore. So I went downtown. I knew I could find one of the girls . . . and I did. She had this private room somewhere, and she took me back there. She started massaging me and stuff. And then she undid my belt and started unbuttoning my pants. I stopped her. I knew it didn't feel right. She asked me if I was nervous, I said no. She asked me if it was my first time, I said no. Then she asked me if I was gay.

[A moment.]

CHAD What did you tell her?

JB I told her, yes. I told her I was gay. I told her I was gay and I was missing my boyfriend.

CHAD You said all that?

JB I think that's the first time I ever said that out loud to someone.

CHAD Even if it was to a prostitute, I'll take it.

JB You're not mad at me?

CHAD You didn't sleep with her did you?

JB No, we didn't do anything. But that's why I went down there. I thought I could . . . I don't know.

CHAD I'm not mad at you. I'm proud of you. You think I didn't have my days where I wished I were straight? Do you know how much easier it would be if we were straight?

JB So fucking easy.

CHAD So fucking easy! We're gorgeous. Girls would be all over us. Do you know how many girls I've disappointed because I'm gay?

JB So many.

CHAD So many! But if we were straight . . .

JB We wouldn't have each other.

CHAD And I wouldn't trade you in for anything.

JB Same.

CHAD I love you.

JB I love you too.

CHAD But you know I'll break up with you if you ever think about cheating on me again . . . even if it's with a female prostitute. I can't believe you almost paid a prostitute for sex.

JB Oh, I still had to pay her.

CHAD For what?

JB I don't know, for her time I guess?

CHAD For her time?

JB Yeah, I mean she did sit there and listen to me talk for a couple minutes.

CHAD Damn, you had the worst therapist and worst therapy session ever.

JB I have something else to tell you . . .

CHAD I swear to God, if this has to do with a prostitute . . .

JB It doesn't. It has to do with me being alone tonight. Did you notice?

CHAD Yeah, how'd you manage that on a work night?

JB I told him I had a date. I told him I had a date with my boyfriend, and I needed the room alone.

CHAD You told your roommate you were gay?

JB Yeah.

CHAD I don't know what to say. What did he say when you told him?

JB He said, "Boyfriend? What are you gay or something?" I told him I was. Then he said, and I quote, "That's cool, I used to watch *Ru Paul's Drag Race* all the time. That shit is funny."

CHAD He did not say that!

JB I swear to God.

CHAD I can't . . . I don't even . . .

JB I know. I was speechless myself.

CHAD So you came out to two people this week?

JB I did.

CHAD Wow. I'm so impressed with my boyfriend right now.

JB Thanks. I've been so nervous about telling you.

CHAD You can tell me anything. You know that.

JB I know. I love you for that.

CHAD About the prostitute though . . .

JB Yeah, can you tap into your forgiveness powers and forgive me for that?

CHAD I might be able to . . . it might take about four or five more candles though.

JB I think I can make that happen. I love you, Chad.

CHAD I love you too, JB.

[End of scene.]

DUBLIN AND BOSTON AND MIAMI: PART 1

[SEAN is on the call by himself humming and scrolling on his phone waiting for the others. ANTONIO joins the call.]

SEAN Tony! My main man. It's good to see your face, man.

ANTONIO Sean-y boy! What's up, dude? Wait, where's Finn?

SEAN I don't know; I texted him ten minutes ago and he hasn't responded.

ANTONIO That's weird. He's usually on like ten minutes before us. I'm the late one. Because as we know, being fashionably late is reserved for the most fashionable. *(gives a Zoolander/Bluesteel look into the camera)*

SEAN *(sings)* Please stop.

[FINN joins the call.]

FINN Hey guys! Sorry I'm late. It's been a wild day so far.

ANTONIO Bro, it's not okay. Our time is precious.

SEAN Antonio joined the call about 30 seconds before you.

FINN Oh, great. So I didn't miss much.

ANTONIO How you gonna do me like that, Sean?

SEAN You've done this to yourself. Hey Finn, is everything okay, dude?

FINN Ahhh. I have big news. Oh, actually, I don't think I'm supposed to say anything for at least a few months but . . . *(shouts off-screen)* Catie! Can I tell them? They won't tell anyone! *(to screen)* Right boys?

SEAN Uh, no? I mean, it's hard to say when we don't know what you're going to tell us.

ANTONIO Honestly, I'm live-tweeting everything now.

FINN *(shouting off-screen)* They said no! Really? Okay! *(to SEAN and ANTONIO)* Okay. We're still really early, so we're not officially announcing this for a little while, but . . . *(takes a breath)*

ANTONIO Out with it, dude.

FINN I'm pregnant! I mean, we're pregnant! I mean, Catie is pregnant and I'm going to be a dad!

SEAN *(sings)* Oh my god!

ANTONIO Woah!

FINN Right?! Isn't it amazing? I still can't believe the words coming out of my mouth. Catie took a pregnancy test a little while ago, which was positive, but she didn't have the doctor's appointment to confirm it until today. We've spent the whole day celebrating. I got sidetracked with the time and just like, . . . joy, which is why I ran a little late.

SEAN This is monumental, man, congrats.

ANTONIO *(seriously)* Yeah, that is big news. That poor kid. *(smiles)* Ahhh, I'm just kidding. That's awesome, bro!

FINN No, Tony, you're right. I am nervous I'm gonna mess that little guy or gal up. But the good news is that the baby will have Catie and hopefully her radiance, kindness, charm, and intelligence will make up for everything I'm lacking.

SEAN   Aw, don't sell yourself short, man. You're gonna be a great dad.

ANTONIO   Yeah . . . you're good at . . . soccer. Or *(says in accent)* "football." You can teach it that. Kids love sports.

SEAN   It? Are you serious right now, Antonio?

FINN   Oh, it's okay. Antonio has never struck me as much of a kid person anyway. I get it. I remember what it's like to be 24 and living that party lifestyle. Kids just seem so far away from all of those good times. I remember.

ANTONIO   Hey, I've got some stuff other than partying in the works. My boss told me the other day he'll be out the door in the next month or so, so I may be movin' on up! Also, Finn, you're like 11 months older than me. Calm down.

FINN   11 months older and wiser. Don't you forget that. But that's cool, mate. I hope you get it!

SEAN   How could he forget something so apparent?

[Finn chuckles.]

ANTONIO   Whatever. At least Sean and I will still have time to have lives outside of kids.

FINN   No, we'll still have time to have these poker nights. A baby can't change a monthly meeting. If moving across the world doesn't affect our bromance, a baby surely won't. Dublin, Boston, and Miami are so far from each other!

ANTONIO   I don't know about that, dude. Remember Jeremy from our study-abroad program? His girlfriend got pregnant and then we never saw him again.

SEAN   Tony, he joined the military and got stationed in Japan. That's why we didn't see him.

ANTONIO   I'm just saying. We live in different places, too.

[Finn looks affected.]

SEAN   How about we play some online poker?

FINN   Yes, but I can only do a quick game since we have a lot to talk about with the baby coming. Catie is on the phone now with her parents, so I thought I could catch up with you guys while she's talking to them.

[Antonio gives Finn a look.]

FINN   Tony, it's not like that. Today is just a special day.

ANTONIO   Whatever you say. But let's get started. I'm ready to take aaall your money! Especially yours, "daddy."

FINN   *(softens)* Aw, can't you go easy on me now that I have a little one on the way?

SEAN   Nope—we leave the kids out of poker night. This rule begins now.

ANTONIO   Yeah, we don't get them involved until we all have them. And I never will, so do the math.

FINN   Fair enough. For now. How much are we wagering again?

SEAN $10 each.

FINN   All right. Daddy needs a new pair of shoes! *(a moment)* Oh my god. I can actually say that now. *(He takes a moment of genuine happiness.)*

ANTONIO   All right, all right. Let's move on. We're all happy for you, but your level of absolute bliss about having children is going to give me nightmares tonight. Let's get on with the game.

SEAN   Tony, let him have his moment. Like my girlfriend always says, "relish in what makes your soul shine."

ANTONIO   Excuse me? Girlfriend?

[Sean smiles.]

FINN   Hold on, is "forever single Sean" seeing someone?

SEAN   *(trying to be cool about it)* I mean, we've been, like, talking for a couple of months and just recently decided to label it. *(smiles, sings)* Sean got himself a girlfriend!

FINN   Mate, congrats. I can tell by that smirk that she's clearly making you happy.

ANTONIO   Happy? Is that what the kids are calling it? *(winks)*

SEAN   That's grade-A disrespectful, Tony. Harmony is a strong, educated woman with thoughts and feelings.

FINN   Don't worry about that. Tony's jokes aren't landing as usual. But we're both excited for you, man. How did you two meet?

SEAN   Well, that's the thing . . . we kind of, haven't met yet.

ANTONIO   Wait, isn't this how you were catfished last time, Sean?

FINN   I'm sure Sean wouldn't be catfished again. You've spoken to her on Facetime, right?

SEAN   So far just over the phone, but I've seen her picture.

[Antonio and Finn react.]

ANTONIO   Oh my god, dude. It's happening again.

SEAN   I knew I shouldn't have brought her up. I knew you guys wouldn't get it.

FINN   Sean, you have to admit it's hard to trust someone you haven't seen. Even if you feel like you have a connection. Especially considering what happened last time. You must understand we are reasonably concerned given the circumstances.

SEAN   Well we haven't seen your baby yet, how do we know it's real?

FINN   Those are obviously not the same.

SEAN   Someone told you the baby was real and you trusted them. That's what I'm doing.

FINN   Sure. I don't want to kill the mood for the sake of arguing. Let's just play poker.

SEAN   I actually told Harmony I'd call her soon, so I may as well go. I can just Venmo you the $10, Finn, since we all know you would've won anyway.

ANTONIO Hey! That's not cool. I win sometimes!

FINN Tony, no you don't. Sean, I'm sorry we upset you man. We shouldn't have been so quick to judge. Let's just play one game.

SEAN Nah, I'm gonna head out. Congrats on your baby, Finn.

[Sean leaves the call.]

FINN That was kind of abrupt, right?

ANTONIO Yeah it was. He was hella defensive.

FINN I get it, but that was still a weird interaction. Anyway, I guess we can't really play with just the two of us . . . unless you want the computer to play too?

ANTONIO Actually, I should probably go. I have some news, too.

FINN Oh yeah?

ANTONIO Yeah. I ordered pizza and my app says it should be here in two minutes.

FINN Wow, do you think you're ready for that kind of responsibility?

ANTONIO Honestly, yes. I've been dreaming of this day since last night.

FINN Wow, well go enjoy your pizza, man.

ANTONIO Thanks, bro. Later. Congrats on getting Catie knocked up.

FINN Thanks, Tony.

[Tony leaves the call. Finn smiles to himself.]

FINN *(to himself)* And then there was one.

[End of scene.]

DUBLIN AND BOSTON AND MIAMI: PART 2

[8 months later. Antonio joins the call first. Sean joins moments after.]

ANTONIO Hey, dude! What's crackin'?

SEAN Not much! I can't believe you were the first on the call! Proud of you, man.

ANTONIO Right? I've had to flex my punctuality more with my new job.

SEAN I heard about that. Congrats on that promotion!

ANTONIO Thanks! Gotta make more money to support my balla lifestyle, ya know? *(quotes Jack Harlow's "WHATS POPPIN" featuring DaBaby)* "spending money in the club like Sam's."

SEAN *(laughs)* That song is great. Almost as good as *(sings "ROCKSTAR" by DaBaby and Roddy Ricch)* "I got the mop, watch me wash 'em like detergent, And I'm ballin', that's why it's diamonds on my jersey . . ."

[Note: the director can update the song/quote in the previous lines to more current music, as long as it has the same theme/feeling.]

[Finn joins the call and Sean stops singing. It's kind of dark and he appears to be in a closet.]

SEAN Finn?

FINN Oh, hey lads. Sorry to interrupt How are you doing? Did I see you got a new job, Tony? Congrats, man!

ANTONIO Thanks, Finn. Are you . . . in a closet?

FINN Oh. Yeah. I am.

ANTONIO Dude, you know you don't have to live your life in the closet. We're all allies here.

FINN Very funny. I'm just . . . hiding from Catie.

SEAN Why would you do that? You love her so much it's actually disgusting.

ANTONIO Yeah, you guys remind me of my parents. *(fake retches)* Ugh.

FINN I know. I know, but all of this baby stuff is getting to be too much. I just don't know if I'm ready to be a dad yet. Catie's due next week and I just realized my cactus died. Like it's really dead. It probably died a month ago and I didn't even realize it. How am I supposed to keep a child alive if I can't even keep a low-sun, low-maintenance plant alive?

SEAN Take a breath, Finn. You're going to do great. Just give that kid love and food and change the diaper every once in a while. My mom says my dad didn't change a single diaper, so you'll already be doing better than he did, and look how I turned out.

ANTONIO Yeah, and a cactus doesn't cry when it needs stuff, ya know? The baby will let you know when to feed and water it or whatever. I've killed like six plants. It's super easy to do. But you rarely hear about dads killing babies.

FINN But you do hear about dads killing babies?

ANTONIO I mean, like once in a blue moon on the news. And when you see the pictures, you're like, "Yikes. That is incredibly tragic but he does look like the type."

SEAN This is unhelpful. You are not going to kill your baby, Finn. You're too full of love and already too full of worry. You're going to be on WebMD like every day making sure the baby is, like, breathing at a normal pace or something.

FINN Thanks, boys. I really needed this. I hated missing our virtual poker nights the last couple of times and the weight of everything has just been piling up. I can't keep putting it all on Catie. She's having a harder time since she's growing a human inside her.

ANTONIO Pregnancy is still crazy to me. Women can just grow extra people.

FINN Right? Catie is amazing. Her moods are everywhere now, and her ankles are the size of hamburgers, but she's honestly a champion and I love her more every day for it.

SEAN See, you have some happy thoughts under all of those anxious ones.

FINN Yeah, I guess you're right. I just need to focus on what I know and what I can control.

SEAN Exactly.

ANTONIO Right, like you know you're lame sometimes but you can't control it.

[Finn smiles.]

SEAN Unhelpful.

FINN No, Tony's right. For once. I am being lame. I'm bringing the group down. How about some online poker, lads?

SEAN Actually, I was hoping I could introduce you to someone.

ANTONIO A version of yourself that doesn't suck at online poker?

SEAN Very funny. I'm actually texting Harmony right now. Would you guys like to meet her?

FINN Definitely!

ANTONIO I didn't know you guys were still together after your trip to meet her in person fell through a few months ago?

SEAN We did take a little break, but we decided that our connection was too strong to ignore. We're trying to plan another trip again next month. This time, I'll be flying to Wisconsin.

FINN Good for you.

SEAN Oh! Here she is!

[A black window opens in the call with a name that says "Harmony." We only hear incoherent noises from her.]

SEAN Harmony? Harmony, baby? Can you hear us?

[Antonio sends the following private message to Finn: "This is still highly suspicious right?" Finn's response: "100 percent." Harmony's video begins working, but the sound does not. She waves and tries to speak.]

SEAN Oh, there you are! Looking gorgeous as always. We can't hear you, though, Harmony.

[Harmony leaves the call.]

SEAN Oh, she just texted and said her Wi-Fi is really spotty right now. She'll try again with our next chat. But at least you got to see her! You can't say she's not real now.

FINN We knew she was real, Sean.

ANTONIO Yeah, even though it is a little suspicious that we didn't hear her voice.

[Sean appears hurt by that comment.]

SEAN Whatever, you don't have to believe she exists. I know she's real and that's what matters.

ANTONIO Dude, I'm just joking. We've seen you post screenshots of your FaceTimes with her on Instagram.

[Finn looks at his phone and reacts.]

SEAN Some joke.

FINN You boys. Oh my god. I'm getting a call from Catie. Should I answer?

SEAN A call from your pregnant wife? I'd say yes.

FINN *(speaking on the phone)* Oh, yeah. Sorry, I'm in the closet. We can talk about why later . . . are you okay? Oh my god. Okay, I'll be right there. *(to Antonio and Sean)* Boys, Catie is having contractions. I think we're going to the hospital now. I have to go!

ANTONIO Dude, you got this!

FINN I can't believe it's happening now. I thought I had more time. I thought I'd be able to spend more time doing things like playing poker and drinking beer and being young with you boys.

SEAN We're still going to do all of those things. Even if you need to take a few weeks or a few months off of online poker nights, we're always a call away, man. And all of those things will be waiting for you.

FINN Okay, okay. I love you boys.

ANTONIO   Bro, we love you, but you need to leave. Like immediately.

FINN   Right. Oh my god. Right. *(takes a breath.)* See you on the other side!

SEAN   *(overlapping)* Good luck!

ANTONIO   *(overlapping)* Sending good vibes your way!

[Finn leaves the call.]

SEAN   That was intense.

ANTONIO   Right? I need to go have a drink just thinking about what he's in for. Should we do something?

SEAN   I don't know if we can do anything for a baby in Ireland when we're in Boston and Miami. Wait, actually, maybe we can see if the hospital has like a flower service or something?

ANTONIO   Yes! That's a great idea, man. Want to go in on a bouquet or something?

SEAN   Yes! How about we call the poker game for today? I'll call the hospital or a local flower shop or something and see if they can deliver.

ANTONIO   Sounds good, man. Let me know if you need my help. I'll talk to you later!

SEAN   See you, man!

[Antonio leaves the call. Harmony logs back in. We can see and hear her this time.]

HARMONY   Hey guys! So great to finally meet—

SEAN   You're too late.

HARMONY   Oh.

[End of scene.]

SEATTLE AND KNOXVILLE: PART 1

[ALEXIA and MEL start their call.]

ALEXIA   Did you get in okay last night? I saw you texted me super late.

MEL   *(yawns)* Yeah. I pulled into the driveway at around 3 a.m., and then sat in my car for 30 more minutes because I didn't want to go inside.

ALEXIA   *(consoling)* Oh, Mel. I understand. You've got a long road ahead . . . well . . . actually behind, now. Hah!

MEL   Are. You. Serious. You're making jokes right now? When I'm exhausted, depressed, and dehydrated?

ALEXIA   Well one of us needs to lighten the mood a little. And drink some water, Babe. That last one is your own doing.

MEL   *(sighs and lifts glass of water to screen sarcastically)* Cheers to your positive attitude.

ALEXIA   Babe. Once you get a good night's rest, I'm sure this will be a little easier.

MEL   You know I haven't slept well since we got the call.

ALEXIA   I know, Mel, but you're still processing. Hearing your mom has cancer isn't easy, and neither is driving from Seattle to Knoxville in two and a half days. . . . Why did you do that again?

MEL   I needed time to think. And to cry by myself. But I forgot how many people can still see you when you're in your car sobbing to Joni Mitchell's *Blue* album. I'd say pretty much half of the country is probably concerned about my well-being at this point, but especially the people of Kansas City. I stopped to get a burger there while I was driving, and this woman saw me wipe my tears away with the bun. It wouldn't have been so bad, but when I wiped the tears away, I also wiped ketchup onto my face. So then I was just this ugly, wet-looking, depressed ketchup monster driving a Hyundai Elantra.

ALEXIA   That is really sad . . . but also kind of hilarious. Why didn't you tell me this when we talked on the phone last night?

MEL   I was embarrassed then, but the shame wore off into a deep bout of indifference and existential crisis.

ALEXIA   That's . . . pos . . . i . . . tive kind of? At least you're sharing your feelings with me?

MEL   Yeah. Thanks for always being there for that, Al. And thanks for being so cool about being long-distance while I help my mom work through this.

ALEXIA   I'd do the same thing for my mom, Mel. And you know I love Wanda. Give her a big ole Rocky Top hug for me.

MEL   Oh, you know I will.

ALEXIA   How is Wanda doing?

MEL   She's really taking it all in stride. But I don't know if she's trying to be strong for me or if she's actually just at peace with it.

ALEXIA   Your mom was always a beam of light. I've never known her to complain about a thing. . . . Which is honestly pretty weird considering who she spawned.

MEL   You had better be talking about my brother.

ALEXIA   *(sarcastically)* Oh, most def.

MEL   Listen, every relationship needs one idealist and one realist. It's not my fault real life can be kind of a bummer.

ALEXIA   You know I need you to keep me grounded, Babe.

MEL   And don't you forget it, Al.

ALEXIA   And don't you forget that you need a little sunshine in your life sometimes. And here. I. Am.

MEL   *(begins quoting from Disney Pixar's FINDING NEMO)* "I forget things almost instantly. It runs in my family . . . well, at least I think it does . . ."

ALEXIA   *(joins in)* "When life gets you down, you know what you gotta do? Just keep swimming."

MEL   "Nemo, newcomer of the orange and white, you have been called forth to the summit of Mt. Wannahockaloogie to join with us in the fraternal bonds of tankhood."

ALEXIA   "Shark bait!"

MEL   "Oooo ha ha!"

[The director is welcome to update these quotes with an older/newer Disney Pixar film that better suits the ages of the actors as something they may have enjoyed in their youth.]

[They both laugh. A moment.]

MEL   Ah. Thank you. I needed one of our Disney quote-alongs.

ALEXIA   Fellow Disney fanatic, at your service.

[A moment.]

MEL   Oh hey, I almost forgot to ask, how is your group presentation coming along?

ALEXIA   Oh, you know, it is going horribly. I thought when I had a real career at a marketing firm I wouldn't have to participate in group presentations as much, but here we are. Here we fucking are.

MEL   Yeah, that is so annoying. If it turns out to be anything short of perfect, it's because of those dummies. Wasn't that Tracey girl helping at least a little bit?

ALEXIA   Yeah, I mean, she thought she was helping, but everything she did was off-brand, so I had to change and correct it.

MEL   Damn. That sucks. You'd think people at a marketing firm would have a clearer concept of branding.

ALEXIA   Right? That's exactly what I was venting with Tracey about until she screwed up and proved to be as worthless as those other corporate punks.

MEL   Well good luck. It's tomorrow, right?

ALEXIA   Yeah, it's at 10 a.m. Pacific. I'll be leading it, so send me good vibes, please!

MEL   You know I will!

ALEXIA   Well hey, I should probably let you go. I know you're in East Coast hours now so it's super late, and I need to finish editing this presentation anyway.

MEL   My body still hasn't adjusted yet, but you're right. I need to at least try to go to sleep.

ALEXIA   Yes. Self-care is so important. Treat that temple of a body right and give my queen some sweet rest!

MEL   *(smiles)* Sounds good. Give Sadie a pat on the head for me. And good luck tomorrow.

ALEXIA   Oh, you know I will. And thanks.

MEL   Love you, Al.

ALEXIA   Love you, M.

MEL   We'll talk again soon, okay?

ALEXIA   No pressure, Mel. I know you're balancing a lot. Call me when you can.

MEL   Thanks, Babe. Love, love.

ALEXIA   Love, love.

[The call ends.]

End of scene.

SEATTLE AND KNOXVILLE: PART 2

[The call begins between Mel and Alexia].

MEL   Hey, honey!

ALEXIA   Hi, Babe!

MEL   Ugh, it's so good to see your face.

ALEXIA   Yours too.

MEL   I mean, it's really nice to see you, though. Do you understand? So. Nice. I love my family but woof. They can be a lot.

ALEXIA   Oh right. Marcus is there now, too, huh?

MEL   Yeah, he got in yesterday. He's such a little son of a bitch.

ALEXIA   Is that really the expression you want to choose right now?

MEL   No, you're right. He's the son of a strong-ass, independent, educated woman. Also, he's an asshole.

ALEXIA   There it is. What's he even up to now?

MEL   Well, he's trying to use my mom's illness as an excuse to bum here and not pay rent. But he says he "really wants to take care of her." Like, oh, is that why you were out all night with your college bros and slept in all day? Because you want to take care of her?

ALEXIA   People in their 20s are the worst.

MEL   No, we rocked in our 20s. Marcus in his 20s is the worst.

ALEXIA   Fine. You got me. How is your mom?

MEL   She's doing okay right now. She had a breakdown earlier today, though..

ALEXIA   Oh, man.

MEL   Yeah. . . . She was looking through some of our old family pictures. We were all laughing and reminiscing. It was actually really nice. We felt like a real family for the first time in a long time. Then she started holding up our old school portraits next to our faces to compare the differences and we were all giggling. But suddenly, her smile clenched up, her face started to flush, and she started to cry. It was like it came out of nowhere. When we asked her what was wrong, she told us the doctor said there's a chance the tumor could continue growing forward, which could make her blind and then she'd never get to see our . . . precious faces again.

ALEXIA   Wow, Mel. That's really heavy. Are you okay?

MEL   I mean . . . not really. . . . I've never seen my mom so torn up . . . so torn up in worry and self-sorrow. I know she is a human, but . . . it's hard to see your heroes like that. *(beat)* I didn't know what to say.

I couldn't say anything. I just held her while she cried into my chest the same way she held me when I would cry from scraping my knee when I was little.

ALEXIA Well I'm sure that's what she needed. A literal shoulder to cry on. How great of you to be able to give that to her after so many years of her giving that to you.

MEL Yeah, I guess. This is just a lot harder than I thought it would be. Having a loved one with cancer makes you confront mortality every day, and it's like, if you don't talk about it, it'll find its way into your conversation or mood or even a TV show that you're watching specifically to forget about it. It's almost as if, if you're not controlling that conversation it will weasel its way into your life and control you.

ALEXIA It's amazing how you can see something everywhere when you're trying not to see it.

MEL Exactly. Shit, Alexia. I'm sorry I've just been pouring all of this onto you. How are you? How was your presentation?

ALEXIA Good. Actually, the presentation was really good. I did it all myself, and it was kind of . . . perfect. Not to toot my own horn.

MEL Nah, girl! Let out those toots! I knew it would be awesome!

ALEXIA Yeah. It was great.

MEL Wait, what's wrong? Why do you seem weird about doing a good job?

ALEXIA . . . They offered me a promotion.

MEL Oh! Wow! Congratulations! That is amazing news! What's bugging you out?

ALEXIA The promotion isn't at my firm in Seattle. It's in Hawaii.

MEL What? You have a branch in Hawaii?

ALEXIA They said they're expanding to Hawaii and they want me to be the first to run that branch.

MEL   No offense, but wouldn't they want a more experienced manager to run a brand-new branch?

ALEXIA   That's exactly what I asked, but they said no. They're trying to target a younger crowd in Hawaii, and they want someone a little younger but with my credentials to do that. The presentation was just the icing on the cake. This has evidently been in the works for a while.

MEL   Wow. That's amazing. I'm so proud of you, Al.

ALEXIA   Mel, you know I'm not going to take it.

MEL   What? Are you kidding? You have to! You've been talking about running your own firm since college. This would probably double your salary!

ALEXIA   I'm already so far from you in Seattle now. I can't be even further from you. What if I need to get there quickly to be with you and Wanda?

MEL   Babe, that's very sweet, but I can't let you do that. My mom isn't going to want that either. Besides, if the tumor continues shrinking through the next few rounds of chemo, I'll be leaving to be back with you again.

ALEXIA   Is that a real possibility?

MEL   *(defensive)* Of course it is. . . . You don't think she's going to get better?

ALEXIA   I didn't say that. I was just remembering what you told me. That if it doesn't shrink and if it keeps growing at the rate that it perhaps did . . . well . . . like you said. Ted Kennedy had that kind of tumor and even with the best doctors in the world . . . he died . . .

MEL   We don't know for sure if it's that kind of tumor yet. There's a chance it was there her whole life and they only recently discovered it. If that's the case, she'll probably be able to live with it for many years.

ALEXIA   Mel, I know. I hope you're right. I just want us to have realistic expectations of where this could lead. Prepare for the worst and hope for the best, you know?

MEL   Hello, I'm the realist in the relationship. You don't think I've thought of that? But my mom is a fighter. She will make it. Take the promotion and I'll be with you in Hawaii in a few months.

ALEXIA   She probably will, but I don't know, Babe. I feel like maybe this just isn't the right time for a big move.

MEL   So you're going to give up an amazing job because you're so convinced that my mom will die?

ALEXIA   *(hurt)* Mel. You know that's not true. I'm just trying to help. I want to be there for you through all of this.

MEL   I'm sorry but you're not helping. And the present is the only time we have. You can't let my mom's illness stop you from living your dreams.

ALEXIA   Dreams evolve. I want us to be family. I'd love to run a firm, but you know our relationship always comes first.

MEL   We will be fine. You, however, won't be if you don't take it. Go.

ALEXIA   Okay. I'll sleep on it for a few days. I told them I'd let them know by next week.

MEL   Well it should be an easy decision.

[A moment.]

ALEXIA   Yeah. I guess I'd better get some rest. Get a head start on the whole "sleeping on it" thing.

MEL   Alright, good night.

ALEXIA   I'll talk to you later, M.

MEL   Talk soon, Al.

ALEXIA   Love you.

MEL   Love, love.

[The call ends.]

End of scene.

SEATTLE AND KNOXVILLE: PART 3

[The call begins between Mel and Alexia. Alexia appears to be in the driver's seat of a parked car.]

ALEXIA   Mel. Mel. Please say something.

MEL   I just really thought she could make it longer.

ALEXIA   Your mom is still here. Go talk to her!

MEL   I really can't right now. I think I'll just break down.

ALEXIA   I'm sure she wants to talk to someone about it. Marcus is fine, but he isn't her daughter.

MEL   He's better at this than me, though. It's so annoying, too. I stay, I help my mom cook, clean, get her ready for the day while he's out doing God knows what, but when it comes to consoling someone, it's natural for him.

ALEXIA   Who did she go to when she broke down with the family pictures?

MEL   I think she probably just cried into my chest because she was near me. And my boobs are like squishy, comfy pillows.

ALEXIA   Your boobs are my favorite squishy, comfy pillows. *(They both smile.)*

MEL   Don't make me smile. This is serious.

ALEXIA   Oh, Babe. I know. But I mean, most people don't know when they'll die. Maybe there's some freedom for her in knowing she has 2–3 months.

MEL   No! It's going to be horrible. We're just going to cry all the time thinking of new things she won't get to be a part of. They'll be so much pressure on how we spend every moment.

ALEXIA   But Mel, what if she had died in a car accident, you know? You wouldn't know in advance. You wouldn't get to spend months with her before she left the earth. She would just be gone.

MEL   Ugh. I know Alexia. I just . . . I don't want her to die. I know that's a stupid thing to say. But I don't know what to say.

ALEXIA   Hey, that's not stupid. That's relatable. And I'm certain that's how your mom feels, too. Go talk to her.

MEL   I think maybe we just both need space right now. What are you doing?

ALEXIA   Oh, I'm on my way to get a first look at the new building.

MEL   I thought they were providing a car for you when you landed?

ALEXIA   Oh, I decided to just rent a car. I'm going to have to get used to driving here anyway.

MEL   Oh. How was the flight?

ALEXIA   Mel, we don't have to talk about my work right now. What's going on with you is a lot more important. When are you going to talk to Wanda?

MEL   I'd really rather not talk about that right now. I can talk to her when we get off the phone. I just . . . need this time. Please. Tell me about your boring flight. I really want to hear about it.

ALEXIA   Okay, Mel. Um, it was super long, but work at least gave me an aisle seat and a drink voucher, so I had a Mai Tai, watched *Toy Story*, and then read a little.

MEL   You bitch. The first one?

ALEXIA   Yeah, they had it streaming on the American app.

MEL   That's the best one. I can't believe you got to drink alcohol and watch a Disney Pixar movie today and I . . . I went to the hospital . . .

ALEXIA   This is why I didn't want to talk about it! Let's change the subject!

MEL   No! Sorry. Was your flight delayed at all?

ALEXIA   No, it actually left on time and arrived early. A girl near me also ordered the whole row snacks because she was coming from Vegas where she won a ton of money. She was a hoot.

MEL   *(sarcastically)* Of. Course.

ALEXIA   What do you want me to say? It was the most pleasant flying experience I've ever had! I just didn't want to rub it in!

MEL   Sorry, it's fine. You're fine. I'm just emotional right now and I miss you. I know I told you to take that job, but I can't believe how far away you are now. It's like I can physically feel how far you are.

ALEXIA   Oh Mel, that's all in your head. We'll be together before you know it.

[Mel reacts. She looks like she may cry.]

ALEXIA   Shit. I'm sorry, Mel. I didn't mean it like that. You know I didn't. I just—

MEL   No, I know. Three months isn't that long.

ALEXIA   That really isn't what I meant, okay?

MEL   Al, it really is okay. I know you didn't say that to hurt me. You're just being realistic.

ALEXIA   Mel, no. That isn't what I meant because . . . I'm not in Hawaii.

MEL   What are you talking about? Are you in Seattle?

ALEXIA   M, I sent you a Snapchat from the airport. You know where I am.

MEL   No.

ALEXIA   You didn't actually believe they'd play Garth Brooks in the Honolulu airport, did you?

MEL   You sent that Snapchat from Tennessee?

ALEXIA   Uh-huh.

MEL   What about your promotion? Today was supposed to be your first day in Hawaii! Did you lie to me about how nice your flight accommodations were?

ALEXIA   Mel, I decided not to take it. I'm on a short list for a few other young firms opening soon across the country, so I'm not giving up on any kind of dream you think I have. This just wasn't the right time, and with my current job, I can work remotely as long as I give two weeks' notice. *(beat)* Most importantly, I couldn't let you do this alone. I love you. *(beat)* And no, I wasn't lying, that was literally the best flying experience I've ever had. I got a free drink and snack and everything was on time. I still can't believe it myself.

MEL   Wait, so if you snapchatted me at the airport all that time ago, that would put you pretty close to here, right?

ALEXIA   *(gets out of the car and starts walking)* Yeah, I'd say I'm getting pretty close.

[A knock at the door.]

MEL   *(holding back tears)* Is that you?

ALEXIA   Come find out for yourself.

[Mel leaves the frame. Alexia's frame goes black. We hear a door open and Mel and Alexia crying. We hear whispers of an "I love you."]

[End of play.]

Acknowledgments

My sincerest thanks to the playwrights who allowed me to read their work during this process. It was a challenge putting this book together given the caliber of writing coming from so many wonderful theater artists. I thank the playwrights who have shared their talents between these pages—without our writers, we would have no theater. (I'll let academics try to debate that one.) In addition, I want to thank Ricky and Dana Young-Howze for suggesting plays and playwrights; to Glory Kadigan, artistic director of the year-long Planet Connections Zoom Festivity; to Liz Amadio and Cosmic Orchid; to Akia Squitieri and the Rising Sun Performance Company; to Miranda Jonte and Back Porch Theatre; to Ria T. DiLullo and Emily Schmidt of The Skeleton Rep(resents); to Reanna Armellino and Hazen Cuyler of The Greenhouse Ensemble; to Craig Houk and the Two Hander Slam; and to all theatre artists who have continued to create, showcase, and celebrate new work during the pandemic and beyond!

I would also like to thank Applause Theatre and Cinema Books, especially senior editor Chris Chappell, for having faith and greenlighting this project, as well as assistant editor Laurel Myers, editorial assistant Barbara Claire, and production editor Ashleigh Cooke for all their hard work and dedication. I also owe a huge thank-you to my agent, June Clark, of FinePrint Literary Management for sticking with me. (This is our fourth book together!)

Sending a big thank-you to Danielle Bienvenue Bray, Dan Bray, and Sadie Bray for reminding me what matters most in this world. And a warm thanks to Jack and Dash for keeping me company while editing this work.

Finally, I want to dedicate this anthology to Angela Hall, a wonderful playwright and screenwriter who passed away this summer. She has had two plays published in the Applause Best American Short Plays series. I hope you seek them out. She is sorely missed.

Playwright Biographies

LINDSAY ADAMS is an award-winning playwright and lyricist. Her plays, *River Like Sin* and *Rattler* were both named semifinalists for the 2018 and 2019 O'Neill National Playwrights Conference. Her play *Her Own Devices* has received two awards from the Kennedy Center and the 2016 Judith Barlow Prize. A song from her new musical *Our Man Harry* (cowritten with Rebecca Nisco) was performed at the Kennedy Center as a part of their Millennium Stage Concert Series. She has received commissions from companies like CLIMB Theatre (MN) and Springville Center for the Arts (NY). Her plays have been produced and developed at Women's Project Theatre (NYC), Theatre Alliance (DC), Keegan Theatre (DC), Actors Theatre of Indiana (IN), B Street Theatre (CA), KC Public Theater (MO), Interrobang Theatre (MD), This Is Water Theatre (TX), The Hub Theatre (VA), Fishtank Theater (MO), Midwest Dramatists Center (MO), and Westport Center for the Arts (MO), among many others. She is a proud member of the Dramatists Guild and has an MFA in Playwriting from the Catholic University of America.

JENNY LYN BADER is a playwright and author whose work has been produced internationally and published by Dramatists Play Service, Next Stage Press, Applause, Smith & Kraus, Vintage, *Lincoln Center Theater Review*, *Plays International & Europe*, and the *New York Times*, where she was a frequent contributor to the "Week in Review." Her plays include *None of the Above*, *In Flight*, and *Mrs. Stern Wanders the Prussian State Library*. Audio plays include *International Local* (Subway Plays app) and *Tree Confessions* (This Is Not a Theatre Company). She performed her solo play *Equally Divine: The Real Story of the Mona Lisa* on Theatre Row, receiving the "Best Documentary One-Woman Show" Award (United Solo Festival). A summa cum laude graduate of Harvard, she cofounded Theatre 167 (Caffè Cino Award, NY Innovative Theatre Foundation). Other honors include the Edith Oliver Award (Eugene O'Neill Center), Athena Fellowship, Lark Fellowship (nominated by Wendy Wasserstein),

Randall Wreghitt Award (TRU), and ThinkFast's Audience Award. She is a member of the Dramatists Guild, Authors Guild, League of Professional Theatre Women, ICWP, Honor Roll, and Playwrights Gallery.

IVAM CABRAL is a PhD in Pedagogy at Universidade de São Paulo. Actor, filmmaker, and playwright, he founded with Rodolfo García Vázquez Os Satyros Theatre Company in 1989. As an actor, he took part in the cast of many shows and performed in more than 30 countries. He has published over 20 books including chronicles, children's literature, and dramaturgy. His works have been translated into Spanish, English, Swedish, and German and published in Angola, Cuba, and the United Kingdom. He also writes for TV and cinema. With Rodolfo García Vázquez he directed the fiction movie *Philosophy in the Boudoir* (2017) and *The Art of Facing Fear* (2021). He is the executive director of SP Escola de Teatro in São Paulo. He also works as a psychoanalyst and curator.

AUDREY CEFALY is an alumna of the Playwrights' Arena cohort at Arena Stage, a recipient of the Walter E. Dakin Fellowship from the Sewanee Writers Conference, and a Dramatist Guild Foundation *Traveling Master*. She is published by Concord Theatricals, Smith & Kraus, and Applause Books. Cefaly's plays, including *The Gulf*, *Alabaster*, *Maytag Virgin*, *The Last Wide Open*, *Love Is a Blue Tick Hound*, and others, have been produced by Cincinnati Playhouse, Florida Studio, Florida Rep, City Theatre, Penobscot Theatre, Gulfshore Playhouse, Merrimack Rep, Signature Theatre, Barter Theatre, Vermont Stage, Oregon Contemporary Theatre, 16th Street Theater, Capital Stage, About Face, Kitchen Dog Theatre, Circle Theatre, Theatre Three, Aurora Theatre, Quotidian Theatre Company and University of Alabama at Birmingham. Her play *Alabaster* received an 11-city Rolling World Premiere, the largest in National New Play Network history.

ERIC EIDSON received his undergraduate degree in Theatre Education and Acting Performance from the University of Northern Colorado and holds an MEd in Educational Leadership from Concordia University–Portland and an MFA in Playwriting from Hollins University. He is currently working on a PhD in Fine Arts–Theatre at Texas Tech University while working as a High School Theatre Teacher. In his spare time, he enjoys spending time with family, playing frisbee, and enjoying the outdoors with his wife, Lauren.

VINCE GATTON is a New York–based playwright and Drama Desk–nominated actor. His full-length play *Alexandria* won Sanguine Theatre Company's Project Playwright Festival 2018, and his short play *Better* was one of the winners of the 2018 Samuel French Off-Off Broadway Short Play Festival. Other shorts have had readings in MTP's annual Cherry Picking at the Wild Project in New York City; *In the Whole History of Hi-Q*, *Better*, and *Hey* were all finalists for the National Playwriting Award at City Theatre in Miami; and another short, *Jam*, won Best Play in the 2015 LIC Short Play Festival at the Secret Theatre in Long Island City. *Wake*, his first full-length play, was a semifinalist for PlayPenn, and a finalist with readings at Dayton Playhouse's FutureFest, Boomerang Theatre's First Flight Festival, and Vintage Theatre Productions' Mystery/Thriller New Works Festival. He received a Drama Desk nomination for Outstanding Actor in a Play for David Johnston's *Candy and Dorothy*, which he also performed at Wellfleet Harbor Actors Theatre in Cape Cod. Other notable acting credits include Leigh Fondakowski's *Spill* at Ensemble Studio Theatre; *Cock* and *Clean Alternatives* at the Kitchen Theatre in Ithaca; *I Am My Own Wife* and *Fully Committed* at Barrington Stage Company; *I Am My Own Wife* again at Coachella Valley Rep (Desert Star Award Nomination) and Two Turns Theatre Company; Taylor Mac's *The Hot Month* at Boomerang Theatre Company; and *The Temperamentals* at New World Stages, standing by for Michael Urie. You can also catch him being himself on a certain rerun of Jeopardy, in the documentary *Married & Counting*, and in the *Pippin* episode of Encore! on Disney+.

MICHAEL HAGINS is an African American playwright, director, fight director, actor, and producer. Michael is a member of Dramatists Guild and an advanced actor-combatant for the Society of American Fight Directors. Michael was born in Brooklyn, New York, but raised in a small town in Florida for his childhood. He has used the racism and prejudice he dealt with at an early age to fuel his writing, which he has done since the age of nine. Michael is an avid lover of Shakespeare (he has done every play in the Shakespeare canon) and has performed, directed, and taken part in over 1,000 plays and films over his artistic career. Off-Broadway: *The Long Rail North* (Soho Rep, FringeNYC). New York Productions: *Basement* (Roly Poly Productions); *Michael Is Black* (Planet Connections Theatre Festivity); *The Renaissance Dueling Plays* (Planet Connections

Theatre Festivity); *The Vengeance Room* (FRIGID Festival). Regional/ Other: *Hit and Match* (Chicago Fringe, Johannesburg Fringe). Outstanding Playwriting—*Hit and Match*, 2013; Outstanding Overall Production of a Solo Show—*Michael Is Black*; winner of Best Playwriting, Best Director, and Best Overall Production of NEPTA Awards for *As You Wish It or The Bride Princess or What You Will*, 2020; Winner—Best Play and Best Streaming Play, Off-Broadway Regional Awards–Hawai'i for *A Shot Rang Out*. Artistic Director, C.A.G.E. Theatre Company

DANA HALL is a playwright, actor, and mental health therapist. Dana has had dozens of plays produced across the United States and internationally. She took home a Best of Fringe award at the Women's Theatre Festival (NC) for her examination of social disparities with the play, *No Justice*. She is the 2022 Femuscript (FL) Monologue Winner performing her original piece *Snowglobe*. Her Halloween-themed comedy, *Don't Lose Your Head*, was published with HEUER 2022. Her best-selling children's book *Beyond Words*, which focuses on inclusivity and kindness, won the Mother's Choice Award in 2020. *New York Journal* recognized her as on their 50 under 50 most influential creators during the pandemic list of 2022. She is a member of the Dramatists Guild, League of Professional Theatre Women, Honor Roll!, and International Centre for Female Playwrights. DanaHallCreates.com Instagram: @DanaHallCreates

ARLENE HUTTON is the author of *Last Train to Nibroc* and *Letters to Sala*. Rubicon Theatre's production of her play *Gulf View Drive* received the 2018 Ovation Award for Best Production. Credits include B Street Theatre, Cincinnati Playhouse, Florida Studio Theatre, Kitchen Theatre, and Washington Stage Guild. An alumna of New Dramatists and member of Ensemble Studio Theatre, New Circle Theatre Company, New Light Theatre Project, and Honor Roll!, she is a three-time winner of the Samuel French Short Play Festival, nine-time finalist for the Heideman Award, Francesca Primus Prize finalist, recipient of an EST/Sloan Commission and NYFA Fellowship. Residencies include the Lark, MacDowell Colony, New Harmony Project, SPACE at Ryder Farm and Yaddo. Hutton's works have been presented at FringeNYC, Off- and Off-Off-Broadway, regionally, in London and at the Edinburgh Fringe. Her scripts are published by Dramatists Play Service, Playscripts, and TRW. She teaches playwriting online for The Barrow Group.

MRINALINI KAMATH's radio play *Stuff*, inspired by the *New York Times* article "The Lonely Death of George Bell," was recorded by Astoria Performing Arts Center. Mrinalini received a Queens Council on the Arts grant to develop her play *Term Limits* and was a Mellon Creative initiative fellow twice through the program jointly administered by the Ma-Yi Writers Lab and the University of Washington School of Drama. Several of Mrinalini's plays and monologues have been published in anthologies. She is an alumna of Youngblood and the Mission to (dit)Mars Propulsion Lab and a member of the Ma-Yi Writers Lab and The PlayGround Experiment. She can be found on The New Play Exchange (https://new-playexchange.org/users/2745/mrinalini-kamath).

ALY KANTOR is a playwright, performer, and teaching artist from Long Island, New York, where she is a creative associate with EastLine Theatre. Her award-winning, internationally produced plays and adaptations focus on women's stories, with a touch of magic, science, history, and/or the uncanny. She is probably not a zombie.

GREG LAM is a playwright, screenwriter, and board game designer who lives in the Bay Area. He is the cofounder of the Asian-American Playwright Collective and a member of The Pulp Stage Writer's Room and the Pear Theatre's Playwright Guild. His full-length epic *Last Ship to Proxima Centauri* premiered digitally at Kitchen Dog Theater in March 2021 and onstage at Portland Stage Co. in March 2022 after winning the Clauder Competition. His full-length play *Repossessed* received its world premiere at Theatre Conspiracy in 2018. His serial play series *Treachery Island* will premiere at The Pulp Stage in 2022. In 2019, he was named a fellow in the Dramatic Arts by the Mass Cultural Council and the inaugural Pao Fellow of the Company One PlayLab. For more about Greg, see https://greglam.wixsite.com/home.

KITT LAVOIE's plays have been performed on all seven continents, including at the Rothera Research Station of the British Antarctic Survey. Plays and musical books include *Sabbatical* (Lincoln Center), *Kiki Baby* (Theater for the American Musical Prize), and *realer than that* (winner, Samuel French New Play Festival). He wrote and produced the acclaimed documentary *Best Worst Thing That Ever Could Have Happened*, about the original Broadway cast of Stephen Sondheim's *Merrily We Roll Along* (*New York Times*' Top 10 Films of 2016, *Playbill*'s Top Five Theater

Documentaries, *Evening Standard*'s Ten Best Arts Documentaries, *Esquire*'s 20 Best Documentaries of All Time). Kitt is artistic director of the Lanford Wilson New American Play Festival and, for 22 years, was artistic director of The CRY HAVOC Company, a new-play-development-focused theater in New York City. He is a member of the acting and directing faculty at the Dobbins Conservatory of Theatre and Dance at Southeast Missouri State University, where he leads the Acting and Musical Theatre Performance programs, as well as at NSKI Høyskole (The Norwegian Actors College) in Oslo. Kitt holds an MFA in directing from the Actors Studio Drama School at New School University and is a member of the Dramatists Guild (Kansas City/St. Louis Regional Representative), the Stage Directors and Choreographers Society, and the Literary Managers and Dramaturgs of the Americas.

LAUREN LYNCH-EIDSON is a Denver-based arts administrator from Clarksville, Tennessee. She has undergraduate degrees in theatre and English from Austin Peay State University and an MFA in arts administration from Texas Tech University. She has had a passion for accessibility in the arts for many years, working at Phamaly Theatre Company in Denver, the nation's longest-running disability-affirmative nonprofit theatre. In addition, she spent several years volunteering in person and virtually for A.B.L.E. Ensemble, a Chicago-based theatre for, with, and by individuals with developmental disabilities. She is also Adjunct Professor at the University of Denver. Previously, she had the privilege of working at Wonderbound Ballet, Chicago Shakespeare Theater, and the Eugene O'Neill Theater Center, among others. When she's not at work, you can find her playing board games, writing, singing with the Denver Women's Chorus, or stealing cuddles from her dog, Harry Pupper, and her husband, Eric.

COLETTE MAZUNIK is a writer and educator living in Denver, Colorado. Her plays include *A Danger to Yourself and Others* (winner of the Gulfshore Playhouse New Works Festival), *Ravening*, and *Shelter in Place*. Short films include *Thanksgiving Dinner* and *Match*. Her short films have been official selections for the Madrid International (Best Story nominee) and the Bermuda International Film Festivals, among others. Her play *The Matthew Portraits* was a finalist in the Samuel French Off-Off Broadway Short Play Festival. She was an inaugural Playwright Fellow at the Denver Center for the Performing Arts and partnered with aerospace engineering scientists at the University of Colorado–Boulder to write about near-earth space debris. As a teacher, she loves to create safe spaces for students to hone their skills and shape their unique and diverse stories. She has an MFA in playwriting from the Actors Studio Drama School at New School University and is a member of the Dramatists Guild. Scripts available at newplayexchange.org.

JOYCE MILLER is currently querying her dark humor memoir, *Almost Rapist.* Published monologues include *How I Became a Millionaire by Selling Jars of My Farts Online* (2022), *Just Checking to See Whether or Not You Have a Body Double* (2022), *The Brave Little Toaster's Radical Manifesto* (2020), *My 28 Years of Heterosexuality Was Just a Phase* (2015), *Recent Hit Pop Songs Co-Written by Influential Feminist Philosophers* (2014), *Casting Call for my Internal Biopic* (2013), *A Creative Writing Professor Shares a Few of His Favorite Writing Exercises* (2012), and *Product Review: The Invisible Backpack of White Privilege from L.L. Bean* (2014), reprinted in the compendium *Keep Scrolling Till You Feel Something: Twenty-One Years of Humor From McSweeney's Internet Tendency* (2019). Plays include *The Handmaid's Dianetics Episode I: Scientolojesus*, *The Handmaid's Dianetics Episode II*, *The Handmaid's Dianetics Episode III: Ofhubbard*, and *The Handmaid's Dianetics Episode IV: Science of Survival.*

J. MERRILL MOTZ (rhymes with "boats") created Paper Soul in 2013 for the MN Fringe, focusing on experimenting with the expectations and misconceptions of solo performance. For the MN Fringe he created and performed *Boxcutter Harmonica, Rewind-A-Buddy, Ding Dong! Sing Song!, The Jackpot Hour With(out) Jack Power, Knifeslingin'!,* and *SOFT*. In the before times, he toured *Knifeslingin'!* to New York, New Orleans, Cincy Fringe, and Central Michigan University. Over the past few years he digitally performed *Rewind-A-Buddy* and created *BRIG*, which won awards for Best 2021 Solo Performance and Best 2021 Solo Horror (respectively) from *The Young-Howze Theatre Journal*. He recently toured *SOFT* to the Cincy Fringe for the first in-person Fringe Fest since 2019. By day Motz can be found watching people's pets around the Twin Cities, by night he's probably a private eye . . . or at least drinking like one.

TORY PARKER is originally from West Virginia, graduated from Centre College in Kentucky, and now lives and works in Louisville. In Louisville, she's worked and performed with Claddagh Theatre Company, the

Chamber Theatre, Bellarmine University, Wayward Actors Company, Derby City Playwrights, Company Outcast, the Louisville Fringe Festival, and director Emily Grimany. As a playwright, her original works, *Twilight Sleep* and *Recommended for You*, appeared in the National Women's Theatre Festival in their 2020 and 2021 Fringe Festivals. She is the co-artistic director of DCSG Theatre, an online theatre company.

BRENDAN POWERS and **RACHEL BURTTRAM** are professional actors and writers. When COVID-19 shuttered theatres across the country in Spring 2020, they hung a curtain and some Christmas lights in their back bedroom closet and *tiny_Theatre* was born. Using playwright-approved material, they present free play readings on Facebook Live each week. In addition, they wrote and produced two online interactive murder mysteries that have been popular with both general audiences and Fortune 500 companies seeking out unique teambuilding experiences.

SHARECE M. SELLEM, a native of Connecticut, is a playwright, choreographer, director, and performing arts instructor based out of New Haven, Connecticut. She was trained by Headlong Performance Institute of Bryn Mawr College in Pennsylvania and Yale University's Practical Approach to Directing Summer Program 2014. Her resume includes performances at Bregamos Community Theater, Long Wharf Theatre, Pride Arts Center of Chicago, Charter Oak Cultural Center, Carriage House Theater, Illinois Voices Theatre, Norwich Arts Center, University of California San Diego, and more. She is the founder and curator of the Quick Quarantined Play Festival (2020) and founder of Vintage Soul Productions LLC and currently resides in Delaware.

TREY TATUM is a playwright/composer originally from the Alabama Gulf Coast. His plays include *ZOINKS!*, a teen detective caper about the opioid epidemic; *Alabama Monster*, his solo show about mental illness, family ties, and creatures that lie just out of sight; and *JALZ*, a remake of the blockbuster movie *Jaws* that examines Alzheimer's disease, end-of-life care and family legacy. Current Projects include *Have Monster, Will Travel*, an audio fiction podcast about road trips, monsters, and the meaning of family. Other productions include a reading at Lincoln Center, inclusion in ANT Fest at Ars Nova, the Samuel French OOB Festival, and a residency at Robert Wilson's The Watermill Center. Trey's play *The River*

Valeo was a semifinalist for the Princess Grace Award. He is the former programming director of The Tank, a nonprofit presenter of the arts in New York City. Trey currently lives in Cincinnati, Ohio, and makes theater and mischief with his wife, director Bridget Leak. Treytatum.com

JORDAN TROVILLION is an American actress and singer. She has appeared in *Detroiters* and *Secrets in the Walls*. She grew up in Michigan and started acting on stage in school, later studying theater at the University of Michigan–Flint. https://www.jordantrovillion.net/

RODOLFO GARCÍA VÁZQUEZ is a playwright, filmmaker, and theatre director. He cofounded with Ivam Cabral the Os Satyros Theatre Company in 1989 and has received the most important Brazilian awards. As a doctoral researcher in Theatre Theory at Universidade de São Paulo, he investigates decoloniality in theatre. He has directed in over 36 countries, such as the United States, Sweden, Germany, South Africa, Cape Verde, and Kenya. He has published over 10 books. As a filmmaker, he directed *Hypotheses for Love and Truth* (2014), *Philosophy in the Boudoir* (2017), and *The Art of Facing Fear* (2021). He is the pedagogical coordinator of the directing course in SP Escola de Teatro and also a visiting teacher in the University of the Arts of Stockholm and Helsinki.

Rights and Permissions

All inquiries about performance and other rights to the plays in this book should be directed to the following contacts:

98 People on Live   Susan Gurman, The Gurman Agency, susan@gurmanagency.com

Baby's Breath   Pat McLaughlin, Beacon Artists Agency, beaconagency@hotmail.com

BRIG   J. Merrill Motz, justmotz@gmail.com

The Cure   Michael Hagins, mchagins@gmail.com

Disappearance of an Activist as Documented by ClassPass Customer Service   Joyce Miller, joycesusannahmiller@gmail.com or P.O. Box 8615, New York, NY 10116

Fish Tank   Aly Kantor, aly.kantor@gmail.com

Guru of Touch   Jack Tantleff, Paradigm Talent Agency, jtantleff@paradigmagency.com

Humans   Mrinalini Kamath, mkamath07@gmail.com

Killjoy, Ohio   Trey Tatum, treytatum@gmail.com

The Last Supper   Lindsay Adams, limericklinz@gmail.com

Life in the Hard Drive   Greg Lam, greg.lam.writing@gmail.com

Protocols   Vince Gatton, vince@vincegatton.com

Ravening   Colette Mazunik, colettes.email@gmail.com

Recommended for You   Tory Parker, toryvgparker@gmail.com

Role Play   www.tiny-theatre.com or 716-812-7693

Stay Awhile   Dana Hall, Magnoliawrites120@gmail.com

This Is Not Business as Per Usual   Sharece M. Sellem, smsellem@vintagesoulproductions.com

Time Zones Apart   Eric Eidson, Eidson.Eric@gmail.com or Lauren Lynch-Eidson, LaurenLeanzieLynch@gmail.com

Together, Even When You're Not   Kitt Lavoie, kittlavoie@gmail.com

Toshanisha—The New Normals   Rofoldo García Vázquez, rodolfosatyros@gmail.com